Praise for (

"Unusually intimate and well told . . . Pomfret paints a compelling and engaging picture of a China in rapid transition economically, socially, and morally."

—Amelia Newcomb, *The Christian Science Monitor*

"[Pomfret] is neither voyeur nor romantic but rather a resident who deeply understands his adopted homeland."

—Lily Tung, *Newsday*

"Anyone interested in understanding the social and political history of China from Mao's reign to the current regime will get it in *Chinese Lessons*."

—Dennise Lythgoe, *Deseret Morning News*

"Pomfret has a firm grasp of big-picture China, but it's his mastery of personal, small-picture stories that remains so riveting."

—Brian Palmer, *Entertainment Weekly*

"At a time when so many books about China are written from a distance—their authors having spent only a short time in the country, if any time at all—thank goodness for *Chinese Lessons*."

—Ian Johnson, *The Wall Street Journal*

"Reads like a novel, complete with conflict, intrigue, illicit sex, convincing villains, and sympathetic, flawed heroes."

—*Booklist*

CHINESE LESSONS

CHINESE LESSONS

FIVE CLASSMATES AND
THE STORY OF THE NEW CHINA

JOHN POMFRET

■   ■   ■

A Holt Paperback
Henry Holt and Company ■ New York

To John D. and Margaret Pomfret

Holt Paperbacks
Henry Holt and Company, LLC
Publishers since 1866
175 Fifth Avenue
New York, New York 10010
www.henryholt.com

Distributed in Canada by H. B. Fenn and Company Ltd.

Library of Congress Cataloging-in-Publication Data
Pomfret, John.
  Chinese lessons : five classmates and the story of the new China / John Pomfret.
    p. cm.
  Includes index.
  ISBN-13: 978-0-8050-8664-5
  ISBN-10: 0-8050-8664-1
  1. China—Anecdotes.   I. Title.
  DS736.P66. 2006
  951.05'8—dc22   2006041211

Henry Holt books are available for special promotions and
premiums. For details contact: Director, Special Markets.

Originally published in hardcover in 2006 by Henry Holt and Company

First Holt Paperbacks Edition 2007

Map art © 2006 James Sinclair
Designed by Kelly Too

Printed in the United States of America
1   3   5   7   9   10   8   6   4   2

Sixty-three history majors from Nanjing University's Class of '82 at Nanda's front gate, winter 1982

CONTENTS

CHINESE LESSONS

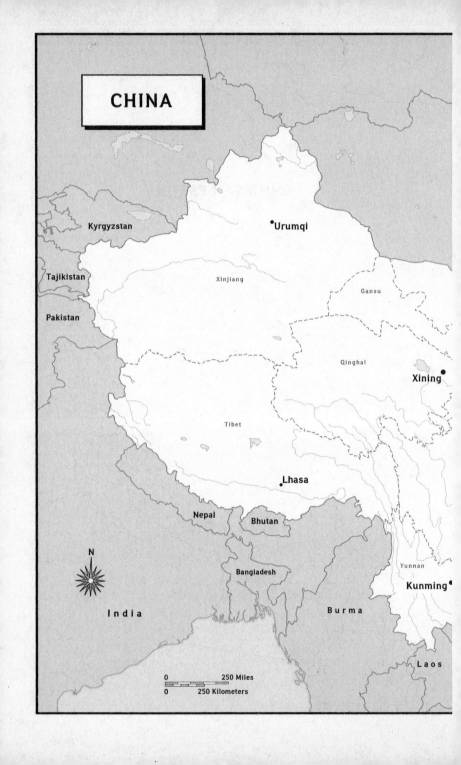

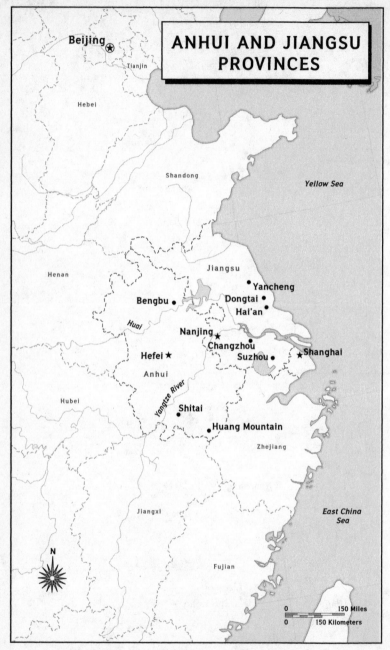

ANHUI AND JIANGSU PROVINCES

Beijing

Tianjin

Hebei

Shandong

Yellow Sea

Henan

Jiangsu

Yancheng

Dongtai

Bengbu

Hai'an

Huai

Nanjing

Changzhou

Shanghai

Hefei

Suzhou

Anhui

Yangtze River

Hubei

Shitai

Huang Mountain

Zhejiang

Jiangxi

N

East China Sea

Fujian

0   150 Miles

0   150 Kilometers

A great number of Pomfret's classmates hail from these cities and towns in Anhui and Jiangsu Provinces.

PART I

SENT DOWN

1

WARMLY WELCOME YOU

At six o'clock in the morning of February 3, 1981, I awoke with a start to the sounds of drums, trumpets, and the squawk of a woman telling me in Chinese to "increase vigilance, protect the motherland, and prepare for war!"

This woman would hound me for the next year, her disembodied voice blasting out of a tinny speaker dangling by a wire just far enough from the bottom bunk that I could not disable it with a broom, yet close enough to wreck my mornings. And not just mine. She was China's daily national wake-up call, broadcast across the country, with the same clanging music and panicky martial message.

Around me, seven Chinese men, ranging in age from eighteen to mid-thirties, all dressed in blue long-sleeved T-shirts and long johns, rustled out of their cotton bedding. As if on cue, they sent up a chorus of phlegmy hocks. Some spat on the floor; others into white enamel teacups. One by one, they slipped on flip-flops, grabbed their metal washbasins, yanked filthy washrags from a jerry-rigged clothesline stretched across the room, and shuffled off to the public bathroom to elbow out a space at a trough of cold water.

I lolled in bed, slowly unfolding my six-foot-two frame from the chin-to-knees position I had to assume to sleep on a five-foot-ten bed. Above me my bunkmate, Xu Ruiqing, lounged, too. Xu (pronounced *shoe*) was the eldest in our room, a thirty-two-year-old Communist Party functionary from a little city sixty miles east of Nanjing. His formal title was

Secretary of the Communist Party Committee of the Students Majoring in History, Nanjing University, Class of 1982—a lot of words that meant he could linger in bed if he wanted, too. Like me and the others in the room, Xu was an undergraduate student, but he had special duties: determining who would get a shot at membership in the ruling Communist Party, and keeping tabs on his fellow students, me included, for any signs of wayward behavior.

I surveyed the room, a dark box with cement floors and dingy whitewashed walls, half the size of my bedroom at my folks' apartment in Manhattan. Crammed against the walls were four bunk beds with gunmetal frames and rice-husk mattresses. The lumpy pillows were also stuffed with rice husks that would stab through the thin cotton cover. Our bedrolls, still in heaps, would soon be folded with military precision. Tacked on the walls were snapshots from home, typically the family arrayed solemnly around their most valuable possession, more often than not a clunky radio.

Eight wooden desks were shoved together in the center of the room, each desk matched with a stool. At head-height, my roommates had strung three wire clotheslines. Wet laundry, scabrous underwear, holey T-shirts, and faded Mao jackets drooped from the wires. From my bottom bunk in the purple darkness of early morning, the lines resembled mountain ridges stretching off into the distance.

The whole scene, lit by two naked low-watt bulbs, looked more like a work camp than university student housing—*The Grapes of Wrath* goes Asian. The only nod to modernity was taped on the wall near my pillow: a picture of New York's skyline and the skull and roses of the Grateful Dead.

I had arrived in China in September 1980 after completing my third year at Stanford University. The United States had established diplomatic relations with China only a year earlier, though contacts between the two countries had intensified beginning in 1971, when Henry Kissinger, then the national security adviser, made a secret trip to Beijing as part of President Richard Nixon's plan to thaw the decades-old cold war with the Communist nation. The two powers then united in a secret and ultimately successful campaign, involving intelligence sharing and gunrunning to rebels in Afghanistan and other Third World hotspots, with the goal of entombing their shared enemy: the Soviet Union.

You'd never guess it from the bare-bones surroundings of my dorm room, but I considered myself lucky to be in China. I'd started to study modern Chinese history and the Chinese language at a time when China was terra incognita. As a twenty-one-year-old American exchange student, I had won a front-row seat at what I thought was going to be the greatest show on Earth: the reemergence of China on the world scene after four decades of self-imposed isolation. Being a student offered opportunities not available to Western diplomats, businessmen, or journalists for the simple reason that the Chinese government didn't much care about us foreign college kids. We could move around more freely, have closer contact with the locals, and, as a result, get a better idea of what it was like to be Chinese.

I had first experienced China through my belly. As a child, Chinese food was one of the first cuisines I was willing to eat outside of hamburgers. I remember, as a nine-year-old during the Vietnam War demonstrations of 1968, hearing students at Columbia University shouting, "Mao, Mao, Chairman Mao!" As I got older, my interest expanded to Chinese history and current events. But I never bought into the notion, then voguish on U.S. campuses, that Mao Zedong had created a worker-peasant paradise in China. My father, a journalist for the *New York Times* before becoming an executive at the company, had imbued in me early the ideas that government is not to be trusted, and that revolutions inevitably crush their own.

By my junior year at Stanford, I had chosen to major in East Asian Studies and had committed myself to finding a way to get to China. At the time, just a handful of Chinese universities had programs for exchange students, and most of those were summer courses. I wanted to go for a year or more.

Through a friend, I contacted a Chinese-American professor working at Stanford's linear accelerator who agreed to write a letter on my behalf to his former classmate, the dean of the Beijing Languages Institute. My plan was first to study language in Beijing and then apply to a Chinese university. In December 1979, I received a letter from the People's Republic, written on rice paper in the curlicued script of a bygone era, with a postage stamp of a monkey-king cavorting on a cloud. "Dear Friend

Pomfret, Salutations!" it began and went on to inform me that I would be welcome to begin studies at the institute the following September. I had learned my first lesson in how things were accomplished in the People's Republic—through connections. The same principle applied to getting my Chinese visa. The Chinese consulate in San Francisco had not received notification of my acceptance to the Beijing Languages Institute. I waited for months, exchanging a stack of letters with the school, until my father came to my rescue. A *Times* editor put him in touch with a Chinese diplomat, Cao Guisheng, who years later would be identified as a top Chinese intelligence officer. Cao agreed to help and in August 1980, I picked up my visa at the Chinese consulate in San Francisco. That first brush with a Chinese spy would not be my last.

Before leaving California, I dropped in at the Asian Languages Department at Stanford. One of my Chinese professors pointed his finger at me and said, "You are going to China. Do you have a Chinese name?" It had never occurred to me that John Pomfret would not work perfectly well in China. The Chinese language, made up of about four hundred monosyllables (compared to English's eight thousand), is woefully limited when it comes to transliterating foreign words and names. The closest one could come to my name would be something like: "Yue-Han [John] Pang-Fu-Lei-Te [Pomfret]."

My professor chose Pan as my new surname. Like my name, it started with *P*. There are only a few hundred last names for all 1.3 billion Chinese, and so it would be that whenever I met a Chinese with the last name Pan, he or she would invariably joke that we were from the same mythical ancestral village. For a given name, the professor chose Aiwen, from Edwin, my middle name. Aiwen means "lover of culture." Pan Aiwen. I thought it was cool. Only later would I learn that Lover of Culture was a girl's name, the Chinese equivalent of, say, Petunia.

In 1980, there were no flights between the United States and China. The way in was through British colonial Hong Kong, the plane swooping for a landing over the tenements that ringed Kai Tak Airport. The next morning I boarded a train for the first leg of my trip to Guangzhou, formerly known as Canton, the largest city in southern China. After an hour, we arrived at the listless border town of Lowu, the last stop in Hong Kong.

Lugging three suitcases and a backpack, I walked over a bridge crossing the fetid Shenzhen River into China.

In 1980, Shenzhen was a network of villages dotted with rice paddies and fishponds, with a population of 280,000. Its tallest building was five stories high; its workers and farmers each produced on average $250 worth of goods each year. A year earlier, the Chinese government had picked Shenzhen as the first of its five so-called Special Economic Zones, where experiments with capitalist-style economic reforms would soon unlock the pent-up moneymaking talents of one of the world's most entrepreneurial peoples.

Once on Chinese soil, I transferred to a train for Guangzhou. The Shenzhen station seethed with travelers hauling merchandise—clothes, canned food, bales of rice—in sacks attached to bamboo shoulder poles that bent under the weight of the load. The scene was a two-tone riot of navy blue and olive green, the color of almost all clothing worn in China. Men with wild eyes and Mao caps surged on board. Absent the Mao cap, I looked pretty much the same.

As a foreigner, I had been placed in first class, where the fans worked, clean white lace antimacassars adorned the seatbacks, and attendants delivered thermoses of boiling water and lidded teacups. The rest of the long train was third class, what the Chinese aptly call "hard seat," where hundreds of sweating, smoking travelers crammed together on benches.

The train clanked past bamboo groves, duck ponds, and village houses blackened by coal dust. I saw men steering wooden plows pulled by water buffalo, women hunkered over knee-deep in rice paddy water, and travelers tottering on clunky black bicycles along dirt paths. This was a view of rural southern China I would come to know well, and one I believed would be everlasting.

After dumping my suitcases at one of the few Guangzhou hotels that catered to foreigners, I went off in search of food. All I had was an address of a famed restaurant and a bad street map. I trudged for hours, getting caught in a downpour, before finding shelter under the awning of a teahouse alongside several couples, all of whom were holding hands. That was interesting; I'd been told that public displays of affection were banned.

As late afternoon approached, families cascaded out from narrow doorways into the streets for dinner, squatting on tiny stools, rice bowl in one hand, chopsticks in the other, shoveling food into their mouths. By the time I found the restaurant, it was teeming with diners. All heads turned toward me, the sweat-stained foreigner. My Chinese was pretty primitive, so I walked table to table with a waitress, pointing to what I wanted to eat. What's that? Snake. And that? Owl. And that? Civet cat.

In my college Chinese textbooks, by chapter three, we had learned "vanguard of the proletariat" and "serve the people," but we never did learn how to say "I'd like General Tso's Civet Cat, please." I chose a plate of shredded chicken with bell peppers, some green vegetables, and a steamed fish, downing it all along with four bowls of rice and an indeterminate quantity of warm flat beer served in bowls. Diners from neighboring tables, their faces scarlet with drink, staggered over to toast this "American friend." That night I learned a new word: *fantong,* literally "rice bucket" or "big eater." To peals of laughter, I repeated it louder and louder. "I am a rice bucket. I am rice bucket." Later on I learned it also meant "dummy."

The next evening, I boarded the train from Guangzhou to Beijing. Back in first class, I shared my berth with a Chinese official in a finely pressed Mao suit. I had brought a small cassette player, and I popped in a Bob Marley tape, explaining in broken Chinese, "This is the music of revolution." Thinking this would earn me some solidarity, I was surprised when he seemed to recoil in horror at the word. I thought he had misunderstood, so I reformulated the sentence. "This is revolutionary music." Again, he looked at me oddly, as if in dismay. After four decades of non-stop political struggle, revolution was probably the farthest thing from his mind.

I wandered back to the hard sleeper cars with their rack-upon-rack of three-level padded black bunks crammed with families and young people. A group of students heading to the university in Beijing asked me to sit down and share some sunflower seeds. A few tried out their halting English on me, as I did my Chinese on them. They, too, had no interest in Bob Marley. They favored the Eagles' greatest hits, until the train police appeared and told me to go back to first class and my new friends scattered with embarrassed smiles.

As the train chugged north toward Beijing, the air grew cooler, the skies brighter. I developed my first crush on a Chinese woman—a train attendant who made fun of my bad Chinese and harangued me for being left-handed. Both would become routine—the crushes and the teasing I took about the way I spoke their language and manhandled their chopsticks.

The landscape out the window changed from tropical rolling hills to flatter, drier plains of yellow dirt. We lumbered through the industrial heartland of Wuhan, crossing the Yangtze River, and then half a day later we left the muddy waters of the Yellow River behind as well. At dawn on the third day we began our approach to Beijing.

Once in Beijing, I made my way, via a rattling Russian-made taxi, from the railroad station to the Beijing Languages Institute, on the northwestern outskirts of town. On the way we passed an enormous square. The driver turned to look at me: "This is Tiananmen!" he shouted, spraying me in his enthusiasm with a mouthful of spittle. I asked him to drive around it once so I could take in the view and the enormous painted portrait of Mao that dominated its northern side.

With their victory over the Nationalists in 1949, the Communists moved the capital from Nanjing to Beijing. They flattened Beijing's old city walls and bulldozed the courtyard houses and shantytown that stretched for a mile in front of the crimson gates of the Forbidden City, for centuries the residence of China's emperors, empresses, and their eunuch aides and courtesans. In place of the shantytown, they paved a four-million-square-foot rectangle; it was called Tiananmen, the Gate of Heavenly Peace. After an hour's drive, the driver deposited me at the school. I dragged my stuff past a series of gatekeepers and under the nose of a twenty-five-foot-tall Mao statue, freckled with coal dust.

The first thing that struck me about Beijing was the vastness of the sky. Hazy blue, it floated above the city in marked contrast to the grayness below—the worn and tired people with their sullen faces, green army trucks, dirty stone houses, and omnipresent propaganda posters. Though Beijing was one of the largest cities in the world, no skyscrapers speared its immensity. The autumn winds were crisp and dry from the north and east, and carried sand and leaves. I learned fast to wrap my head in a scarf before heading out the door.

Half of the students at the institute were foreigners studying Chinese: Italian Communists, Pakistanis seeking secrets to China's A-bomb, Iranians and Iraqis (they fought continuously), white-robed Arabs, French intellectuals who walked around carrying ashtrays, Germans with their Karl Marx–wannabe beards, Americans who crooned Motown loudly and off-key in the common showers, and hundreds of Africans, many of them in forced exile. The rest of the students were Chinese, studying a Babel of foreign languages, from English to Bulgarian.

Most of the Chinese hoped to study overseas. That fall I edited fifteen college applications on behalf of my new Chinese friends to Harvard, Yale, Dartmouth, University of Chicago, Columbia, and Stanford. The applications were hand-carried to Hong Kong and mailed there to avoid censors, spies, and jealous colleagues who with a word could derail the plans of a lifetime.

The personal statements I transcribed were my first inklings of the toll exacted on ordinary Chinese by the Cultural Revolution, when Chairman Mao shut high schools and universities and declared war on educated Chinese. As youngsters, these students had secretly nurtured ambitions that were not only lofty but outright illegal. They were brave, a bit reckless even, steeled by miserable childhoods. All were familiar with political repression, mostly as victims, occasionally as perpetrators, and sometimes both. Their lives, so devoted to books in the beginning of the 1980s, were, in fact, tinged in blood. Competition for a university place in 1977, when they had tested into the institute, was the most intense it ever had been and ever would be in Communist China's history. For each spot at a liberal arts college in China, there were sixty-seven test takers.

Kuang Da, a brilliant linguist, had spent six years in a shoe factory. Zhang Hua, a willowy southern girl with eyes as big as walnuts, had witnessed the beating death of her father and then watched Red Guards push her brother out a third-story window, crippling him. Wang Kegang, with movie star looks, had planted wheat for three years. Wang's personal statement described the transformation of an idealistic boy, who worshiped Chairman Mao, into a hardened young man. "I have a scientific outlook on life," he wrote, that taught him "people's desire for power, money and comfort are boundless. I see the meanness in life. Never again will I allow myself to be cheated by charismatic preaching or political superstition. I will let none of this stop me as I seek my goal." He could have been writing for his whole generation.

The American universities ate these stories up, starting an educational love affair that would see more than three hundred thousand Chinese study in the United States, often on scholarships, over the next several decades. Kuang ended up going to the University of Chicago; Wang to Yale; Zhang to Smith.

Wang even spent a summer with my parents, working the quintessential American immigrant job—running rides and taking tickets on Coney Island.

My first impression of the Chinese at the Beijing Languages Institute was how skinny they were. Foreigners studying at the institute were not allowed to live with Chinese, so for me the best way to meet them was to play pickup basketball, introduced to China in 1896 by American missionaries. Despite its imperialist pedigree, Mao loved basketball; it was the only Western sport not banned during the Cultural Revolution.

Courtside, the Chinese students would peel off layer after layer of clothes; a blue or green Mao jacket, a brownish gray sweater, an off-color white shirt that hadn't been washed in days. Finally, a thin, blue long-sleeve cotton sweatshirt came off to reveal the bony body, all ribs and elbows. They wrapped their belts two, sometimes three, times around their sylphlike waists. Caloric intake in China in the early 1980s was at the same level as it was in the 1930s. Although greatly improved from the decades immediately following the 1949 revolution, the Chinese diet was almost devoid of protein and fat. Perpetually hungry, my friends would jostle in line for access to the best dishes in the dining hall, wolfing down the glop in seconds.

As my first semester drew to a close in December 1980, the institute conducted a singing contest for the Chinese students, foreshadowing the karaoke craze that would sweep the country a decade later. One group of students, dressed in overalls, strumming guitars and banging soda bottles together for rhythm, sang the old minstrel favorite "Plantation Boy." In the middle of the song, a waiflike woman minced up to the mike and, swaying like a Hollywood starlet of the 1940s, tempted the audience with Beijing's very tame version of a come-hither look. Their pitch was perfect, even though they were tone-deaf to the song's racist connotations. Another group of students penned their own lyrics to the tune of a Chinese propaganda ditty, "Study Hard!"

Everyday there is nothing
Nothing to go after at all
Except soy bean milk and onion pancakes on Wednesday morning
But then 20 people cut in line
Our classes are ridiculous
We must study on our own
Maybe tomorrow things will change

The party member judges did not approve. First prize went to a group of straitlaced students in Mao jackets singing "Jingle Bells."

As my Chinese improved and I met more people from within the institute and beyond, I was struck by the deep hostility toward foreigners among Chinese in authority. There was a lot of talk of friendship but very little to be found. My minder at the institute, a diminutive Maoist named Mr. Bi, read my mail and monitored my contacts with Chinese students. The watchman at our dorm forced Chinese visitors to write down their names and addresses, which were then handed over to security personnel. Politically, it was much safer for Chinese to be hostile than to be friendly. Those brave enough to talk to foreigners were often treated harshly and criticized by fellow Chinese, yet they still took incredible risks just to meet me. Not that I was particularly special, but to them I embodied something—a carefree life and access to a freer world—that many of them wanted.

One evening I found myself in Beijing's tiny downtown at a dance in the Beijing International Club, where elderly tourists from the American Midwest mixed with the elite Chinese who had the connections to get past the guard at the door. I had come with Wang to celebrate his admission into Yale. As I boogied to the Clash, Wang sidled up to me. "I want to be like you," he squealed, hugging me impulsively on the dance floor. Nearby, security service agents clumsily snapped their flash cameras, documenting the faces of the partying Chinese.

Another evening, I was strolling out the door of my all-male, all-foreign student dormitory when a Chinese girl entered. The gatekeeper burst out of his little room by the door. "You shouldn't be here," he screamed, the veins bulging in his neck. The girl stared steadily at him and kept walking. He made a note in his log and went back to his pipe and his radio. A week later, I learned that the girl, a friend of an African student, had disappeared.

Daily life for me in China was that of a zoo animal. The fact that I used my body more than my hands on a basketball court, had a large nose, and slept naked became subjects of conversation. This last habit was of special interest because, as I learned first in public baths and later with roommates, Chinese would employ the skills of a contortionist to avoid exposing their private parts. One American woman spent a year rooming with a Chinese woman and never saw her legs above her knee.

Cultural clashes occurred nonstop; we called them "China moments." One day in the fall, I was invited to a friend's apartment for dinner. When

I arrived, the night guard stopped me and told a blatant lie: my friend was not in. There was no way to call because people had no phones, and I couldn't scale the brick walls because they were too high. I erupted at the gatekeeper, mangling my Chinese in a fit of futile histrionics.

"I get angry here," I wrote in a letter home to my parents, "a weird almost uncontrollable rage, a rage that makes me want to break up restaurants, push people, scream and yell, smack into people on my bicycle as they cross the street with their heads down."

For pocket change, I landed a job teaching English at a computer institute for sixty dollars per month, not as bad as it sounds when you consider that a meal of twenty fried pork dumplings cost less than a dollar. My students were in various stages of patching together their lives following the Cultural Revolution. One of them, Liu Bin, lived by the school gates in a one-room brick shack with a packed mud floor and a corrugated tin roof secured by cement blocks. On occasion, he would invite me to his house, where his wife would cook Moo Shu Pork and other northern specialties. We ate around a folding table, two people on stools and one on the bed. I didn't realize until later that it was costing them upwards of a month's salary to feed us, and that each time I was invited, Liu had to receive permission in advance from the Communist Party secretary at his workplace.

At Liu's home, I would play with his six-year-old daughter and listen to his stories of being deported during the Cultural Revolution to grow wheat on a farm near the Russian border. Liu hated the Communists and felt that he had lost half of his forty-two years to the vagaries of their destructive political campaigns. A man in a hurry, he was fueled by a ferocious anger and the conviction that he was a victim owed his due.

Yet my existence in China wasn't always nerve-wracking, and, as I left Liu's house and cycled back to the language institute through Beijing's darkened alleys, an electric, irrepressible sense of joy would spread over me. I felt giddy at being in China, learning to survive and thrive in an alien environment. China was as close as I could imagine to living on another planet. Though it had some of the elements of modern life, even those reflected China's long isolation and profound weirdness—a nuclear-armed power whose people lived in unheated hovels.

I attended my Chinese language classes at the institute four hours a day, six days a week. Our teachers were strict matronly types who often seemed bewildered at the prospect of instructing young men and women from countries that just a few years ago had been portrayed as avowed enemies of the Communist regime.

Chinese is a strange language for an American. While it has English's subject-verb-object sentence structure, the use of tones to impart diverse meanings makes it completely different. Mandarin Chinese has four tones, but thousands of words have the same pronunciation *and* the same tone, and are differentiated only by their written characters, of which Chinese employs somewhere north of ten thousand. The sound *li*, for example, can mean 172 different things, among them "present," "power," "pear," and "profit." To clarify a word's meaning, speakers would often scribble out the character in question on their palms, using their index fingers, often with a balletic flourish, as an imaginary ink brush. I thought this was marvelously inefficient.

I liked the way it felt to speak Chinese—the elegant rise and fall of the tones, the sensuous way my tongue flitted about my mouth, and the economy of a language that needed very few words to say a lot. Speaking good French demands control of one's lips; American English relies on an open mouth; but Chinese can be spoken perfectly even through clenched teeth. "Picture your tongue as a butterfly," one of my instructors would say, and there it would be, flapping against my mouth and banging against my teeth as I sought to harness it and speak Chinese.

Chinese is full of idioms that refer back to arcane bits of history. I enjoyed memorizing these and found them a great way to impress my Chinese friends. The idioms also revealed that Chinese shared a barnyard bawdiness with American English. My favorite was "taking off your pants to fart"—wasted effort.

I gave myself over to a compulsive studying style that involved shouting (the only way I could hear my own voice) along with tapes of sentences recorded for me by my Chinese friends. Each time I came across a character I did not know, I scribbled it down on my palm, transferring it later to a flash card, which I would review throughout the day when I found myself waiting in lines. This happened frequently because just about everything was rationed.

After three months at the institute, I took a college entrance test. I had heard that Nanjing University had a president who was allowing foreigners to live on the "Chinese side," in other words, together with Chinese students. It was a policy that no other major university had instituted and that the school would end a few years later. I passed the entrance exam and in February 1981 arrived at Nanjing University at the start of a new semester.

To its students, the university was and is known as Nanda, a contraction of the first syllable of *Nanjing* and *daxue,* the Chinese word for university. Nanjing, I soon learned, was a far sleepier town than Beijing, its broad, leafy streets lined with French poplars, its buildings made from yellow bricks. Until the late 1970s, the tallest building in the city was ten stories high. In contrast to the Stalinist monstrosities in Beijing like the Great Hall of the People and the Revolutionary History Museum on Tiananmen Square, Nanjing in 1981 looked much as it had in 1949, when the Nationalist government fled in defeat. The Nanjing branch of the Bank of China, where I had an account, was located in a building with squeaky 1930s wooden ceiling fans and a grimy Greco-Roman columned facade in dire need of sandblasting.

I was assigned a room on the first floor of a shabby four-story dormitory. I heaved my stuff down the hall and pushed on an open door. Eight young men were there; seven turned out to be my roommates. Two were listening to a Japanese tape. Another two were huddled over a board game called Go, using light and dark pebbles. One was perched on an upper bunk reading a magazine. Another, in the bunk below, was patching his washbasin with a rusty spackling knife. The remaining two scribbled in their journals. As I walked in, one man, with his back to me, started complaining: "China is so backward, eight people squeezed in such a dump."

"Ai-yo!" came a warning cry from the back of the room. I'd been spotted. Everyone stood up immediately, exchanging nervous looks. They were expecting me. "You must be Pan Aiwen."

The man approaching me looked middle-aged, although I would find out that he was just past thirty. He introduced himself as Xu Ruiqing, the class party chief, "but you can call me Old Xu," he said, giving me a lifeless handshake. He wanted me to call him Old Xu because he'd instantly sized up that I was younger by a few years. The others deferred to him, which I thought was out of traditional Confucian respect for an elder, but later, of course, realized that it was because he was the party connection. As I inched farther into the room, my head got snagged in a soggy, low-lying pair of long underwear dangling from a wire strung across the room.

"Sit down, sit down," Xu said. "This is going to be your bed." He guided me to an empty bunk beneath his, next to the window, a choice location given the wet clothes and garlicky stench in the room. My new roommates continued to stare at me. Nothing furtive. They just gawked. "Can he talk?" asked one. Another stared at my feet. "Look at his shoes. So big."

I had gotten accustomed to Chinese surrounding me, their heads cocked sideways, mouths agape, apprising my looks, my nose, my eyes, hair, and clothes. It was always "Can he talk?" as if Chinese was the world's sole tongue. It never seemed to occur to them that I could understand what they were saying about me. In my four months in China, I had often been unnerved by being privy to what every stranger thought about me. I had thought somehow that Nanda was going to be different. "Hey," I said, looking at them, trying my hand at a joke, "the monkey speaks."

One, a burly boy, smiled and laughed loudly. "Warmly welcome YOU," he bellowed in English. We all laughed. The ice had been broken.

The eighth man in the room, the one who had griped about their cramped quarters, turned to go. On leaving, he clumsily stuck out his hand. "I am Zhou Lianchun," he said, formally pumping my hand, his eyes avoiding mine. "You are the first foreigner I have ever met."

2

THE SLAP

Not only was I the first foreigner Zhou Lianchun met, in time, I would become the only friend who would learn his entire troubled story.

On a beastly summer day in 1966, in the countryside of northern Jiangsu Province, 250 miles from Nanjing, a hundred farmers lined up at the threshing grounds of Production Team 7 in the Shen Kitchen Commune. The threshing ground doubled as a village square, surrounded by dilapidated single-story houses fashioned from mud, bricks, wooden beams, and gray roof tiles. Chickens and pigs had free rein of the place, hunting for grain and other tidbits. Zhou (pronounced *joe*), a gangly eleven-year-old boy with a shaved head and raggedy cloth shoes, was twelfth in line.

"Thwack." "Thwack." The line moved forward. "Thwack." Thwack." It inched forward again.

Zhou reached the front of the line. A middle-aged woman, blood seeping from her nose and ears, faced him on her knees. He pulled back his right hand and, as the others ahead of him had done, smacked the left side of her face—*Thwack*—then slapped her again with his left hand. *Thwack*. The sweat from her cheeks stung his skin.

Zhou and his neighbors were carrying out party policy. Earlier that spring, on May 16, 1966, the Central Committee of the Communist Party issued a document heralding the launch of a political campaign, a "Cultural Revolution," calling for a purge of undesirable influences from abroad and from China's past: capitalism from the West, Communist revisionism from the Soviet Union, and what Chairman Mao called "feudalism" from ancient China.

Mao Zedong launched the Cultural Revolution as a way to regain power in the wake of the disastrous "Great Leap Forward," his economic program of the late fifties, which had brought China to the verge of collapse. In Zhou Lianchun's region, families were herded off their land onto communal farms, where everyone was forced to eat together in a large dining hall. Private farm plots, the most productive element of the region's agriculture, were outlawed. Villages became "production brigades." Thirty production brigades were slapped together to form the Shen Kitchen Commune, with a total population of about thirty thousand people. In a frenzied attempt to increase steel production, the party demanded that all commune members hand in their woks and wheelbarrows to be smelted in backyard furnaces.

One of Zhou's cousins died of starvation; another newborn cousin was abandoned in swaddling clothes at the doorstep of the party committee and never seen again. Zhou and his family survived on weeds, seeds, and the runny gruel served at the communal canteen. Whenever they sat down to eat, Zhou recalled later, he would cry at the sight of the paltry meal before him. The bodies of the malnourished swelled with fluids. People told stories of cannibalism. Nationwide, more than thirty million died of starvation.

Born in a village near the town of Dongtai not far from the coast of the Yellow Sea, Zhou was the son of a peasant and a woman the Chinese referred to as a "borrowed belly." Zhou's father had brought her into the house after his wife discovered she couldn't have children. The "borrowed belly" had first given birth to a girl in 1948. The family nicknamed her Little Brother Lover in the hope that it would move fate to provide the family with a son. Seven years later Zhou was born. His given name, Lianchun, means "eternal spring"—a choice straight from the fields. He called his birth mother Little Mama and his father's wife Big Mama. Big Mama had bound feet and doted on the boy.

The family's house bordered fields crisscrossed with irrigation ditches fed by the San Cang River two hundred yards away. In the sultry summers of north Jiangsu, Zhou and his buddies swam in the river and caught fish and freshwater shrimp. As a boy, he exhibited an entrepreneurial streak and a taste for adventure, and by age eight, was selling radishes and sand crabs, which the Chinese treasured as a delicacy.

The only fertilizer available in Zhou's region came from what the Chinese called *fen*—a character that depicts a shovel and two hands—in other words, freshly harvested human excrement. All Chinese learn to give wide berth to the night soil cart—a horse-drawn tub with a hole on the top from which wafts a pullulating stench—but collecting crap was a popular vocation for boys, akin to a paper route in the United States. Human waste doesn't make particularly good fertilizer, but barnyard manure was rare, so Chinese peasants had long ago learned to make do, slathering *fen* on their fields, despite the danger of spreading hepatitis and other diseases.

When it came to shoveling shit, Zhou was particularly eagle-eyed. "There's a boy, carrying a spade and a basket searching along the alleyways of a village," Zhou wrote years later in an account of himself. "From his concentration, you'd think he had gotten out of bed at the crack of dawn to search for a lost wallet. In reality, he is looking for a pile of shit. And when he finds the steaming mountain of crap, the expression on his face is as if he has won the lottery."

Zhou showed me this essay in early 2004 after I'd traveled to Nanjing to see him. I finished reading and looked at him. "Nice hobby, huh?" he joked. I was also entrepreneurial when I was a kid. I had a paper route for three summers and sold homemade yogurt to the tenants of my apartment building in Manhattan. But gathering turds for profit? There were even political risks. Showing any entrepreneurial flair was routinely criticized as "walking the capitalist road."

At the end of the Great Leap Forward in 1961, the party formally blamed the famine on Mother Nature, not Mao's policies. (To this day the official Chinese name for the period is "three years of natural disasters.") Political euphemisms aside, Mao withdrew in a huff, and more pragmatic leaders, among them a man named Deng Xiaoping who would later open China to the West, ended Mao's policies and got the economy back on its feet.

Mao didn't just shuffle meekly into retirement. He could not destroy his rivals by accusing them of incompetence; they had, after all, put food back on the table. The one thing he could do was to label them enemies of his revolution. He ordered that China's high school students be organized into something he called the Red Guard, which he would soon use as the muscle of his new revolution. Raised in a society that celebrated violence, with no memory of a freer life before the revolution, China's youth had been taught to be unwaveringly loyal to Mao and to fanatically hate "class enemies."

In August 1966, Mao's lieutenant, Lin Biao, told them what to do. "Although the capitalists have been overthrown," he said in a speech reprinted throughout the country, "they still plot to use old thought, old culture, old customs, and old habits to corrupt the masses, subjugate the hearts of the people to accomplish their goal of restoring their rule." The order called on the Red Guard to destroy these "Four Olds."

That month the party committee in Zhou's production brigade, which had a population of about one thousand, formed a Red Guard committee of twelve. The number was not accidental. China was mobilizing for a war—against itself—and Chinese infantry squads have twelve soldiers. Urban Red Guard units donned red armbands, but in Zhou's backwater commune only the chieftains could afford them. In Zhou's group there were eight representatives from production teams, one teacher, two local Communist cadres, and Zhou, representing the students.

Zhou's father had pushed him to study hard in school, and he had excelled, graduating from elementary school the previous spring. But a high school education was a luxury solely available to those recommended by the party. In Zhou's class, only a relative of the principal and the son of the production team leader had continued on to high school. At eleven, Zhou was tall for his age, his skin bronzed by the sun. His father's plans for Zhou that summer had been for him to work the fields and harvest corn. Instead, he sowed revolution.

Zhou and his Red Guard unit went from village to village beating people who belonged to one of Communist China's five lowest castes: former landlords, rich peasants, counterrevolutionaries, bad elements, and rightists. These categories of so-called class enemies go back to the late 1920s when young Communists fanned out across the country and assigned class labels to many families. The majority of Chinese were lucky enough, due to the abject misery of their lives, to be labeled as "poor peasants" or "proletariat," sparing them from harm. However, anyone considered to belong to the five evil castes was subject to execution, at worst, and, at best, continued intimidation, beatings (called "reeducation"), and other violent punishments. Class labels would stick with families for decades.

Such was the case of the middle-aged woman savaged at the village threshing ground. A few days earlier she had stopped her son and another farm boy from fighting by slapping them both. Under the twisted logic of the Cultural Revolution, she was automatically in the wrong, because her family had been labeled "rich peasant," while her son's opponent came from a "poor peasant" family. Zhou's Red Guard committee decided to teach her a lesson. They mobilized the whole production team, about one hundred people, to give her a taste of her own medicine—hundreds of slaps as she knelt in the village square. After the beating, the woman refused to admit she had done wrong.

"Eat shit," she screamed at her assailants. "Eat shit!"

Zhou was then dispatched to a nearby outhouse to collect shit in a wooden bucket and dilute it with water. The Red Guard chief took a wooden ladle and poured the runny concoction down her throat. She kept quiet after that.

Over the next weeks and months, Zhou and his gang smashed Buddhist temples, forced monks to walk around with boulders on their backs and garbage cans on their heads, defaced wall paintings of Buddhist gods, covering them with a coat of red paint. When that dried, a propagandist arrived and painted portraits of Mao on top.

In their search for counterrevolutionary contraband—books, photographs, jewelry, knickknacks, anything representing Mao's "Four Olds"—Zhou's team overturned mattresses, peered inside fireplaces, and rooted through vats of preserved vegetables. If there was a phoenix or a dragon carved into the ancient eaves of the house, they would hack it off, because those images were considered "feudal." They sifted through the contents of shelves and cabinets and confiscated gold, silver, and all jewelry, which the party had labeled "bourgeois." If their targets refused to hand over items, such as good clothes, cotton cloth, or even unwoven flax, they would expropriate it. Zhou's team pocketed the swag or distributed it among friends; it was state-sanctioned theft, a redistribution from one group of have-nots to another.

Zhou remembered being particularly impressed by the bonfires of books. But he did not destroy any of the books in his own home. That was left to a cousin and his older sister, who, in an effort to show the family's revolutionary zeal, ransacked the house, placed the old, bound volumes in piles, and lit the pyres themselves. Zhou hid ten novels from his relatives, wrapping them in a flax bag and stuffing them in an underground vault where his family stored sweet potatoes for the winter. Three years later, when the Cultural Revolution abated for a time, he disinterred them. All but one—a collection of Chinese literature published by Beijing University—had rotted. Zhou kept it. To this day, it smells of mildew and dirt.

Zhou felt immense pride to be on the Red Guard team and to be playing, as he thought of it, with the big boys. Never mind, of course, that he had demonstrated counterrevolutionary behavior by hiding those few books. Like all Chinese youth, the first sentence he'd learned in school was "Long live Chairman Mao!" To be carrying out the chairman's orders gave the precocious eleven-year-old a powerful sense of purpose and self-worth. "The more ruthless we are to enemies, the more we love the people," the team would chant together.

In early September 1966, his gang of Red Guards mercilessly beat an old man accused of once having been a landlord. That same day, fearing more torture, the old man killed himself. But the guards weren't finished. They gave the corpse to his three sons, demanding that the boys parade it around the village. Then they told the boys to chop the body into three pieces and place them in pigpens. If any of them had refused, they all would have been dubbed "evil spawn of the feudal class" and destined for persecution.

A primary target of Mao's Cultural Revolution was the family, the last bastion of traditional Confucian culture. While previous campaigns had sought to gain control over people's thoughts, now the idea was to destroy the fundamental characteristic of the Chinese: loyalty to parents, siblings, and ancestors. Alienating individuals from their families would, in Mao's view, turn the Chinese into people with a single allegiance—to the party and its leader, Mao himself, who was, according to a party song, "the people's esteemed and beloved father."

The Cultural Revolution was particularly damaging because for centuries morality in China was rooted in a veneration for the elderly and the family tree. People didn't disgrace themselves in the eyes of God; they did so in the eyes of their forebears. It's hard to conceive of a greater moral transgression in Chinese society than to dishonor a father's body, as those three boys were made to. But Mao was determined to create a new morality by cutting ties between this world and the past. Brothers were pitted against sisters, children against parents, wives against husbands. People were expected to report on those dearest to them because it was they alone who knew the most private thoughts of their loved ones. China was turned into a society of snitches. The stool pigeon became a hero of the revolution.

Zhou's Red Guard group relied on such informers. One late August afternoon, a village gossip told the group that his relative's family was committing a serious offense: burning paper money as part of a centuries-old ceremony to honor ancestors. It was the Festival of Hungry Ghosts, when the gates of hell open and ghosts wander the earth. The Red Guards burst into their house, dragged out all nine family members, and strung them by their feet from trees that lined the banks of a nearby reservoir. There they beat them. Zhou was frustrated that he couldn't get a good punch in; each time he hit one of the dangling victims, the body would spin. They were left hanging until late evening.

Zhou recounted these stories to me over a lunch of beef noodles in a modern Nanjing coffee shop called Magazine—a two-story glass and faux marble structure with sofas and waitresses wearing baseball caps. It was early autumn, and young couples were sitting around us, smoking cigarettes, drinking fruit tea, and chatting. Their mobile phones rang to disco beats, guitar riffs, and James Bond movie theme songs.

I had heard and read countless stories from the victims of Chinese political campaigns. But before Zhou, I had never met anyone who acknowledged being a tormentor. "In China," Zhou said, "no one admits to torturing, and everyone says they were victims. But do the math. If we have so many victims, we've got to have a lot of torturers." Zhou admitted to having no pangs of conscience for menacing neighbors, relatives, and teachers. "I did what I was told and, being eleven, I liked it," he said. I had never heard that before either. To me, his unvarnished honesty was blood-chilling. He shared these feelings with me because I was his classmate. "You need to understand this," he lectured at one point, "to understand where we've come from."

There is a destructive logic to persecution campaigns. In order for them to continue, vast amounts of time and energy are needed to replenish the circle of victims. Chinese had long been schooled in the arts of torture; they could recall the beatings, beheadings, and other abuse visited on class enemies at the onset of the revolution. Those who were too young had read about it in school. They all knew "the jet plane," in which a victim was forced to bend over, stand on one leg and stretch out his arms like a Soviet MiG for excruciatingly long periods of time; "the big hang," in which a victim was dangled upside down; and "the tiger bench," in which a victim's thighs and knees were lashed to a bench and blocks of wood shoved under his feet until ligaments tore up and down his legs. The forced feeding of feces and intensely spicy peppers added another dimension to the suffering.

The persecution of urban educators and intellectuals that started in June 1966 would eventually give way to attacks on old class enemies and Communist officials accused of "walking the capitalist road," whatever that meant. Fresh out of targets by 1968, the Cultural Revolution then zeroed in on people with simple trades: carpenters, bricklayers, paper makers, cobblers, tailors, and barbers.

In 1968, Zhou, now thirteen, was given a group of eleven people on whom to undertake "thought work," a common euphemism for torture and humiliation. One of those on the list was Big Mama, who, while not his biological mother, was the woman who had raised him as her son.

Big Mama worked as a simple peasant in the fields. But to make extra money for her family, she also did seamstress work in the village. Before the Cultural Revolution, she used the money she made to buy Zhou, the boy in the family and her favorite, books and little presents.

Zhou took up the task of denouncing his mother without the slightest hesitation. In front of his Red Guard troop, he criticized her profession as "capitalist" and dismissed her gifts to him as examples of a "petty bourgeois sensibility." Face-to-face with the woman he loved most, the teenager demanded that she acknowledge her errors. Under the watchful eye of his revolutionary elders, Zhou forced her to spew a Maoist catechism that neither of them quite understood. "The party is always correct. Long live the Dictatorship of the Proletariat. Long live Chairman Mao."

This went on for days in the public threshing ground. After each session, Zhou and his mother would return home together. She would cook dinner for him and the rest of the family, never talking about what went on during the daily public humiliation. Zhou never actually hit or made Big Mama kneel on pebbles or glass. He didn't need to. He had learned how to make her quake with fear using simpler methods—baring his teeth, using a wild stare. Big Mama cowered on a pile of straw as Zhou lambasted her for giving a party official a one-cent discount when she repaired a hole in his Mao jacket.

During his discourse in the Nanjing café, Zhou paused and asked me a question: "How do you think a society where that type of behavior was condoned, no, not condoned, mandated, can heal itself? Do you think it ever can?" I said Chinese were forever telling me, an American, how much stronger their family values were than those in the United States. Zhou smirked. "Don't believe the hype."

3

BROKEN WING

In early June 1966, Guan Yongxing was practicing Chinese characters in her sixth-grade class when nature called. She grabbed a blank piece of rice parchment (Chinese villages had no toilet paper) and sped to the outhouse—a wooden shack over a pit in the earth—outside her rural commune school.

A classmate stopped her. "Don't waste that blank piece. Take this one," she said, handing the diminutive eleven-year-old, whom everyone called Little Guan, another piece of paper, this one with writing on it.

When she returned, her classmates were waiting: "Little Guan used a paper that said 'Long live Chairman Mao' to wipe her ass!" they chanted, blocking her way.

Her father, who was the principal at the school, was summoned by the teacher to discuss the incident. Little Guan said she had not noticed what was on the paper, and besides the proof was already submerged under a pile of shit. "Who cares about a piece of scrap paper anyway?" Little Guan's father scoffed.

This is the way Little Guan's nightmare of the Cultural Revolution kicked off, with a toilet run. Two days later, the Guan family awoke to find their house in a hamlet inside a place called White Pasture Commune plastered with posters accusing Little Guan's father of opposing the Communist Party, socialism, and Maoist thought and of teaching his children to be reactionaries. What began as a malicious childhood prank had mutated into a serious political inquisition: not of Little Guan but of her father. It would last ten years.

Little Guan's father told her not to blame herself for that day. An educated man and a tough principal, he'd already been in the sights of the illiterate peasants then gaining control of their commune. "My family was fated to enter hell; that piece of paper just opened the door," Little Guan said later. But her sense of guilt was inescapable.

Little Guan's father had fallen afoul of the Communist system once before. In 1957, when Chairman Mao encouraged Chinese intellectuals to criticize the excesses of the Communist Party during the so-called Hundred Flowers Movement, Little Guan's father took the bait and spoke out. A year later, Chairman Mao ordered his minion, Deng Xiaoping, to crack down on the malcontents. Little Guan's father—and hundreds of thousands like him—was branded a "rightist" and banished with his wife to the countryside, where he became principal of the small school. In 1962, Little Guan would be "sent down" to join them there—a form of internal exile inflicted on millions of Chinese families.

In 2004, I went to see my classmate Little Guan. On a three-hour bus ride from Nanjing, we made a pit stop at a highway rest area. An old woman who had been sitting next to me disembarked and went off to the bathroom. After five minutes, the driver honked his horn and prepared to go. I noticed that the elderly lady had not returned and asked the ticket taker if she perhaps had transferred to another bus. No, I was told, she had not, but we were going anyway. The bus pulled out, leaving the old woman behind.

As I waited for Little Guan in front of her office, I read a poster on the wall. The sign was from the police, seeking information about a woman in her early twenties whose dismembered body had been found near a street known for its bars and brothels. She had dyed blond hair, had been wearing a Giordano miniskirt and a top that read "Go Wild."

Guan Yongxing was born in 1955 in the seat of sleepy Hai'an County, 170 miles northeast of Nanjing. A local soothsayer had predicted that Little

Guan's mother was going to have a boy. The delivery—at home in her parents' bed—was a difficult one, and Little Guan was born unconscious. "It's just a girl," her mother remarked to the midwife who was reviving her. "Don't waste your efforts."

Female infanticide was always an accepted part of China's rural life because girls married out of the family and therefore did not support their parents in their old age. Still, Little Guan was resuscitated and was given the name her grandfather had picked for a boy: Yongxing (Eternal Stars).

Little Guan's parents were betrothed in 1942, when her father was eleven and her mother was nine. This was typical among the landed gentry. Her father's family was prominent in Hai'an County before the Communist Revolution. They had owned land, small workshops, and stores. At the entrance to the family's courtyard house, visitors could pick up a ball of opium and a pipe and retire to the back for a smoke—a sign of the solid standing of the Guan clan, much as a well-stocked wine cellar connotes status in the West.

With the Communist victory, the party confiscated the family's land, businesses, and savings. Her grandfather, an opium addict, was put on a tough-love rehabilitation program. It was one of the signal achievements of the Communist Revolution: to eliminate, virtually overnight, the scourge of opium addiction in a country where one quarter of the male population used the drug habitually. Many in the Guan family were educated, so the Communists ordered them to become teachers because the need was so great. Fewer than one in ten Chinese could read.

Little Guan's mother was one of the most beautiful women in the county, with the lithe waist and pearly white skin favored by the Chinese. At five-foot-six, she was tall for a Chinese woman. (Little Guan would top out at five feet.) Raised on imported milk powder, well educated, and accustomed to being spoiled, she did not look kindly on other females, including her daughter—a common attitude in a culture where the idea of imperial concubines vying with one another for the emperor's favors was a model for women's relationships. Since a woman's sense of importance was linked to giving birth to males, the arrival of Little Guan did nothing to enhance her mother's position. It just added another mouth to feed.

By contrast, Little Guan's father, uncle, and particularly her grandfather adored her. She spent the first years of her life raised by her uncle and grandparents in Hai'an while her parents lived in exile.

Her grandfather treated Little Guan like a boy and spoiled her, just as families spoiled their boys. This wasn't all that uncommon. Routinely, families would sublimate the longing for a male heir by raising a daughter in ways reserved for boys. Around the house, she was called "young master." Her grandfather took responsibility for washing Little Guan, wiping her after she went to the bathroom and pulling her thick black hair into pigtails. He allowed her to sit at the men's table during the Spring Festival banquet, and he encouraged her to recite to guests stories from *The Romance of the Three Kingdoms*—a fourteenth-century set of tales of heroic derring-do. This was a skill that would serve Little Guan well later in life, when she was a teenager and had no money. In exchange for retelling one of these ancient tales to a boat crew, she earned free passage to and from home. As an adult, she grew into a fine public speaker. Her one weakness, she felt, was that her upbringing as dictated by her grandfather did not teach her how to *pai mapi* (pat the horse's butt), the Chinese idiom for kissing ass.

In 1958, when Little Guan was three, her mother gave birth to a boy named Yonglong (Eternal Dragon), bringing to an end Little Guan's fairy-tale upbringing. Overnight, she was relegated to the family also-ran as her parents and grandparents focused their resources on the boy. What's worse, they openly predicted that Little Guan, who had contracted small-pox in 1956 and was constantly ill with colds and fevers, would fall prey to an early death.

In the spring of 1960, as the Great Leap Forward was ravaging China, Yonglong, then two, contracted bacterial meningitis, which his grandparents mistook for a common cold. One afternoon they tried feeding him fish—a rare treat which the Chinese believed had medicinal properties. Little Guan remembers watching her brother as he lay motionless on a wooden plank, his tongue feebly licking his parched lips. The grandparents took him to the hospital, where he died.

Little Guan's grandfather sent a messenger to her parents' village. The letter intimated that it was Little Guan who had died, not her younger brother. Her grandfather figured this would cushion the blow.

The next night, Little Guan's parents arrived at Hai'an. According to Chinese custom, if a death occurs away from the home, the coffin should be placed outside. Her parents entered the family's courtyard and saw the casket. Recognizing that it was too small to hold their daughter, they collapsed in tears. Little Guan had climbed out of bed to greet her parents, but when she heard them crying at the discovery that it was not she who had died but her brother, she scurried back under her covers and wept.

In 1962, Little Guan was forcibly moved to White Pasture Commune to join her parents. The commune was accessible only by river from Hai'an, forty miles away. Since 1949, the central government had instituted a rigid system of internal controls that used domestic passports to prevent anyone from leaving the area where they were assigned to live. With their move to White Pasture Commune, the Guan family permit had been switched from a coveted urban permit to a rural one, the equivalent of a life sentence to a hardscrabble backwater existence. The family of five— Little Guan's mother had subsequently given birth to two more daughters—spent the first two years living in a room attached to the mud-walled schoolhouse where the father taught.

When they were finally given permission to build their own house, it was a three-room brick structure with a kitchen in the back and a pit for a toilet. The family raised pigs and grew vegetables, chrysanthemums, a peach tree, and grapes.

Despite his *bad class background,* the clunky Chinese term used to describe his spotty political history, Little Guan's father managed to finesse the system for a while. He arranged to get the county government to supply his village with electricity so he could power his radio and record player—two luxuries he had lugged with him after being banished from Hai'an. During the Cultural Revolution, Red Guards confiscated his LPs and used them as spittoon lids—a fitting end for what the Red Guards called "the music of the stinking bourgeoisie." The Guans would eventually lose the radio and record player, again to the Red Guard.

Life was particularly hard for Little Guan's mother, who had seen her status collapse in less than a decade from the flower of the county to the wife of a rightist exiled to the boondocks. She blamed Little Guan for her misfortunes: losing a son, the decimation of her reputation, and even the wayward policies that were ravaging the country and its people. "In the last life, I owed you something and now you have come back to demand repayment," she told the girl.

The Guans were easy targets. They were educated and relatively sophisticated. Little Guan stood out in the village for her clean clothes and the bows in her hair. Her classmates looked up to her for her citified ways. By fourth grade, she was class president. But the advent of the Cultural Revolution gave them license to despise her.

For months after Little Guan's bathroom incident, her father was confined to a village school that had been converted to a camp for political prisoners. Sometimes he would be allowed to return home; sometimes weeks would pass between visits. Though it was his "feudal ways" that earned him punishment, it was, paradoxically, his feudal talents that spared him from worse torment. When Guan's jailers discovered that he could paint Mao portraits and write in well-formed characters, he was put to work churning out revolutionary posters. He was not beaten. When other "bad eggs" like himself were wheeled out for "struggle meetings" or forced to march through the commune, heavy wood planks that read "counterrevolutionary" dangling from their necks, Guan instead wore a placard of lightweight cardboard. Guan let his experience be a lesson for his daughter. "You never know when your skills will come in handy," he told her.

Pilloried as a class enemy at age eleven, Little Guan began carrying a bucket of stones to class. If villagers or students attacked or insulted her, she would pelt them. Nonetheless, she returned home each day with fresh bruises from pummellings by the classmates she once led.

Little Guan's humiliation grew so unrelenting that she refused to go to school. Commune leaders then ordered her to work in the fields of White Pasture Commune—even then a harsh punishment for a child. "Class enemies like you don't deserve an education," one of the leaders of the Revolutionary Committee barked at her. Dispatched to pick cotton and spread chemicals and fertilizer, she was regularly burned by the insecticide that leaked from the tank strapped to her back.

In August 1966, Little Guan's mother discovered that she was pregnant again. A doctor of herbal medicine examined her tongue, felt her pulse, and pronounced it was a boy. Here was her chance to replace the son she had lost, to fulfill her responsibilities as a wife and deliver a male to help her with the backbreaking work of feeding her family. But with her husband incarcerated in the reeducation camp and three mouths to feed, Little Guan's mother decided to travel to Hai'an to have an abortion and undergo sterilization. She left Little Guan in charge of her five-year-old and three-year-old sisters for two weeks.

One night as the three girls slept together, a long, fat snake plopped from the rafters of their cottage onto Little Guan's stomach. "In the moonlight, I saw a snake coiled up as big as a washbasin," Little Guan wrote in an essay years later. One sister was awakened by the sound and wanted to turn on the light, but Little Guan shushed her. "I lay there quietly as the snake, as thick as a bottle, slithered by my pillow, up the wall and out of sight."

Little Guan had stayed calm in the face of danger, neither screaming nor crying. The experience marked a watershed for her. As the world that she knew continued to implode around her, her thoughts would often return to her triumph over the snake. In every other aspect of her life, Little Guan saw defeat and maltreatment: at school, at home, and in the fields. Her victory over nature gave her courage and hope.

A few months later, in the winter of 1966, Guan's father was dispatched to a May 7 Cadre School, a prison camp near Hai'an named after the day that Mao called for the establishment of institutions devoted to cleansing deviant political ideas through hard labor. Except for short visits home, he would spend the next four years there. As the eldest child in a house with no male breadwinner, Little Guan was under even more pressure to work harder and longer in the fields.

In September 1968, almost two years after removing herself from school, Little Guan was ordered to return. At first she was overjoyed, especially at the prospect of finding something new to read. Red Guards had ransacked her family's house shortly after her father's incarceration and carted away their books. The only book that had survived was a collection of one-thousand-year-old poems from the Tang and Song dynasties that her father had hidden inside the book jacket of a volume called *Mao's Works*.

Arriving at the schoolhouse, she realized she'd been led into a trap. The teachers and children had gathered in the dirt school grounds for a struggle session. That day's target was none other than her father—their former principal. "You will take the lead," an official from the commune's Revolutionary Committee commanded Little Guan. "Do you have anything to say?"

Little Guan stood still for a moment but quickly realized what was expected of her. In the faintest of voices she said: "Down with Guan Huailiang. Down with the reactionary Guan Huailiang. I am his daughter, Guan Yongxing."

"Louder," the official commanded.

"I hereby renounce my father. From now on I will not use his last name. I reject him as my father. I will take the name Chen Haijing."

"Louder!" the students screamed.

"I reject Guan Huailiang as my father! Down with Guan Huailiang!"

As Little Guan chanted, she understood, if only vaguely, that she was violating not only the love she had for her dad but also a central tenet of her upbringing: reverence for her elders and ancestors. Her classmates chimed in, "Down with Guan Huailiang! Down with Guan Huailiang!" With their fists pumping the air and their red kerchiefs flapping, they jumped with excitement. Little Guan wept. The official ordered the children back into the classroom and Little Guan took a seat by a window. As she looked out, she could see an older student approach the schoolhouse, whip out a knife, and carve into a wooden beam, "Reactionary Little Guan." Little Guan's classmates watched and giggled. She burst out of the classroom. "Son of a dog," she yelled, "what are you doing?

"Hit me," Little Guan screamed, striding toward the boy. "Go ahead, hit me! If you can't even hit me, you're not even as good as the sperm of a pig! You were raised by dogs!" The look on the boy's face passed from leering pleasure to panic and fear as he stared at his tiny adversary. Everyone came out of the classroom to watch. He ran off.

A few weeks later, just as school was letting out, a crowd gathered on the dirt road that ran in front of the schoolhouse. As Little Guan hurried to see what was going on, someone shoved her from behind, and she crumpled on the ground. "Reactionary!" the person yelled at her. A pain shot up her left arm so powerful that she almost fainted.

Little Guan staggered to the village clinic. The doctor refused to treat her, since she was the daughter of a man with political problems. But the hospital chief helped a bit, slathering her arm with red balm and binding it in a primitive sling of dirty gauze. Little Guan returned home. Her mother yelled at her: "How could you hurt yourself when we need you to do work around here?" One week later, she still could not lift her left arm. Even as she slept fitfully because of the pain, she continued to work in the fields. Fearing more beatings, Little Guan again quit school and, at least to her mother, stopped speaking about the pain.

Four months passed. Little Guan's father was allowed to return home for Chinese New Year celebrations, the first holiday he'd spent with his family in more than two years. Seeing his daughter's injury, he took her to a hospital, where he found a doctor willing to treat the daughter of a "class enemy." The news was not good. The elbow had been dislocated. Because Little Guan had not had it set, it had begun to calcify. The choice was either to break the arm and reset it, or to leave it as it was, hanging limp by the girl's side. The doctor explained that breaking and resetting the arm would be very painful and might not work. Little Guan's father decided to do nothing.

Little Guan and I sat in her apartment as she told me this. It was our first of more than a dozen conversations. Night was falling. We'd talked away the afternoon and hadn't switched on the lights. Outside the traffic was reaching a rush-hour crescendo—buses, trucks, and taxis honking at once. In the looming darkness, Little Guan unsheathed her arm from the sleeve of a blue silk vest. To this day it remains crooked, a broken wing. She still can't lift heavy objects, and it bothers her when the weather changes. She looked at it and patted it with her other hand: "It helps me to remember."

4

FATHER'S LESSONS

Trouble spread like a fever throughout that hot China summer of 1966. In early August, the weather in Nanjing was particularly stifling, which is saying something for a city known as one of China's furnaces. Muggy, one-hundred-degree summer air enveloped the city, locked in by hills to the south and east. The Yangtze offered no relief, its lazy brown flow moving turbidly to the Pacific, three hundred miles downstream.

At dusk on August 3, a group of students and teachers from Nanjing Normal University descended on the home of Wu Tianshi and Li Jingyi and forced them out to the street. The couple, both prominent educators in Jiangsu Province, had been dining in pajamas and flip-flops because of the heat. None of their seven children, including their youngest son, my classmate, Wu Xiaoqing, then fifteen, was at home to witness what followed.

Nanjing Normal University is the city's second-ranking university, just down the street from Nanda. Founded by American missionaries in the early twentieth century as Jinling Women's University at about the same time that American donations were building Nanda, Nanjing Normal's curriculum focused on educating young Chinese to become teachers.

After clapping the couple's heads into wooden yokes, the students frog-marched them several blocks to the Nanjing Normal campus. Along the way, the attackers jostled and hurled abuse. Wu Tianshi's arm was broken. In a field at the center of the campus, they were trundled up onto a makeshift stage, joining several other university officials and teachers who were also bent under the weight of their own yokes. Somebody on the stage barked, "The meeting to struggle the members of the black gang will begin." The students took turns smearing their captives with ink and then beating them with whatever was handy. Someone slammed a garbage can on Li Jingyi's head. Barely conscious, the couple was then bullied off the stage and paraded through the nighttime Nanjing streets.

Somewhere along the way, both fainted from pain and exhaustion. Their captors then dragged the two across the ragged pavement, tearing the flesh from their legs. Li Jingyi, fifty-three, died on the street, her neck broken by the yoke. Several students peeled off from the group and dumped her corpse back where the ordeal had begun a few hours earlier, at her home. They weren't finished with Wu Tianshi.

The gang returned him to the stage, which faced a hall where Wu had lectured on classical Chinese literature and education. Lashing him to a chair, they broke his back. The students punched him, puncturing his bladder. When he fell off the chair, they jumped on him and fractured both of his legs. Throughout, Wu insisted that he had never opposed socialism or the Communist Party. "What kind of person are you?" his captors fired back at him. "I am Chinese," he replied, prompting them to intensify the torture. Two days later, he died in the hospital; he was fifty-six. His autopsy report lists six broken bones, a brain hemorrhage, and massive trauma to his internal organs.

The deaths of Wu Tianshi and Li Jingyi marked the first murders of the Cultural Revolution in Nanjing. One thousand miles away, on that same day, another band of students and teachers beat to death the vice principal of a Beijing high school, the first killing in the capital. At dawn two weeks later, before a crowd of a million, the thug who had led the Beijing killing was granted a public audience with Chairman Mao on the terrace above Tiananmen Square, the same spot where Mao had declared to the world the success of his revolution on October 1, 1949. "From the Red East there rises a sun," the crowd in Tiananmen serenaded the Communist leader, "from China there appears a Mao Zedong." Over the course of the next few months, Mao would preside over similar rallies in Tiananmen Square in front of more than eleven million Red Guards.

At Nanjing Normal, the Red Guard gang that killed Wu Xiaoqing's parents named themselves the 8-3 Rebel Division, for August 3, the date of the murders, and erected a statue of Mao, precisely 8.3 meters tall, to mark the spot where Wu Tianshi had been killed.

At Nanda, I knew Wu Xiaoqing as Old Wu. His nickname made sense because even at university, he seemed more careworn than the rest. Old Wu told me about his life over numerous meals and meetings in Nanjing. Our classmates knew his story in its broadest outlines, but few, if any, knew the details. The Chinese don't like to dwell on their tragedies, especially those involving state-sanctioned murder and state-enforced dishonorable behavior. One classmate, a close confidant of Old Wu's, admitted to never having heard the story. "It'd be too hard to take," he said.

Each time Wu and I met, he'd recount more of the tale of his parents' deaths with a deadpan delivery, so matter-of-fact it seemed that he was speaking about someone else's family, not his own. For me, his seeming indifference, even after four decades, was incomprehensible. It differed so much from Little Guan's true grit and Zhou Lianchun's in-your-face honesty that it made me wonder whether the Chinese system had robbed Old Wu of his capacity to express or even feel hurt.

At the time of his parents' death, Old Wu was living in a place called Waterfield village, about fifteen miles from Nanjing. He had gone to the countryside for the summer, responding to the revolutionary call, issued by Mao himself, that urged urban youth to learn from the peasants. On August 10, a week after the killings. Old Wu and his classmates had just finished irrigating rice paddies by pedaling a waterwheel when one of his classmates spotted two friends cycling past. His classmate waved them down, and together they returned to the warehouse where Old Wu and the others had been staying.

Wu's classmate asked them how the Cultural Revolution was proceeding in town. "Great!" one of the teenagers gushed. "Now the old revolutionaries are facing new problems! We've been told to eat up, skip classes, and change the world!

"Some groups of university students have denounced enemies of the revolution," he enthused, "slapping dunce caps on their heads and parading them through the streets. A few days ago students from Nanjing Normal University beat up this guy, the head of the province's educational department, and his wife. And guess what? They died!"

And so Old Wu learned his parents had been murdered—from two boys raving about it a week after his parents' bodies had been cremated. Old Wu stayed silent, his mind blank. He didn't cry; he sat there stunned. His classmate pulled the two boys outside and told them who Old Wu was. The two boys came back into the warehouse and approached Old Wu. "Friend," one of them murmured, his tone softened markedly from the holy-cow gusto of a few minutes ago. "For sure, your mother is dead. Your father was sent to the hospital so we don't know. We just heard rumors. You'd better go home."

Old Wu had known his father was in trouble, but he could not imagine that both his parents would be killed. Old Wu's father was one of the senior Communist Party stalwarts in Nanjing, having joined the party in the 1940s as a leading educator. In a sign of Wu Tianshi and Li Jingyi's hopes for their new country, they had named Old Wu, their youngest son, born in 1951, Xiaoqing (Sunny Dawn) for the dawn of a Communist China.

By 1960, Wu's father had become chief of Jiangsu Province's education department, a high-level post. Old Wu's mother, Li Jingyi, had also risen within the party to become the deputy secretary of the party branch at Nanjing Normal University. In 1961, during a period of relative thaw following the end of the Great Leap Forward, Wu's father published an essay that praised the industriousness of ancient scholars and put him on a collision course with ultraleftist Maoists. In an internal party document a few years later, the Maoists argued that by looking kindly on ancient scholars, Wu Tianshi had betrayed his proletarian and peasant masters. For this he was labeled a "representative of the feudal-capitalist educational line"—a meaningless phrase but one with deadly consequences.

For a while, party criticism of his father was kept private. The family continued to live in their spacious quarters—a two-story house with parquet floors, a fireplace, and indoor plumbing that before the 1949 revolution had been the home of a Nationalist government official. But as word circulated that he was under a cloud of suspicion, Wu's father holed up at home to avoid potential assailants or uncomfortable confrontations with his colleagues. He rarely left his room on the second floor of his home and would venture outside only to get an occasional haircut. He stopped going out to fill the prescription for sleeping pills he used to quell his bothersome insomnia, dispatching Old Wu to the hospital instead. Doctors there gave Old Wu fewer and fewer pills out of concern that his dad would kill himself.

Born in the early years of the twentieth century when the Qing Dynasty was collapsing, Old Wu's father believed that communism offered the brightest future for China. His faith in the party and above all his faith in Chairman Mao were unshakable. He was, therefore, certain that he would escape punishment and that the party would determine that he was, indeed, loyal to its creed. An old party comrade would call Wu Tianshi daily to bolster his spirits. Old Wu and his brother would often eavesdrop on their conversation from a downstairs line. "You have to stand up to it," his father's friend would urge. "We've stood up to worse purges before, right?" Within a year, the friend would be murdered, too.

By May 1966, Chinese newspapers had begun publishing the names of officials whom the party apparatus had formally criticized. Wu Tianshi's name appeared in an article in the July 14 issue of Jiangsu Province's *New China Daily*. The article was his death sentence. The next day posters with large Chinese characters went up on the walls near Nanjing's universities criticizing Wu Tianshi by name. Old Wu came home from school and was told by his mother that he and the rest of the children would have to denounce their dad publicly as well. So that night, with their father upstairs in his room brooding, Wu and an elder brother spread large sheets of white paper on the dining room table, took out their father's calligraphy brush and ink, and scrawled in giant characters, "Down with the Feudal Capitalist Education Line of Department Chief Wu." Old Wu took charge of the calligraphy because his characters were more muscular than his brother's.

While the boys worked on the posters, Li Jingyi hovered nearby to ensure that her sons' wording was sufficiently harsh. "Call him a black hand," she urged them under her breath so her husband would not hear. If the posters didn't pass muster, she'd be doubly vulnerable—for abetting her husband's crimes against the revolution and for the added offense of using parental bonds to dilute the revolutionary fervor of her children.

For Old Wu and millions like him, self-protection demanded that he denounce his own kin. To this day, he seems serene when he says he does not feel guilty for what he did. Justifying his actions with a shrug, he explained, "That is what everybody did at the time to get along." He paused, then ended the discussion with the catch-all Chinese idiom used to rationalize even the gravest of errors. "*Mei banfa,*" there was "no way out."

Upon hearing that his parents were dead, Old Wu left Waterfield village for Nanjing. His elder sister met him at the door to their home. He could tell by her red eyes that their parents were gone. "Is it true?" he asked. She nodded. Old Wu felt what he described as "a heartrending sense of pain, an inconsolable grief." After he washed his face, his sister told him what had happened without going into details. She did, however, instruct him about how to respond to questions about the deaths.

"Just say your mother died of high blood pressure and your father of chronic hepatitis," she commanded. Acknowledging that Red Guard units had killed their parents would put the children on the wrong side of the revolution and would open them up to further persecution. Two of Wu's brothers had returned home as well. No one spoke. No one cried. "It was like we were waiting for fate to arrange the next step," Old Wu said.

Red Guards commandeered the family home as their headquarters, kicking the children out onto the streets. Old Wu and two older siblings kept on the move, staying in different hovels across Nanjing. One of his elder sisters took on the mantle of both mother and father. The children scavenged for food. Old Wu, the youngest of seven, ached for his parents, especially his dad, and would often recall an afternoon he had spent as a young boy with his father. His father had taken Old Wu on his rounds, visiting poor schools. Old Wu watched the ease with which his father interacted with the peasant teachers and their peasant pupils. Though highly educated, his father did not put on airs. "He loved them," Old Wu said. "He really loved his country."

Old Wu was always a quiet boy; in high school he didn't like public speaking. His father's death magnified his reserve and saddled him with an inferiority complex that has lasted to this day. "Never again would I seek to make a spectacle of myself," he told me. "I was the spawn of a black hand then, and in a way I've felt like one ever since."

In December 1968, Mao issued the directive ordering educated urban youth permanently to the countryside for "reeducation" by China's peasants. The Red Guard was forcibly disbanded. In all, 18 million young city dwellers would be "sent down" to the countryside to live with the rural poor with no idea when or if they would be allowed to return home. They became known as the "sent-down" generation. Old Wu's brothers and sisters were scattered to different parts of the country.

For the next four years, Old Wu lived in a village 150 miles north of Nanjing, sharing a shack with two other "sent-down" teenagers from the city. The trio lived off the food they grew and the meat of stolen dogs, the pelts of which they bartered for pork. In 1969, border clashes erupted between Chinese and Soviet forces along the banks of the Amur River. Chairman Mao instructed his people to prepare for World War III. Old

Wu fantasized about a giant conflagration. "Chaos would have given me a way out of my life," he reasoned. He shared this fantasy with friends. Someone reported him to the production brigade, and Old Wu was harshly criticized. After that, he was even quieter than before.

In September 1971, Mao's annointed successor Lin Biao disappeared. The circumstances surrounding Lin's death remain clouded to this day but the Chinese government holds that Lin had planned to assassinate Mao, that the plot was unearthed and that Lin died in a plane crash in Mongolia while fleeing to the Soviet Union. Lin's removal allowed for the return—for several years—of less radical officials and for the posthumous rehabilitation in 1972 of some victims of Red Guard violence. Old Wu's father was one.

His father's rehabilitation allowed Old Wu to escape from the miserable farming village in which he was living and enlist in the People's Liberation Army, a plum opportunity that offered shelter from the tempest of the Cultural Revolution. With his fears of World War III, the military was one sector of society that Mao dared not destroy. Old Wu eagerly exchanged the grinding poverty of the countryside for the unrelenting boredom of the army. Three years later, in 1975, Wu was invited to join the Communist Party, and he leaped at the chance—again because it would improve his life. There was a condition: Wu would be accepted, the army told him, only if he had a "correct" understanding of why his parents died. Following his elder sister's advice, Wu wrote in his application that his father had died of chronic hepatitis and his mother of high blood pressure, and he added the requisite denouncement.

"My parents made mistakes, and you must criticize mistakes," he wrote. "They refused to transform their worldview. They carried out a revisionist line that hurt the people and the party. This criticism was totally necessary and very timely. We understood the revolutionary masses hated revisionists, so the result was completely understood and we can't criticize it."

He ended: "The Cultural Revolution is great!"

Old Wu's application for party membership was approved. He felt no remorse for joining an organization responsible for his parents' murder. "I know I wrote lies. They made me write lies," he rationalized. "But a party membership helped improve my life." Old Wu had learned a pragmatic lesson from his father's tragic life. On the stage at Nanjing Normal, Wu Tianshi had stood up for his principles, insisting that he was a good Communist, and got it in the neck. In the People's Republic of China, Old Wu concluded, principles didn't matter. Survival was the key.

5

BLACK BRICKS

Old Wu's Faustian bargain with the party was one way to deal with the vagaries of life in China. Zhou Lianchun had another. In 1968, Chinese army troops, mirroring a nationwide trend, swept into Zhou's hometown of Dongtai and the Shen Kitchen Commune to quell the chaos and factional fighting between competing Red Guard units. With a certain level of order restored, the soldiers returned to barracks and the mayhem of the Cultural Revolution abated. A year later, schools in Zhou's commune reopened after a five-year hiatus. During this long break from the classroom, during which he had tormented his neighbors, relatives, friends, and teachers, Zhou had done no studying—no math, no science, no grammar, no history. The only thing he had done, other than working the fields and "making revolution," was read—furtively.

At fourteen, Zhou returned to school. Even by rural standards, it was bleak. The schoolhouse had mud floors; students who didn't bring their own stools had to stand. The curriculum was a patchwork of the pedagogical and the ideological. In Communist China's early years, following the Soviet Union's example, the emphasis was on hard science. When the Cultural Revolution started, schools were shuttered and the Soviet focus on science was pilloried. When they reopened in 1969, schools were ordered to stick closely to functional subjects in tune with the masses, which meant subsistence farming. Math consisted of figuring how much cotton could be harvested on a one-acre plot; physics, of studying tractors, electric motors, and water pumps. Zhou's chemistry course involved a daylong trek to a brewery. No one studied English or other foreign languages.

Zhou graduated from high school a year later. Lacking any connections to continue his education (entrance to vocational school, like university, was limited to students recommended by party apparatchiks), he was put to work in the fields. Each winter and spring from 1970 until 1976, Zhou and the other men in his village performed forced labor for the state just as peasants had done for centuries. The work consisted of dredging riverbeds and repairing the commune's irrigation system. In the summer, Zhou worked in bare feet. In the winter, he wore straw shoes. The ice on the San Cang riverbed pierced the straw and slashed his feet.

During the spring, the men dug irrigation ditches. Zhou rose each morning at 4 a.m. and joined a line of men carrying lanterns, the lights undulating like a dragon into the distance. They dug until 7 a.m., broke for a spartan breakfast, labored until noon, had a bowl of cold rice porridge and preserved vegetables, then worked straight until 9 p.m. Staggering home each night, Zhou felt like a walking corpse. Men on his work team (and they were all men, since the women were responsible for cultivating crops) frequently had to be carried away after collapsing from exhaustion and malnourishment. Twenty-five years after the revolution that was ostensibly waged to free them from abject poverty, peasants like Zhou still toiled as the menial servants of distant, cruel masters.

Zhou's diet consisted mainly of corn, carrots, and sweet potatoes, never meat. To this day, he becomes nauseous at a mere whiff of those vegetables. When there was enough food, the workers' only pleasure was to make bets over who could eat the fastest or consume the most. One of them gobbled two pounds of pig fat in five minutes.

Though still in his teens, Zhou had a good reputation as a laborer and could keep up with the men in his work brigade. But he wanted to stop digging ditches. To do so, he needed someone with influence in the party.

One day in the fall of 1972, the party chief approached Zhou with a proposition. He wanted to introduce him to a young woman. Party secretaries often played the role of matchmaker. Besides, Zhou, who was now seventeen, was at the age where peasants were usually engaged.

The party secretary told Zhou that if he agreed to court the woman, he would recommend Zhou for a place at a university. If the university did not accept him, the secretary had a consolation prize. He promised to appoint Zhou to lead the brigade's Communist Party Youth League office, a position that would get Zhou out of the fields and move him a big step toward entry into the party and a better life. Either way, Zhou's life as a peasant drudge would be over. As a kicker, the secretary promised to help Zhou build a house by procuring the necessary bricks, roof tiles, and straw.

All in all, it was a remarkable deal. The only catch was the woman. Zhou wasn't told much about her. During lunch with her family, he learned that she was twenty-two, five years his senior. The house she shared with her parents was primitive even by Zhou's peasant standards. The food at lunch, while plentiful, was lousy. Zhou sensed something wasn't right. The party secretary pushed him to propose to her, showing up at Zhou's house during the winter and spring labor periods, singing her praises to Zhou until one or two in the morning. "It might have been normal to stay up so late in the big city," Zhou recalled, "but we had work to do."

The secretary recruited others to pressure Zhou. They all stressed the same thing: Zhou had a lot to gain from marrying the young woman. What did it matter if he didn't particularly know or like her? Zhou saw things differently. He loved literature and had devoured whatever novels he could find by Balzac, Tolstoy, Flaubert. He wanted the sort of romance he had read about, not a business deal brokered by a party boss. He wanted out of the fields, but unlike Old Wu, Zhou was not inclined to accept a deal with the devil to get there. Over the next year, to appease the party secretary, Zhou met with the woman a few more times, but had little to say to her. Though he had never kissed a girl, he recognized that there was no spark. Zhou made sure to bring along a chaperone each time he visited because he did not want to find himself accused of stealing a kiss. Such a charge, by itself, would have precipitated a shotgun wedding.

Zhou couldn't help noticing that even though the woman's house was a dump, her family never seemed to lack for food, especially rice and meat, both of which were rationed. One day he was walking near her house when he bumped into a worker from the party secretary's office. Zhou struck up a conversation with the man, who told Zhou that he had just delivered rice to her home. "The party secretary can't do this himself," the man whispered, "because then everyone will know."

"Know what?" Zhou asked.

The man smiled.

Zhou pieced together the story. The woman and the party chief were lovers. In exchange for sex, he had arranged a job for her at a small factory in the commune and guaranteed her family a steady supply of food to supplement their rations. The party secretary was already married, of course, and so had promised to find her a husband to help cover up his infidelity. Having chanced upon Zhou, a boy angling for a way off the farm, he thought he'd made a match.

Zhou told the chief he would not marry the woman. The chief was enraged. "Little Zhou," he said, wagging his finger at the boy, "you've been reading too much and you've forgotten how to be decisive. You should know when to act, but you've become a book idiot"—the Chinese term for a bookworm.

The "book idiot" nickname stuck, just as Zhou was stuck with hard labor. Many of his old high school classmates had succeeded in leaving behind grunt work to become teachers or commune administrators. With their elevated social standing and new clothes, they ignored their erstwhile buddy as they rode their new bicycles past him on the village's rutted paths. On the surface, China was a classless society that glorified physical labor and preached an egalitarian creed of solidarity. In reality, the "narcissism of small differences" suborned any Maoist idealism; the petty distinctions between an impoverished peasant and a destitute country schoolteacher were large and telling. Schoolteachers had status. Peasants had none.

Zhou made one more stab at getting off the labor crew by volunteering for the People's Liberation Army. He needed the party secretary's consent, which was not forthcoming. The only option left was to accept fate and put down roots. Zhou applied for aid to build a house, but again the secretary cut him off, denying him the normal allotment of bricks and roof tiles. Without the secretary's help, Zhou had to collect the materials by himself.

The coast of the Yellow Sea at Dongtai, winter home to many of the world's red-crowned cranes, is not famed for its dramatic scenery. Hundreds of miles of mudflats and maritime grasslands extend into the misty distance. Fishing villages nestle along the banks of brackish waterways, rich in crabs, shrimp, and clams. In winter, the wind, laced with salt from the sea, whips through the marshes.

Zhou spent the winter of 1976 along the coast, living in a tent with Big Mama and a hired hand, harvesting grass to trade for bricks and roof tiles. Zhou and Big Mama studiously avoided any discussion of the Red Guard criticism sessions of the past. They just scythed grass.

By the end of the winter, Zhou had amassed more than seven tons of grass, enough to swap for the ten thousand bricks and three thousand tiles he needed to construct his home. But his labor was not over; he had to transport the harvest to the brick kilns. Zhou rented a flat-bottom boat and filled it with bales of grass. He then harnessed himself and two day laborers to the craft. Like mules, they hauled the boat up a skinny, eight-mile towpath, inching forward under the weight of their load. It took five trips to deliver all of the grass. At the end of that winter, Zhou's face, whipped raw by the winter wind and shrouded in a full beard, seemed to have aged decades. One villager, in a mistaken gesture of respect, called him "Granddad." At twenty-one, Book Idiot Zhou looked fifty.

Zhou took four months to build his house and it was the best in the village, fashioned from high-quality black bricks and wooden beams he cut himself. His attempts to better himself by getting out of the fields had been thwarted, yet he was plainly not content to live as other peasants did. He used cement instead of mud for mortar and laid down a brick floor, refusing to walk on dirt like others in his village. For years, Zhou's handiwork stood as a silent rebuke to the party secretary who lived two doors down in a house made from cheaper red bricks.

That same winter, as Zhou was harvesting grass in the Jiangsu marshes, a political storm was brewing in Beijing. On January 8, 1976, China's longtime prime minister, Zhou Enlai, passed away.

Zhou Enlai was Mao's right-hand man, revered as a Communist saint for his wisdom, culture, and restraint. Though he was celebrated for having saved a few senior leaders and their children during the Cultural Revolution, in truth, Zhou's moderating effect on Mao's worst instincts was exaggerated and his deification undeserved. Nonetheless, because Zhou's death allowed for public expressions of bereavement, it gave average

Chinese the pretext they needed to express a desire for political change and an end to Maoist tyranny.

The Chinese commemorate the dead on Qing Ming, the third day of the third lunar month. Young and old pray to their ancestors, sweep their graves, and offer plates of food and pyramids of fruit to the ghosts of the dead. In 1976 Qing Ming fell on April 2. A few days before the festival, students from Nanda broke into the school's maintenance shop, stole a barrel of tar, and headed for Nanjing's central train station, where they painted train carriages with slogans mourning Zhou Enlai's passing and mocking Mao's wife, Jiang Qing, an aging, former B-movie actress from Shanghai, who had been caught on state-run television smiling during the memorial service.

By the time the graffitied train carriages rolled into the capital, hundreds of thousands of people had heard the news, word spread by what the Chinese called the *xiaodao xiaoxi* (news from the alley), in other words, the grapevine. People laid wreaths at the Monument to the Revolutionary Heroes, a 120-foot-tall granite obelisk, in the center of Tiananmen Square.

By April 4, up to half a million ordinary citizens had flocked to Tiananmen Square to honor Zhou Enlai and, more obliquely, to release a deep reservoir of anti-Communist feeling. Never before during Mao's rule had a protest of this magnitude occurred, and it was happening in central Beijing at the physical nexus of Communist power. Mao's henchmen swung into action. Armed with clubs and tools, the goons were dispatched to the square to forcibly remove the demonstrators. Hundreds were beaten to death.

Mao moved quickly following the crackdown, again purging his old comrade, Deng Xiaoping, labeling him a "capitalist roader." Back in Shen Kitchen Commune, Deng's fall was good news for Book Idiot Zhou. The commune announced that it would hold study sessions to attack Deng. The party secretary gave Zhou a two-week reprieve from agricultural labor and sent him to the commune's headquarters to study "anti-Deng theory."

Zhou used the break to hobnob with commune officials, who revealed they were planning to open a school for each of the commune's twenty-eight production brigades. They needed teachers. The test to become a teacher consisted of reading aloud from a newspaper. Zhou passed and was given a job in a newly opened high school. Zhou still had to fulfill his quota of farmwork for the commune, but, after many dark and wasted years, his prospects were brightening. He had his own house, and his job as a teacher put him, for the first time, into the cash economy, earning currency rather than commune credits and ration tickets. True, there wasn't much to buy with the money, but having a salary put him a big step above his fellow peasants.

On September 9, 1976, Chairman Mao died. Amid unprecedented national mourning, Mao's handpicked successor, Hua Guofeng, was convinced by powerful elements in the military to arrest Mao's widow and the rest of the "Gang of Four," including Shanghai party leaders Zhang Chunqiao, Yao Wenyuan, and Wang Hongwen. Within a year, Deng Xiaoping, twice-purged, had been rehabilitated. By 1978, he had outmaneuvered Hua to take the reins of power, though Deng knew enough not to assume the title of party chairman. Deng formally took a secondary position, as a vice premier, but he was, and would remain for twenty years, China's paramount leader.

In October 1977, the Shen Kitchen Commune's loudspeakers crackled with a report from the capital: at a meeting on education it was decided that university entrance examinations, which had been suspended since 1966, would be reinstated. The party also moved to get educated Chinese out of jail or internal exile and back to work. The party was trying to make up for its excesses. Starting in 1978, it gave jobs, houses, and pensions to 2.7 million victims of its political campaigns. Like Old Wu's parents, tens of thousands of murdered officials were rehabilitated posthumously as well.

Zhou was determined to pass the college entrance exam, though he knew it would be far more difficult than the quiz he had taken to become a teacher. He spent the next two months filling in the huge gaps in an education that had stopped at the end of sixth grade. In early December 1977, Zhou took the exam, which covered Chinese, history, geography, and mathematics. There was a foreign-language section that did not count toward the total score. Though he did well in most subjects, he scored only 5 out of 100 in math and failed.

Zhou decided he'd given it his best shot, and did not want to take the test again in July 1978. Years of losing out to politically connected children and run-ins with the party secretary had hardened him into a fatalistic young man without illusions or self-confidence.

Big Mama was eager to exploit this moment to marry off Zhou. She arranged an introduction to a worker in one of the commune's factories. Lin Fei was pretty and, like Zhou, had scraped her way out of the fields. She arrived at their first meeting in her work clothes, simple blue cotton pants and a fading blue jacket. To Zhou, that meant she did not put on airs. Zhou, who still held fast to his ideals about romantic love, came away with a favorable impression. Though they had never held hands or spent a minute alone inside a room together, after six months Zhou and Lin Fei were engaged.

But Zhou's elder sister, who was eleven years older and had attended a teacher-training program before the Cultural Revolution, rejected her younger brother's decision to junk his dreams of bettering his life. One evening early in 1978, she came home to speak with Zhou and found him reading a translated Russian novel under the wavering light of an oil lamp. "Why aren't you studying?" she asked.

"I don't want to," Zhou replied. His sister had brought a suitcase with her. Her parents assumed she was planning to stay the night. She wasn't. Inside were her high school textbooks, all for Zhou.

"I never burned these," she informed her little brother with a smile. "And unlike your smelly books, these were saved in a safe place."

Under her watchful eye as well as the prodding of his father, Zhou began to cram again. During the day he worked the fields and taught school; at night he studied. He lost weight and his hair fell out in clumps. Several days before the test, Zhou boarded motorized transport for the first time in his life, riding a bus fifteen miles to Dongtai's tiny downtown to take the test a second time. He was twenty-three.

This time, Zhou aced it, his math score jumping up from 5 to 46. His total score was 399.5 out of 500—the highest in the commune. A mark of 330 was enough for a place in a leading university.

China's college entrance process seemed designed to maximize stress. Students applied to university and picked a major before they took the entrance exam, leaving them without the benefit of knowing their results before they submitted applications. If they applied to a top school and selected a popular major but got a middling score on the exam, they would not have a real crack at their second choice. Zhou split the difference, aiming high by applying to Nanjing University, but choosing an unpopular major, history, which had a lower minimum score. When his test result came in, he felt sure he would be admitted. But the university kept him waiting.

Zhou's acceptance letter finally arrived on October 10, 1978, giving him four days to report to school before the start of the semester. He packed a small canvas bag of clothes, including a blue Mao suit that had been washed so many times it was bleached white, and a padded cotton jacket he'd worn for five years. His parents and fiancée (he and Lin Fei had postponed their wedding until after Zhou's graduation) saw him off at the bus station. He was leaving the fields at last.

6

A MEAT PIE FROM HEAVEN

I had heard my share of Cultural Revolution stories, but when I tried to conjure images of Book Idiot Zhou's or Little Guan's lives during that time, I always seemed to fail. Their experiences were totally foreign to me. As a city kid, I knew nothing of the countryside. At sixteen, when Zhou was digging ditches and Little Guan was hiding out at home, I was smoking reefer under the Brooklyn Bridge and mooning U.S. Navy ships plying the East River.

Then, during the winter of 2002, I journeyed to China's border with North Korea to do a story on the famine that had killed at least 2 million people in the "hermit kingdom." My classmates and others of their generation had always drawn an analogy between yesterday's China and today's North Korea led by Kim Jong-il, a paranoid megalomaniac with a bad hairdo. With the help of Korean-American preachers working on the Chinese side of the frontier, I met a dozen North Korean refugees, malnourished, sickly, and scared. I will never forget one brother and sister. We found them minutes after they had sneaked over the snowy border into China. Despite the bitter cold, they were dressed in rags. My escorts drove them to a safe house, where they fed and bathed them. I walked into the room, and the pair stared straight at me and began to shake visibly.

"Are you here to eat us?" the girl asked. She was serious.

To avoid beatings and humiliation, Little Guan had spent almost two years away from school. She had continued planting rice, spreading fertilizer and insecticide, and tending her pig. In 1969, she worked 285 days in the commune's fields. While farm laborers her age were awarded 3 work points a day—equivalent to less than ten cents—Little Guan was awarded 2.8, docked 0.2 work points because of her father's political failings.

In the winter of that year, Little Guan's life took a turn for the better. One day, two sympathetic teachers, who themselves had previously been labeled "rightists," stopped by her family's compound with physics and math textbooks and a proposal for Little Guan. They understood why Little Guan was skipping school, and suggested that she continue her studies on her own, visiting the school once a month for tests. Such treatment wasn't entirely unheard of; political victims would often look out for one another.

Little Guan's test scores were the best in her school. She knew, however, that good test scores did not mean much. In order to continue on to high school, she needed a recommendation from the Revolutionary Committee. Given Little Guan's bad class background, she was not likely to get it.

Still, Little Guan kept studying. Throughout the spring and summer, she studied at night with her legs in a vat of water to protect them from the village's ravenous mosquitoes. During the day, she labored in the fields. Little Guan wasn't doing this purely for the joy of learning, but rather to pursue a lifelong goal of going to a university. When she was six and living in the county seat, a girl next door had won admission to Beijing's famed Tsinghua University, the country's best science and engineering school. Long ago, Little Guan had decided to be just like her.

Little Guan's unrelenting diligence and success in her studies was a remarkable act of will, especially considering her outcast status. She knew that under the current rules in China no one of her ilk would win a place in a university. But she was undeterred. Little Guan had seen enough change in her short life to understand that nothing was permanent.

In mid-1970 Little Guan's father came home for good after four years of "reeducation" at the May 7 Cadre School. Thousands of such camps had been established in 1967 to remold errant bureaucrats and academics through hard labor and ideological indoctrination. As he did before, Guan had managed to avoid beatings and the harshest physical labor in the prison because his calligraphy and painting skills were useful to the members of the propaganda squad. The irony of using a confirmed rightist to do their proselytizing seemed to have been lost on his tormentors.

Upon his return, Guan wasted no time lobbying his old friends to get his daughter into high school. The village had recently switched party sec-retaries and the new man, a former Red Army soldier, had no interest in his daughter's political background. He asked the teachers a simple ques-tion: "Whose test scores are the best?" And with that, Little Guan, now fifteen, was allowed to attend high school.

Six days a week she would march the three miles to and from school. When she returned home at 7 p.m., she would head to the rice fields to complete by torchlight her quota of farm work for the commune. She spent Sundays in the rice paddies, her family's vegetable patch, or muck-ing out the pigpen.

Little Guan graduated from high school in early 1973, first in her class. Even so, she was denied the reward she most sought—a place in college. The lingering stigma of her father's political problems ruled that out. She resorted to a fallback plan: teaching elementary and middle school in White Pasture Commune. Still, she needed approval from the local party committee, which had fallen under the control of the descendants of those deemed in 1949 to be "poor peasants." A meeting was called and, one by one, the peasants stood up to denounce Little Guan.

"Who wants someone with counterrevolutionary thoughts teaching our children?" asked one. "Look at her, she doesn't even look like a peasant girl," yelled another. "She's a stinking capitalist miss," hissed a third. "She's going to teach our children bad lessons. She's going to ruin my kids."

Little Guan returned to the rice paddies. Now eighteen, she was rated by her local cadres as fifth best in rice transplanting out of the sixty women on her production team. She worked so hard her nose bled. When she stuffed rags into her nostrils to stanch the flow, blood would dribble from her mouth.

Little Guan's ambition ebbed away, leaving her all but resigned to a life-time of peasant labor. She did, however, vow never to marry anyone from her commune. Marriage to a local would mean losing any hope of leaving White Pasture Commune and regaining her old residence permit in Hai'an, where she'd lived when she was a little girl. She also promised herself never to bear children. Being born into the peasantry was, for her, the worst fate imaginable.

In her free time, Little Guan began to tutor the women of the produc-tion team, teaching them how to write their names. Female illiteracy was widespread among the generation born before the 1949 revolution, particularly among women in the countryside. The same "poor peasants" who had quashed her dream of becoming a teacher were among those she tutored. In the classroom, these women took a shine to Little Guan. The "stinking capitalist miss" became "the girl who could reform her thoughts."

In September 1973, the commune needed to fill the post of chief of its Women's League, a largely powerless party group charged with overseeing women's issues. Little Guan, as one of the few with even a modest education, was considered a top prospect. She was eager for the job; if she got it, she might regain her city residence permit and leave the farming life behind. One problem loomed: only a member of the Communist Party could serve as the chief of the Women's League.

Little Guan was not in the party, nor had she much hope of getting in since children of "class enemies" were not welcome. Unlike Old Wu, she didn't have people in high places lobbying on her behalf. However, one day in October 1973, the secretary of the commune's party committee came to the Guan house. He entered without knocking. The secretary, a broad-shouldered man in his forties, with rough hands and tobacco-stained teeth, found Little Guan alone in her parents' bedroom.

Putting his arm around her, he told her that he wanted to "foster" her entry into the party. Little Guan tried to move him out of her parents' bedroom, but he refused, keeping his arm around her shoulder. "We can have our heart-to-heart chat here," he said with a smile. "Right here."

Little Guan pushed him away.

He came closer; she pushed him away again.

"Don't you want to enter the party?" he said softly. "It's not nice to be unfriendly."

Little Guan wriggled free and stumbled into the other room. "I don't need this type of fostering," she told him. The secretary followed. He slapped on his Mao cap, looked at her sternly, and left.

Word spread quickly. By dinnertime, Little Guan's father had heard his daughter had declined an offer to enter the party, though he had not heard why. He was furious with her for turning down this chance to better not just her own situation but also the family's. In the midst of his outburst, she silenced him.

"If you want me to become the Women's League chief, I will kill myself with sleeping pills," she screamed. Her father let the matter drop, and with it, his own hopes to leave the small village to which he'd been banished seventeen years before. To this day, Little Guan feels that fate dispatched the cadre from the committee to her house that day to remind her that she would never fit into the party's world or adapt to its ways.

Concealed behind the uniform Mao suits and unisex hair styles, sexual aggression was seething unchecked throughout Chinese society. Party officials routinely seduced girls and women who needed favors, sometimes raping them. Sleeping with the party secretary was the best, and often the only, way a city girl who was sent down to the countryside could wangle permission to return home. It was also a key route by which peasant girls—like the young woman Book Idiot Zhou's party secretary wanted him to marry—got out of the rice paddies and into factories or clerical jobs in the communes.

For years, Little Guan's father had told her that communist propaganda was wrong, that the capitalist world was not awaiting liberation by China's selfless cadres, and that the party had not constructed a workers' paradise on earth. The older she got, the more Little Guan agreed with her father's version of reality. Her commune would routinely hold propaganda meetings during which peasants would be asked to depict the horrors of life before the revolution of 1949 and how that contrasted with the current good times. Invariably, the discussions would end up taking a wrong turn, the peasants recounting tales of hunger and starvation during the Great Leap Forward when the party was very much in control. Little Guan had always been told that China before the revolution was a feudal hellhole. But her own conclusion was that the times of greatest suffering and violence came after Mao's ascendancy, not before.

Wisely, Little Guan kept her opinions to herself, leaving her able to catch a lucky break or, in the rural patois, a "meat pie from heaven." A nearby school needed a teacher. This time, the revolutionary committee, now stacked with the women whom Little Guan had tutored, had no objections.

As a teacher, Little Guan was compelled to join the Mao Zedong Thought Propaganda Team attached to her former production team. In the autumn of 1974, they were ordered to conduct a campaign against superstition; Little Guan volunteered to write an essay decrying fortune-telling. Since the revolution, the Communists had succeeded brilliantly in eradicating organized religion, but the activities of all manner of traditional fortune-tellers, feng shui geomancers, soothsayers, and healers thrived under the radar. These spiritual advisers remained central to all sorts of deeply embedded social rites, particularly in the countryside: choosing names, wedding dates, the site and positioning of a house. The party battled these beliefs, stressing their feudal and antiscientific nature, but it didn't get very far.

Little Guan decided to seek out a fortune-teller in another commune, someone who would never have heard of her. The usual price for having one's fortune told was one *mao*—less than a penny—but this oracle with a straggly beard and prominent moles, charged double. She figured she was being set up for a scam.

Little Guan entered the small hut where the withered sage held court. She was directed to a small bamboo stool. The man wore Coke-bottle glasses but could barely see. He toyed with the hairs on his chin. "You are crippled," he stated, "and you had a bad birth."

"Go on," she replied.

"You lost your brother. You're good in school." Growing uncomfortable at what she took to be his uncannily good guesses, Little Guan lied. "No, I am illiterate," she answered.

The old seer mumbled something and made a pained noise. "Don't lie to me," he snapped. "Let me give you some advice. Don't get married. You are going to college when you are twenty-three."

"I can't go to college," Little Guan cut in.

"There will be changes," the old man insisted. "It's definite."

"The man who will marry you will be to your south," he added. "And when you get a job, remember this: you will have an easy time going to the capital, but if you go someplace else, it will be tough."

The session was over. Little Guan exited the hovel with the giddy feeling that the half-blind soothsayer might be right and that the party's remonstrations against superstition and fate were wrongheaded and, worse, not consistent with being Chinese. The fortune-teller had given her renewed hope that her life might yet change in fundamental ways, something the party hadn't done in years. She returned to the propaganda team and told them she could not write the essay.

Little Guan's visit to the fortune-teller initiated her belief in one of the basic tenets of Buddhism: the overpowering role of fate in human lives. The truisms of Maoist thought were meant to explain the vagaries of life. In reality, they were the source of the twists of fortune that had caused Little Guan's father to be imprisoned and the family banished to the countryside. Fate—her own fate—became something Little Guan could worship, and something to explain why she and her family had been tormented. Little Guan came to see that her own fate and that of her country were inextricably linked.

Little Guan was walking to school one morning when the loudspeakers, which hung from trees in each village, crackled with the news that China was reinstating college entrance exams. Little Guan began to tremble uncontrollably. "All sorts of feelings welled up in my heart," she later recalled. "The hair on the back of my neck stood on end. I stood like I was dreaming. 'I am going to college,' I thought. 'The fortune-teller was right. I am going to the university.'"

The government ordered that the first entrance exam be held on December 2, 1977, just two months hence, citing an urgent need for young, smart graduates to fuel its "Four Modernizations" campaign to improve agriculture, industry, science and technology, and national defense. Little Guan's principal did what he could to stop her from preparing for the test. If Little Guan left her teaching job, it would mean that the principal's status would drop. With her, he had enough teachers to run a high school; without her, his school would revert to being a junior high. He denied her request for time off to study.

Little Guan did exactly what millions of other prospective college applicants did; she hid her intentions and studied on the sly. She wasn't just worried about her boss. There was the question of face. People would laugh at her if she failed. Also, there was the inborn Chinese reluctance to divulge one's plans for the future. Employers, colleagues, even friends, motivated by simple jealousy, routinely smashed any dreams for a better life. This is true even today. The best policy is to keep mum about any ambitions, however humble they might be.

Little Guan had moved out of her family's house and was now sharing a room with three other teachers. At 6:30 a.m. every day, the teachers gathered in the schoolyard to do exercises, following along with instructions broadcast over a crackly loudspeaker. "One, two, three, four," it squawked, "touch your toes! Prepare to fight the imperialists, Long live the Communist Party!" By 7:30 a.m., school had begun. With no time to study in the morning, Little Guan concocted a story saying her family needed her to work nights by torchlight in the fields.

Each evening she left school at 10 p.m. and walked three miles home, arriving an hour later. Her mother would have a bowl of rice with a small serving of diced greens from their vegetable patch waiting for her. The Cultural Revolution now over, her mother had softened toward her eldest daughter and was even supportive of Little Guan's ambitions. Little Guan would study until 2 a.m., sleep until 5 a.m., and then get up and walk back to school, arriving there in time for revolutionary jumping jacks.

Little Guan had no idea what to study for the entrance exam. So she guessed. She knew the test would be divided into six parts: Chinese, mathematics, geography, history, politics, and the foreign-language section, which didn't really matter. To prep for politics, Little Guan finagled dozens of copies of the *People's Daily,* the main newspaper of the Communist Party, so she could study its editorials. When the editorials contradicted one another, which happened frequently, Little Guan memorized the one that seemed more hard-line Maoist. For history, she pored over old high school textbooks, published fifteen years before because no history books had been written since then.

Little Guan still worried that someone in authority would bar her from taking the exam. A rumor circulated that test proctors would look for calluses on the hands of students to ensure that they were laborers and not "stinking intellectuals." Little Guan went to the chief of her production team and got a stamped document attesting to the fact that she had done physical labor.

The exam was given at the county seat in Hai'an. Little Guan arrived the day before and spent the night at her uncle's house. She studied until 2 a.m. Her uncle woke her at 6 a.m., gave her a thimbleful of grain alcohol to calm her nerves and two steamed buns stuffed with meat, and sent her on her way. Throughout the two-day-long test, Little Guan's desk rocked because the legs were uneven. She discovered that she'd forgotten an eraser. A monitor kindly passed her his.

Little Guan should have failed the physical examination that followed. Still susceptible to nosebleeds, she had a bad case of anemia. Her left arm was crooked and considerably weaker than her right. To this day, China does not allow anyone who is handicapped, sickly, or afflicted with a congenital disease to attend regular universities. But Little Guan charmed the doctor, who was a rightist like her father. With a pat on her shoulder, he passed her.

The next month a letter came to Little Guan's school announcing her acceptance to Nanjing University. The school cooks banged pots and woks. The principal was noticeably less pleased, even if there was no way he could stop her now.

Little Guan was the first student in her commune to be accepted by a major university. She rushed home to tell her parents. They already knew. The postman had guessed the contents of the letter and announced the news as he rode his bicycle toward her school. Arriving home, Little Guan found her father in the courtyard with an orange. He peeled it and, as a rare treat, gave her half. The next day, Little Guan brought candy to school and handed it to her students. Traditionally, Chinese dole out sweets during a wedding banquet. "This is not for marriage," Little Guan told her pupils. "It is for something even more important."

PART II

LOVERS AND COMRADES

7

BITTER LOVE

Song Liming, the Romeo of Nanda's class of 1982, lost his virginity on a hot July day to an Italian exchange student named Antonella Ceccagno. The two lovers lolled in bed in Antonella's room in Building 10 of the Foreign Students Dormitory, drunk with a relationship that both had waited months to consummate. Then came a knock on the door.

In the midafternoon shadows, they exchanged looks of horror. Antonella staggered to the door. "I get up but my legs are shaking," Antonella wrote in *Stories between Two Cultures,* a memoir of her days in China published in Italy. "They'll be able to read it on my face that we were doing the most forbidden thing. They'll put him in jail. My Chinese roommate probably told them. You really get paranoid living in this country. I open the door slowly and lack the courage to look them in the eye. Before me stand a pair of shiny black boots that end in a pair of green military pants. Mother help me, this is it!" Just one month earlier a Chinese woman caught making love with an Australian was sentenced to three years in prison.

The boots and military pants turned out not to be attached to a Chinese cop but to an earnest Japanese student, dressed like a tough guy, who was searching the dorm for a classmate. Even so, Antonella's legs continued to shake, and the cold sweat that had broken out on Song's back would not dry.

China was changing, but not fast enough for my classmate Song Liming. In 1979, the year after my classmates entered Nanda, relations were normalized with the United States. Western businesses were beginning to seek investment opportunities. A Singaporean investor committed to building a thirty-story five-star hotel to anchor Nanjing's downtown. On the street, the sexless pixie haircut was no longer de rigueur for women. Men, too, were exuding a rakish, if somewhat emaciated, charm.

Song knew he was charming, too. His finely shaped lips, infectious smile, and impish laugh qualified him as "simpatico," in the words of Antonella and her Italian girlfriends at Nanda. Song fancied himself a cross between a Chinese scholar and a nineteenth-century European intellectual. He was scruffily hip, his scarf jauntily thrown around his neck, his PLA-issued bookbag dangling off his shoulder. His greatest desire, he would say, was to be a free man.

Born in 1959, Song emerged in the wee hours of the morning, giving his literal-minded dad the idea for his name, Liming—Daybreak. Song's hometown, Yancheng, was and remains a down-at-the-heels city near the shores of the Yellow Sea in Jiangsu Province, 250 miles north of Nanjing, not far from the village where Book Idiot Zhou was raised.

A small-time official in the grain bureau, Song's father jumped on the Maoist bandwagon at the start of the Cultural Revolution, joining a radical faction of the Red Guard that took its name, the Eager Gallopers, from a poem by Chairman Mao. Song's father did his patriotic duty by leading struggle sessions against teachers, professors, and other "enemies of the revolution," parading them through the streets, beating them, and forcing them to endure hours of public interrogation, criticism, and humiliation. For a petty functionary, it was the highlight of his life. Song's father then spent several years interrogating and brutalizing fallen party members at a May 7 Cadre School similar to the one where Little Guan's father was held. Song's dad was equally violent with his family, and, as the eldest of two sons, Song bore the brunt of frequent beatings from a man who, like many Chinese parents, relied on his in-laws to raise his four children. Song's father would show up at their house in a drunken rage to whip his son, using a belt that he double-wrapped around his body like so many skinny Chinese men.

Like many officials who tried but failed to become a member, Song senior loved the Communist Party with the wounded intensity of a spurned lover. Even after the end of the Cultural Revolution and the arrest of the

Gang of Four, he insisted on the party's infallibility. One day in the mid-1980s Daybreak Song and his father were at a public bath where someone asked the aging bureaucrat why he still supported the party.

"Well," he replied edgily, as if it was common knowledge, "everything the party did was correct."

In 1975, at age sixteen, Daybreak Song was sent down to the countryside. Unlike Little Guan or Old Wu, Song remembers life there as generally pleasant. He worked at a silk farm. When he had the choice, one year later, to return to Yancheng or spend another year in the fields, he decided to stay. Getting out from under the arc of his father's belt was a pleasure that not even the tedium of growing mulberry leaves for silkworms could erase. Song spent his second year in the countryside studying for the college entrance examination in a mud-brick hut lit by an oil lamp. He passed.

Song and I were sitting in a trattoria in Rome in early January 2004. The last time I had seen him was twenty-two years before, the day I had left Nanjing. The waiter approached and, figuring the white guy was a better bet to speak Italian, looked to me to order. I spoke no Italian. Song's was just fine. "The American imperialist will have fried artichokes and pasta with pecorino. I'll have bacon and tomato pasta," Song joked. Looking at me, he smiled. "I am still Chinese, you know. We don't like cheese."

As we sipped a spirited Chianti, Song mused that living in Italy was not really that different from living in China. Like China, Italy is a nation with a troubled recent past, one of bad politics, tax cheats, and crazy traffic. Exiled or not, he was at home.

My classmates entered Nanda during a heady period as the country shed its puritanical Maoism in favor of a mixed bag of economic and social reforms. Peasants were allowed to grow crops on private plots, sell them at private markets, and keep the money they made. In the cities, the seeds of a free-market economy sprouted. Private restaurants, barbershops, and shoe cobblers opened their doors in Nanjing. Nanda students frequented a small privately owned eatery that served delectably greasy pot stickers quaffed down, when they had it, with Five Star Dark Beer.

In the spring of 1978, a motley collection of foreign students—Canadians,

Yugoslavs, French, and Japanese—adventurously held the first dance at Nanjing University since 1966. Less than two years later, the first big batch of American exchange students since the revolution in 1949 would arrive.

Everyday life was still buffeted by political winds from Beijing. As a way of battling for control over the direction of the country, factions within the party leadership launched a succession of contradictory political campaigns whose eerie effect reverberated through the campus. One week, foreign students would host a party that Chinese friends would attend, where dancing was allowed, and boys would appear with their hair over their collar. A few weeks later, we would announce another dance, and no one would come. A new circular had been distributed: no more social contact with foreigners, no more dancing. Male students were commanded to get haircuts and women could no longer let their raven locks hang free.

For Daybreak Song and my other classmates who had survived the depredations of the Cultural Revolution, university life stretched their minds farther than they had ever been before. Though the classes were often numbingly boring (every research paper had to begin with a quote from Chairman Mao), these students, who on average had missed six years of education due to closed or dysfunctional schools, displayed a pent-up idealism and curiosity about the outside world unrivaled in Communist China's history.

In the Chinese dormitories, lights went out at 10 p.m. But long into the night, hundreds of students would crowd the ill-lit cement hallways and malodorous, sodden bathrooms to study. Even during winter, they would huddle outdoors, wrapped in their blue or green cotton-padded overcoats, reading under the eaves of the school's infirmary, where the lights stayed on all night.

Neither of his parents had graduated from high school, so Song's family had no books in their house except for several volumes of the *Quotations of Chairman Mao*. Until he was twenty, he had never read for pleasure. After he entered Nanjing University that was all Song did, and he had a lot to choose from. Passed around in dog-eared mimeographed copies was literature the likes of which had not been seen since before 1949. China was witnessing a creative explosion of poetry, short stories, and plays as young and old sought to make sense of the pain of the past and to express their hopes and concerns about the future. Foreign works, banned for more than a decade, also took the country by storm. The biggest hit among Song's classmates was *Piao,* or Floating, the Chinese name for *Gone with the Wind.* The students in the history department had one copy that they read in two-hour chunks blocked out through day and night. It became a common excuse for showing up late to an early-morning class: "I was doing the graveyard shift with *Gone with the Wind.*"

It's understandable why people who grew up among horrific chaos and suffering would identify with *Piao*'s backdrop of war and dislocation. But what made the American novel so popular was the sappy, quixotic story line of love *nearly* conquering all. That romantic pessimism struck a deep chord among my classmates, who viewed themselves as tragic and called themselves China's Lost Generation. While most Americans finish the book thinking Scarlett will prevail and wind up getting Rhett in the end, the typical Chinese reaction was that she and her love were doomed.

While my classmates lost themselves in the antebellum South, history was exploding outside the gates of the university. A new general secretary of the Communist Party, a diminutive reformer named Hu Yaobang, was appointed on February 29, 1980, and a new premier, Zhao Ziyang, was named in September. Zhao was a particularly interesting choice; he had come from the inland province of Sichuan, where his free-market experiments in agriculture and industry had resulted in huge economic growth for the region known as China's rice basket.

In November 1980, the government put the Gang of Four on trial, accusing them of persecuting to death 34,800 Chinese and wrongfully imprisoning 729,511 others—lowball figures but nonetheless the first step the government had made toward rectifying the crimes of the Cultural Revolution. True to her thespian roots, Mao's wife, Jiang Qing, exhibited a melodramatic truculence during the televised trial, calling her accusers "fascists" and agents of Taiwan, which prompted the judge first to order her to shut up and, when she refused, forcibly remove her from the proceedings. My classmates were initially riveted by the trial, especially Madame Mao's outbursts. But as the proceedings wore on, it became obvious that this was more a Stalinist show to strengthen the party's hold on power than a process to herald the introduction of political accountability. On

January 25, 1981, the verdicts came down: Jiang Qing was sentenced to death, although she was granted a two-year reprieve during which time she could "repent." Madame Mao never repented, but neither was she executed. She committed suicide in custody in 1991.

Behind the scenes, Deng Xiaoping was solidifying his control. He had maneuvered his protégés to the top of the party and the government and by 1978 was running the People's Liberation Army as chairman of the Central Military Commission. In the summer of 1981, to finalize its break with the past, the party's Central Committee issued a report that blamed Mao for "leftist" excesses, such as his belief in the need for a permanent revolution. The report concluded that Mao was 70 percent correct and 30 percent wrong in the way he ruled. This was kid-glove treatment for a man responsible for the deaths of more than 30 million of his countrymen, but nonetheless a clear sign that the days of ultraleftist policies were over. Song and other classmates pored over the report, though none of them had any delusions that it meant the party was ready to embrace Western-style democracy. "Only socialism," the report concluded, "and socialism alone can save China."

Because the government had made no substantial investment in education for more than a decade, Nanda was in bad shape. Occupying several square miles in the Drum Tower District, the campus was situated inside a gated compound that had changed very little from the 1920s, when the school was run by American missionaries.

Students were housed in cement block dorms built in the 1950s. They were packed eight or ten to a room, sleeping on bunk beds with their belongings shoved into trunks below. Chunks of cement would randomly break off and fall from classroom ceilings and dormitory walls. The school had one dirt playing field; a running track of black pebbles and coal chips; and a gym with buckling wood-plank floors. Only upperclassmen could use the library, but it was impossible to find books there because the card catalog was in shambles. There were no copying machines.

Song was elected to be our class representative to the Youth League—a major step on the way to party membership. His responsibilities included spying on his fellow classmates, functioning as a lookout for ideological wavering and what the party described as "anti-social behavior": dancing, drinking, and sex. But when Old Xu, our class party boss who slept above me, approached him with an offer to consider applying for party membership, Song politely demurred. Freedom, which Song so avidly sought, didn't square with party group-think. Song did not believe in Marxism-Leninism and, more to the point, it seemed to him that all party members did was spend hours in tedious meetings, "uniting" their thoughts. Song used a favorite Chinese circumlocution to spurn Xu's advance, explaining that he was flattered at the suggestion of entering the party, but he did not believe he was worthy.

Song's position as Youth League representative had benefits, including the chance to live with foreign students. This meant that Song could swap his Chinese dormitory bunk for a bigger bed in a bigger room that he would share with just one roommate. He would also have hot showers whenever he wanted them, instead of once a week, and lights out at his leisure instead of at 10 p.m. So Song moved over to the foreigners' side and I later took his bed in the Chinese dorm, in his opinion an act of supreme stupidity.

In her memoir about life at Nanda, Antonella described their achingly slow, circuitous, and often infantile courtship, marked by veiled hints of love and paranoia about his safety—all unfurling against a backdrop of the end of her year in China and her fast-approaching return to Italy.

It's hard to overestimate how extraordinary their romance was. Antonella was the belle of Nanda, to my eyes a younger version of Sophia Loren. Voluptuous, with a husky voice, lilting accent (in any language), and a slinky sensuality, she was pursued by men of all races and nationalities. Chinese guys looked at women like Antonella in abject terror. Few male undergraduates were ever alone with female students and hadn't a clue of how to put the moves on one. At dances, boys danced with boys and girls with girls; on campus, boys held each others' hands, just like the girls did. Song was exceptional. He might have been a blushing Romeo, but he was a Romeo nonetheless.

Song expressed his feelings not by touching Antonella or telling her directly but by penning poetry and giving her nicknames. He bashfully announced that if she would not go on a school trip to an old shipyard on the outskirts of Nanjing, then he would not go, either. He glued into her diary the lyrics of a song, written in the 1940s, which had only recently been rereleased. "The girl is the needle and the man is the thread," ran the refrain, which young Chinese considered tantalizingly suggestive. "Ah, two people and only one heart." On a forest walk, Song scampered up a tree, captured two cicadas, and handed them to Antonella. In the West, we'd call this the juvenile-suitor-scares-girl-with-bugs routine. But for Song, the insects possessed a deep meaning and gave him an opening to flaunt the profundity of his culture, or, rather, the profundity of his understanding of it. In 1076, a Chinese poet wrote a line that was famous for centuries:

Though far apart, we are still able to share the beauty
of the moon together

The character the poet used for "moon" resembled the character for "cicada," so the bug became a symbol for those celebrated lines. Song was, if elliptically, attempting to tell Antonella that love could bridge their different cultures. She hadn't a clue what he was trying to say.

"My smile of appreciation must have seemed a bit forced today; I wonder if Song noticed," she wrote. "There's nothing I can do about it because I find holding cicadas somewhat revolting. I've never received one as a present before and I'm just glad he didn't present me with a handful of frogs."

Antonella's attempts to light sparks fizzled as well. She felt Song's thigh under a table at a restaurant, and he avoided her for a month. The pair went to a movie, and he disappeared right after it ended. When they found themselves alone in her room, she reached out and touched him, and he moved away. The couple went for a walk in the park, and she summoned up the courage to tell him she liked him. Song then changed the subject, and for two hours they chitchatted until Antonella finally brought the topic back to love. Song acknowledged he liked her and said he did not want to hold himself back. But even then, she wrote, the evening ended with a whimper. "After such a long and difficult declaration the free embrace I expected is not there. Our hands brush, vaguely."

Antonella asked a Chinese girlfriend to analyze Song's intentions. She laughed at the naive Italian: "He's written you poetry and given you a new name, how can you doubt his love?" But Antonella was looking for passion, not poetry. Chased by many men, she was completely befuddled about how hard it was to get this one.

Antonella could not share these frustrations with her Chinese room-mate. Indeed, relations between the two women were strained. One night, Antonella returned a day early to Nanda from a trip to Shanghai. Because there were hardly any phones, she had no way of telling her roommate she was coming. The door to their room was locked. She knocked and heard muffled noises inside. Antonella sat on the stairs and waited. After a long delay, her roommate emerged, sheepishly motioning Antonella to enter. Her roommate's face was crimson, and her roommate's boyfriend was sitting like a statue at her desk. "We've been studying geography," she said.

The next morning Antonella's roommate, who usually kept quiet, ranted about how she was sure Antonella would denounce her and she would be kicked out of Nanda. The rules were clear: premarital sex was forbidden; those discovered would be expelled (and forever shamed). Antonella tried to reassure her. It may be like that in China, but she was not Chinese. In Italy no one would think twice if they saw you in your room with your boyfriend. Sex was a private issue. Her roommate was not convinced.

A week later, Antonella was summoned by the dean of foreign students, who explained that her roommate wanted to return to the Chinese dormitory. Her excuse was that Antonella had expressed contempt for the Chinese. The dean must have noticed Antonella's look of incredulity. Contempt for the Chinese?, Antonella thought. She was falling in love with one of them. The dean realized the accusation was ridiculous and apologetically sent her away without her roommate's wish being granted.

The roommate's rationale was twisted but typical of the tactics Chinese used to protect themselves. To Antonella's roommate, schooled in the brutal logic of Maoist vilification campaigns, attack was always the best defense; a false accusation could nullify the effects of a true one. If Antonella had later denounced her for sleeping with her boyfriend, the roommate would have argued that it was a lie that demonstrated just how much contempt Antonella did in fact have for Chinese people. This was a society where the simple act of snuggling with your boyfriend could spark a convoluted train of false accusations and bad blood. The Chinese observed that Western freedoms and directness created simple and unsophisticated people; it was half put-down, half praise. They were tougher on themselves: "It's hard to be Chinese," went a popular lament.

Despite the clash of cultures, it was easier for Song to spend time with Western women than it was for Western men to be with Chinese women.

In the early 1980s, Chinese girls and women were routinely punished for consorting with foreigners. Some were dispatched to labor camps, like the woman caught with the Australian and accused of hooliganism, a blanket charge that covered everything from homosexuality to traveling without state permission. Others were fired from their jobs.

Chinese society viewed sex in stark terms. Men always got the better of an activity that was generally accepted to be both brutish and short. Chinese women would summarize what sex was like with Chinese guys by clapping three times and yelling, "Finished." Society was so uneasy about sex that it took an official pronouncement in the late 1970s before most men and women would dare to hold hands publicly.

On July 16, 1982, Antonella and Song ate dinner together and then returned to her room. Antonella's roommate had gone home for the summer holidays, so the couple kissed. "The cuddling is difficult because we'd like to let ourselves go further but can't," Antonella noted in her diary. Two days later in the afternoon, they ended up locking the door and making love. Four days after that, Antonella returned to Italy. Before she left, she gave Song a gift of two caged canaries. "A typical Chinese present," she wrote, "or at least close to my idea of what two Chinese lovers about to part might give one another. In Italy I would never have thought of giving a gift like this."

In 1994, as Antonella prepared to publish her diary, Song read it and wrote a short commentary on what he called the "uncertain dance of two people from different cultures." "No woman had ever expressed her love to me, and I never imagined a woman so beautiful could fall in love with me," he wrote. "I loved her but didn't dare express my love; the closest I could get was to express myself through an Oriental way of loving.

"This story may seem incredible to a Westerner, and truthfully, many modern Chinese youth may find it strange," he continued. "In those days university students were forbidden from wearing jeans, having long hair, having dance parties, and loving each other. The changes we've undergone are so great that after reading this diary I look back on how we lived and ask myself: Was it really like that?"

8

PARTY ANIMAL

If Daybreak Song was the model of a new type of Chinese learning how to be comfortable with himself and the world outside China, Ye Hao was the opposite. Ye (pronounced *yeah*) was one of my roommates my second semester at Nanda, and every time I entered the room, he would jump to his feet and remain standing for minutes, smiling unctuously. This was an awkward routine considering the tiny space we were crammed into. If everyone stood up each time I entered the room, we would have been sardined. When I got up to leave, Ye would stand again, flashing me a brown-nosing smile, rendering any normal conversation impossible, which I guess was his goal. Ye did not want to face allegations that he had become too close to a foreigner. He avoided anything that might get between him and his application to join the party.

Beneath the formality, I knew little of Ye Hao. In contrast to some of my roommates, who would crawl into bed with me and share their darkest secrets, Ye Hao kept his distance. He had grown up in a township called Jurong just a few miles from Waterfield village, where Old Wu first learned that his parents had been murdered. He was a small but graceful boy, gifted at sports, with excellent balance and perfect teeth. Ye's parents named him Hao (Bright) as a sign of their faith in communism.

The son of a lower-level official in the grubby township, Ye, like Daybreak Song, escaped the hardships of the Cultural Revolution. Ye's father knew how to play the system. When called upon to criticize colleagues or turn them in, Ye's father did so with requisite but limited relish. When asked to protect friends or relatives, he demurred politely, preferring to save himself and his immediate family. When his sister was beaten and jailed after Red Guards found old novels in her house, Ye's father cut her off.

As with Old Wu, the lessons Ye learned at his father's knee were critical to his future. To make it, his father taught him, one must keep in lockstep with the Communist Party. Do not let ideas about right or wrong affect your relationship with the party. To get things done, his father instructed, you need to learn how to judge people. If someone can be useful to you, cultivate that person. If a person can't help you, you needn't waste your time.

In July 1977, Ye took the first university test and failed. A year later, he made it, testing into Nanjing University. By the middle of his first year, Ye had applied for membership in the Communist Party. He set about cultivating Old Xu, my bunkmate and, as the class party secretary, the man who held the keys to party membership. Each week Ye took him out for a glass of warm soybean milk—a palliative for the hepatitis Old Xu had contracted a few years before. Ye helped Old Xu obtain medicine and plied him with information about what other classmates were thinking and doing. Ye even moved into our room so that he could be closer to Old Xu.

"Ye made me feel like I was very important," Old Xu later recalled. "He really knew how to brownnose."

During his free time, Ye would stroll the streets of Nanjing. Although it was a faded remnant of its cosmopolitan heyday of the 1920s, Nanjing was far better than Jurong. Ye decided he would do anything to stay in the city after graduation.

Nanjing, the name means "southern capital," is a city where Chinese traditionally went to lick their wounds while barbarians from the north carved up their country. In medieval times, it served as the capital during six short-lived dynasties when northern China was occupied by nomadic tribes from beyond the Great Wall. Nanjing was also the capital at the beginning of the Ming Dynasty in the fourteenth century and then again during the two decades preceding the Communist Revolution.

A crossroads for plunderers and poets, emperors and colonialists, Nanjing was a safe house for Chinese culture, home to great painters and writers and the sing-song girls who worked the flower boats and brothels that lined the Qinhuai River snaking through the city. Nanjing is the setting for China's greatest novel, *The Dream of the Red Chamber* by Tsao Hsueh-Chin, a tale of love, sex, and reincarnation amid the declining fortunes of a great family. Through the centuries, Nanjing has been pillaged, burned, rebuilt, forgotten, and rebuilt again. In the fourteenth century, the first Ming ruler emptied the city of its citizens, exiling more than three hundred thousand to the far corners of the empire. A hundred years later, a repopulated Nanjing was celebrated as one of the most beautiful cities on earth. In the 1920s, an American architect laid plans to rebuild the city as a modern capital, a melding of Washington, D.C., and Paris, France. First, Japanese aggression in the late 1930s (culminating in the Rape of Nanking, during which an estimated three hundred thousand Chinese were slaughtered in one month), and then the Communist Revolution put an end to that.

In his walks around Nanjing, Ye dreamed of transforming the city yet again, imagining himself condemning buildings, cutting deals with foreigners to open new factories, amassing power, wealth, and women—grandiose schemes for a boy from a backwater. Though such dreams were now possible in China, Ye shared his ambitions with no one. At college no one talked about what they wanted to do. Students who were trying to enter graduate school overseas kept their plans to themselves, hiding college applications under their mattresses, scurrying to their mailboxes when none of their classmates were looking—much as Little Guan kept her studies to herself as she prepared for the college entrance exam. My classmates snooped on each other, read each other's diaries, feared and suspected one another—an expression of the deep mistrust they perfected during the Cultural Revolution when they were pitted against their parents, siblings, and friends. Knowing that most people could and would use any information, false or otherwise, to hurt others and help themselves made trust, not to mention close friendships, a rare commodity.

Despite the persistent paranoia, Ye Hao and his classmates did develop pastimes at Nanda. During the Cultural Revolution, individual hobbies and interests had become potential liabilities. The casual associations that make up everyday life—a pickup soccer game, a pottery class—were imbued with dangerous political significance. So for self-protection, people isolated themselves and buried their hobbies.

But with the fall of the Gang of Four, the government began to back off from its full-court press on the lives of ordinary citizens. In November

1978, Deng Xiaoping announced that "tai chi is good," ending years of persecution for people who practiced the ancient slow-motion martial art. Boxing, which had been banned for decades because it was "bourgeois," was again allowed, and clubs opened in major cities. Nanda arranged sports competitions. The winner of one track meet, held on March 23, 1982, won a jar of chicken chili paste. The runners-up got bookmarks or bars of soap.

The early 1980s saw the first expression of a new kind of Chinese nationalism—not the rote sloganeering sort demanded by Maoism but something more powerful. In November 1981, the women's national volleyball team won the world championship in Japan, triggering near riots throughout China.

I was eating pot stickers and drinking warm beer with Daybreak Song and a few other friends at a small, privately owned alleyway eatery when we heard a cacophonous roar that accompanied the news: this was the country's first world championship in any sport. We dropped our chopsticks and headed to the main road, where we were confronted with a moving mass of tens of thousands of young people bearing Chinese flags. Ye Hao was in the crowd marching gleefully. "He's going to report on everyone he sees," Song predicted. Sure enough, according to Old Xu, he did. The victory was all the sweeter for the people of Nanjing because it was inflicted on the Japanese in Tokyo. Hatred of Japan was the deepest, most persistent feature in China's approach to the outside world.

Along the way we bumped into several more classmates. I turned to look at several of them, and they were crying. "The Chinese have stood up," one of them kept yelling, the same expression Mao Zedong used in 1949. Indeed, all around me, young men were weeping. I was dumbfounded. One volleyball victory was all it took to release years of pent-up passion?

Ye was known among his classmates as a tenacious competitor. He excelled at cards, especially the Chinese version of gin rummy. It involved lots of bluffing, and Ye's skill at faking out his classmates earned him the nickname "Big Bluffer."

One day in April 1980, a senior party official on campus called a meeting of party members and applicants to respond to a spate of essays that had appeared the year before, taped on a wall in Beijing. The most provocative among what were called the Democracy Wall essays was one penned by an electrician named Wei Jingsheng, titled "The Fifth Modernization." It argued that, along with the party's new push to modernize China's industry, agriculture, science, and national defense, the country needed a "fifth" modernization, democracy. The party crushed this attempt at free speech, which had come to be called the Democracy Wall movement. Wei was arrested and sentenced to fifteen years in prison on charges including "counterrevolutionary incitement." Other essays claimed that China's youth were facing a crisis in belief.

A professor named Lu Minghua chaired the meeting, telling the assembled party applicants that no such crisis existed. He then went around the room, asking his students what they thought about the issue. The students repeated his words automatically. "Yes, teacher, there is no crisis of belief." Ye, to the surprise of those listening—especially the note taker, who copied Ye's response verbatim—launched into a speech.

"I am very excited," Ye said, his dainty hands placed on the table in front of him, "because I am requesting permission to enter the party. The Gang of Four caused the youth to doubt the party. By deifying the party's leader, it decreased the party's prestige. Party members also used their membership to gain personal benefits, and this hurts the party, too." Ye paused, looked around the room, and continued.

"But we must acknowledge that without the party, there would be no new China," he said, parroting a line from a propaganda jingle always playing on state-run radio. "This proves the greatness of the party. China suffered decades of foreign aggression. Every time we fought back we failed. Only under the party have the people become the masters of China. Although we are poor and backward, we are no longer oppressed. Taiwan's economy may be stronger than ours, but it's a subsidiary of the imperialists. The American economy may be rich, but that nation's spirit is weak. We believe firmly in communism."

Ye ended his disquisition. The room was silent. One participant remembers thinking: "This guy really is the Big Bluffer. Why couldn't I have said that?" It was a perfect statement, even if no one thought for a second that Ye believed a word of it. But what did that matter? Ye had grasped the formula; he knew what the party wanted to hear, and deftly worked in all the requisite buzzwords and slogans. Within a year, shepherded by Old Xu, Big Bluffer Ye had entered the Communist Party.

Ye's party membership changed his life. In the past, membership in the party meant self-abnegation and sacrifice. Party members were supposed to be those willing to serve China in ways others couldn't or wouldn't: fight floods, settle the forbidding western territories, volunteer to help bring education and economic growth to the poor in the countryside. After Old Wu's father joined the party in the 1930s, he spent more than a decade in poverty, teaching Communist soldiers and agitating for the revolution behind enemy lines. But now party membership meant something other than absolute self-sacrifice: it was a leg up. In 1978, when my class matriculated, we had four party members out of sixty-three history majors. Over the course of their four years at Nanda, ten more students would enter.

Ye looked at the party as a ticket to a better life. In addition to being assigned a job at least in Nanjing, membership would give him access to perks beyond his imagination, including travel to New York, Venice, Washington, D.C., Sydney, and his fantasy town, which would prove to be Ye's favorite, Las Vegas. But Big Bluffer Ye had motivations beyond simply bettering his lot. He sought not only to be an agent of his own fate; he wanted to be an agent of change, to transform his society. He also wanted power. To get that, party membership was key.

At our reunion in 2002, Ye explained his motivation for entering the party and government service and not becoming a historian.

"Nearing graduation I was faced with a choice. I could do research and spend my life studying, but I realized that my life was short," he said. "I wanted to do something real. Something important. I wanted to change the world. Time has proven that my decision was correct."

Once in the party, Ye stopped hobnobbing with his party mentor and roommate, Old Xu. No more weekly soybean milk, no more medicine. Big Bluffer Ye didn't have friends, just "comrades." He moved out of our room and began running with another crowd.

When Ye graduated, he was assigned to a position in the party's Organization Department in Nanjing. The Organization Department was a critical party bureau, which controlled important party and government jobs. A popular bit of doggerel described working there: "Go in lockstep with the Organization Department, and they'll organize a promotion for you every year."

9

OUTSIDE THE GATES

Big Bluffer may have been angling to get into the party, but I was angling to party. Used to the hectic social life of an American university campus, I wanted the same in China. Most of all, I wanted to fall in love.

On March 24, 1981, authorities at Nanda posted a sign on the university's main gate banning all dance parties on campus. The political atmosphere was tightening again; student leaders from various departments were told to contact the university office if they wanted to have a get-together of any sort.

Operating as we always did somewhere outside the suffocating control of the authorities, the foreign students at Nanjing University nonetheless decided to throw a party. To make space for dancing, we pushed away the tables in the special dining hall reserved for foreign students. To the tunes of the Talking Heads and The Cars, we gyrated and slam danced. Only a few Chinese students came, but several townies from "outside the gate" showed up.

I never figured out who invited Fay. At one point during the night, I was crossing the room with an armful of beer bottles, and a woman I didn't know flicked at them nonchalantly with her fingertips. I deposited the beers with my friends and asked her to dance.

Fay had the most talkative pair of eyes I had ever seen, and with them she could get anyone's attention. She also had mastered a way to show off the lithe body underneath her Mao suit. She wanted to get out of China and figured that a relationship with a foreigner was the best way to do it.

She wasn't the least bit deterred by the fact that women around the country were getting arrested for doing the same thing. We danced throughout the evening and chatted a bit. "Do you like to climb mountains?" she said. I imagined this as a Chinese pick-up line and was titillated by its possible interpretations. We made a date to head the next day to Purple Mountain, the site of the tomb of Sun Yat-sen, the founder of modern China.

I surprised my roommates by rising early and not telling Old Xu where I was going. He usually asked, in a friendly way, and I usually complied. But this was my first date with a Chinese girl. I was not going to let anyone know.

Fay was unemployed. She had finished high school but had not passed the college entrance examinations, leaving her no choice but to live at home with her parents. The daughter of an officer in the People's Liberation Army, she did not want the army job that her father had arranged for her and preferred going to parties with a growing crew of Nanjing artists and foreign groupies. She had tried her hand at studying English and dance but lacked the self-discipline to master either. Barely twenty, feeling as if her youth had been hijacked by Communism and Mao, she exhibited a knee-jerk nihilism that I found bewitching. China was still a tough, repressive place, yet Fay just wanted to have fun.

At the bus terminal, her eyes took hold of me and directed me onto a bus. I felt like I was in the middle of a romantic spy novel. I had never dated anyone "illegally." I also had never dated anyone in another language. Fay was wearing brown polyester pants with a tacky sheen and a green Mao tunic, but to me the outfit was as revealing as a negligee. In the months that I had been in China, I had become adept at seeing through ill-fitting garments and past lackluster colors to the woman beneath.

We got off at the end of the line, and Fay headed up the trail while I followed five steps behind. As we entered the woods, she slowed her pace and I caught up. It was a gorgeous day, and a cool breeze wafted through the trees. For the first time since I had been in China I heard birds chirping. In the 1960s and '70s, the government had ordered its people to kill birds in all cities as part of a muddleheaded policy to be more modern. Their mass extermination prompted an insect population boom—flies and mosquitoes, mostly. So next, the party assigned each family a quota of insects to kill.

We walked and talked as we hiked to the top of Purple Mountain. At one point, Fay stumbled and I held out my hand. She grabbed it and did not let go. Her hand was cool and smooth, her fingers long and lean. I interlocked my fingers with hers.

We came to a clearing and stood face-to-face. I was thinking I should kiss her when out from the bushes popped a man with a camera. He took our picture and ran off. Before I could pursue him, Fay squeezed my arm: "Don't you dare."

"Who was that guy?" I asked.

"He's probably a dog's leg," she said.

"A dog's leg?"

"A police officer or someone working for them," she said. In China, the cops weren't called pigs as they are in the West; they were dogs. A pig, worshipped for its meat, was invariably a term of endearment.

Fay and I met often. Because we could not call each other, each date concluded with the details of where we would meet next. One favorite place for kissing was a dark alleyway near Nanda that ran by a hospital built with American money before World War II. At night the facility's crematorium would burn the day's dead, leaving a fine dust to settle on the walkway where we'd meet. It was gruesome, but we were left alone. We would kiss in a corner, or I would stretch Fay out along my parked Flying Pigeon bicycle, the seat and the handlebars digging into her back. The winter months were the best because our heavy clothes provided us with a measure of protection, allowing us to make out without too much fear of security agents recognizing me. To conceal my big nose and brown hair, I would don a hat and a surgical mask, which Chinese wore when they had colds, and we could ride our bicycles to even more secluded places on the outskirts of town. We couldn't check into a hotel; even though there were always empty rooms, I lacked the necessary official permission. Plus we weren't married. I became adept at picking out police uniforms in a crowd. I worried about Fay, whether the police would visit her and take her away.

Once security guards caught us kissing in the grass of a lakeside park near closing time. "You're one of us! You're one of us!" they screamed at her, as they moved in for an arrest, their nightsticks cocked. Fay turned to me, cool as ice, and spoke in gibberish. To the guards, it must have sounded like English. I then translated, explaining to them that she was a Chinese American. They let us go.

I was mesmerized by Fay and our world of stolen kisses and groping through winter clothes. While other Chinese women would shuffle and had bodies with no curves, Fay walked like a dancer and exuded an untamed sexuality. Living with seven guys, however, I had no place to take her to be alone. We would snuggle for endless hours outside—in alleyways and parks.

Part of me wanted to be Chinese. I dressed like they did, in blue workers' pants and an itchy brown woolen sweater; I ate what they ate; tried (and failed) to curse like they cursed, and tried (and failed) to mumble their language like they did. Fay was my entry. By loving her, I was getting into China, just as she was trying to get out.

Fay opened for me a new world of artists, workers, and struggling young people whose views of China differed from what I heard in my dorm. My classmates were generally satisfied with the pace of change, which made sense since they were the ones who were poised to benefit. But the people Fay introduced me to had none of that patience; they knew about Western freedom, and they wanted it, now.

One day, one of my classmates spotted me taking Fay to the movies. Word got around fast. My relationship piqued the interest of Old Xu, who had noticed that I wasn't spending much time in the dorm room or participating in class activities. "You seem preoccupied, Little Pan," he observed, using my nickname, "Are you in love?"

Old Xu regularly tried to get me to divulge Fay's identity. He angled for clues, inelegantly inserting little questions into our otherwise everyday banter. What did her father do? What neighborhood did she live in? What school did she go to? What was her major? Old Xu was on a mission.

Xu's own thoughts were a mishmash. He would often tell me that all Chinese were schizophrenics and would point to his own life as an example. In the early 1970s, when he was working as a propaganda chief at a government bureau in Changzhou, sixty miles from Nanjing, his job was to denounce Deng Xiaoping and his "capitalist thought." A few years later, when Deng returned and the Gang of Four was arrested, he led the pro-Deng campaign. Xu would back anyone as long as it meant keeping alive.

As Old Xu intensified his quest to unmask my girlfriend, I realized that I had a way to get him to back off. In those early days of the reforms, foreigners could buy a wide variety of products—sugar, bicycles, rice, cotton—that were rationed for Chinese. I quickly became Xu's ticket to a better life or, at least, a well-stocked larder. Every month or so, Old Xu would find me alone and present me with a shopping list of things to buy for him at Nanjing's Friendship Store, which was open only to foreigners or Chinese with foreign currency or a new type of bills that began circulating in April 1980.

A dead ringer for Monopoly money, Foreign Exchange Certificates were issued by banks in exchange for hard currency, such as U.S. dollars. My Chinese friends and roommates coveted FECs because it allowed them to shop at Friendship Stores. We foreigners wanted People's Currency, or *renminbi,* because with it we could buy pot stickers at a street-side stall, not to mention other necessities, at rock-bottom Chinese prices. Few ordinary shopkeepers ever came into contact with FECs and so would often refuse to accept them.

Living with Old Xu gave me my first important lesson about corruption of everyday life and especially the importance of doing favors. In the beginning, I bought things for him because I wanted him to like me. Later on, I became more no-nonsense about the exchange, realizing that if I ran his errands, he would stop asking about Fay and allow me to have semi-normal interaction with my friends. But if too much time had passed between trips to the Friendship Store, Old Xu would squeeze me for information about Fay or question my friends about the nature of their interactions with me.

Once, when I felt Old Xu was pushing me too far, requesting ten pounds of sugar and a bicycle, I snapped. I told my Chinese friends that he was calibrating his surveillance of me according to whether or not I bought him off. By revealing his small-scale black marketeering, I'd given my friends juicy ammunition. True to form, they reported the information to officials, prompting an investigation that yielded no evidence but resulted in a black mark on Xu's record. By ratting out Old Xu, I, too, had entered the snitch culture.

As word of my girlfriend spread, so, too, did my supposed "expertise" on relations between the sexes. On the eve of the Spring Festival vacation in 1981, all of my classmates had returned home except for me and Bing, a waiflike doctor's son from Sichuan and one of the youngest in the class.

Sometime after the lights went out, Bing, who slept in the bunk across from me, crawled into my bed. Having become accustomed to a certain level of physical intimacy between men—hand-holding, walking arm-in-arm—I made space for him.

Bing told me the story of his courtship with the daughter of an actress in his hometown. His parents were against it because her parents had been persecuted during the Cultural Revolution, which tainted them with the tar brush of a bad class background. Bing's parents had little faith that China's reforms would stick and expected the pendulum of history to swing again. But Bing believed in "free love," as he called it, and trusted that the bad days would not return. "What should we do when we are alone?" he asked, twitching his legs. "I've never kissed a girl. You know these things. What does your girlfriend like?" He snuggled closer. Was he angling for a demonstration?

"Well," I said, "the key is to get her to relax. And touch her softly." When he began playing with my chest hair, I nudged him out of bed. I had wondered about Bing's sexuality. But people were so repressed that they could barely discuss heterosexual sex, let alone homosexuality. To the police, homosexuality was a crime. Psychologists labeled it a disease. Asking Bing if he was gay would have been like inquiring if he was psychotic.

Sexual tension was high at Nanda. Of the sixty-three people in my class, whose average age was twenty-three, only three had kissed a member of the opposite sex. One roommate, Old Ma, seemed to ejaculate every night.

"Goddammit!" he would bellow each morning. "I rode the horse again!" employing the slang term for nocturnal emission.

One of the university's most popular courses was the art appreciation class because it offered an opportunity to gape at slides of nude paintings. You could always tell whenever the class had been held because the graffiti in the men's bathroom would suddenly veer south. "Sex is the highest form of human happiness," read one proclamation. "Don't girls have sexual desire?" asked another. One student, with trademarked Chinese formality, wrote, "Forgive my forthrightness, I want sexual intercourse!"

On the evening of March 10, 1981, so many students packed the class at Nanda's main auditorium that they broke the doors. The class was split in two: Tuesday evenings for humanities majors and Fridays for those in the sciences. One evening a group of my classmates organized a guerrilla squad to infiltrate the Nanjing Institute of Fine Arts and sneak a peek at a nude painting session. The Peeping Toms returned with flushed faces and satisfied smiles. One lay on his bed, moaning, "Goddamn, goddamn."

When the lights went out, my roommates would rate the school's cutest girl. One cold night, as we shivered under our cotton blankets, the guys concluded that the belle of the school was a biology student. "She might be a bit too showy," one roommate said. "She wears dresses in summertime, and it doesn't seem like there's a bra. Those things are swinging up and down; it makes my heart race." The next night, the conversation turned to the ugliest girl, who, it was agreed, could be found in the Chinese and philosophy departments. The top four were known by nicknames: "Rotten Winter Melon," "Duck Butt," "Big Flat Face," and "Short Stool."

When my parents came to visit me in China, at my suggestion they smuggled in three copies of *Playboy* for my classmates. Within a week they had disappeared—the men divvying up all the nude shots, while the more studious among the bunch tried to work their way through the jokes. Chinese were captivated by the more open sexuality of Westerners, which they viewed with a mixture of jealousy, fascination, and fear—an obsession that continues to this day. My male classmates' single most vivid memory of me is that I slept naked even in winter. Early one morning, before the loudspeaker by our window began blasting martial music and paeans to Karl Marx and Chairman Mao, one of my roommates peeled back my covers to ogle my penis. "Is it really bigger than ours?" he said, moving in for a closer look. The back of my hand caught him squarely in the face, sending him flying away from my bunk and onto an adjacent desk. The room erupted in peals of laughter. "Good shot, Little Pan," someone cheered.

After the appearance of the poster banning unsupervised dances, the university began holding weekly get-togethers chaperoned by teachers and Communist Party officials. Compared to our parties, these affairs flopped. Under the watchful eyes of teachers and party members, men danced with men, women with women. If by chance a mixed couple appeared on the floor, everyone snickered nervously.

Of my classmates, only one, Qian Yu, really knew how to dance. His specialty was a cartoon version of John Travolta in *Saturday Night Fever.* "Dee-suh-ko, dee-suh-ko," he would mutter under his breath in the dorm room, wiggling his hips with one finger above his head. Many of my classmates hailed from village hamlets and knew only the "Loyalty Dance," which they were compelled to perform during the Cultural Revolution to show allegiance to Mao. The choreography was fairly simple: chest pounding, arm raising, foot stomping, and all the while shouting, "Long live Chairman Mao!" Western-style dances, like Qian Yu's, were viewed with a combination of horror and fascination.

"In my heart I criticize the dances," one classmate wrote in his diary. "I think people who like to rub up against each other—boys and girls—are dirty. I feel very uncomfortable watching it. It is a capitalist way of living, but I still want to go to see the dances. I am fascinated by it. The lights in the dining hall, the music. I dislike them but I am so curious."

China was emerging from the long night of thirty years of isolation from the rest of the world, and my classmates had that and so much else on their minds. At 10 p.m., talk would range from the nature of beauty (is there such a thing as Marxist beauty or capitalist beauty?), to history (was it China's fault that foreign countries carved up the country in the nineteenth century?), to the events of the day, which they heard on the Voice of America's nightly broadcast. "The topic for discussion tonight in the dorm was prostitutes and lovers, and also freedom," read the diary entry of another classmate. A few weeks later, talk turned to the crushing of the Democracy Wall movement in Beijing. Then American power. Then American democracy.

In early 1982, Premier Zhao Ziyang declared on the one-channel national TV station that the month of March would be designated "Civilization and Courtesy Month." Everyone in my dorm room sensed that another political campaign was afoot. Orders to oppose gambling and "feudal superstitions," to get haircuts and bathe regularly, to refrain from sneezing and nose picking (at least in front of other people) were handed down—none of which made the slightest bit of difference. Prohibitions followed against spitting, littering, and public urination. At Nanda, the movement was kicked off by a deputy university president railing against the tide.

"These days I have noticed some male students grow their hair so long that from the back they look like girls but from the front they look like men," he said. "Not man, not woman. What's beautiful about that?" "Look at us," he continued, pointing to himself and other dowdy party functionaries on the dais. "Neat, clean, and simple. That's what's called beautiful." The crowd laughed.

"Out there in society some people say that when it comes to hygiene, the university is not as good as an elementary school." More laughter. "Some dormitory rooms are so smelly, you can smell them from the street. You walk into the dorms and there is this stench." The laughter had become guffaws.

"Not only does it smell bad, it also smells sour." The crowd cheered. "The tops of some beds look like a junkyard." The cheering intensified. "When students go to the bathroom the dump doesn't go into the hole and the pee misses the pond." And with that, the deputy president was laughed off the stage.

After we'd been dating for about three months, Fay and I decided to travel together to Tibet. Given that police routinely arrested Chinese women for consorting with foreign men, traveling together was risky; traveling together to Tibet was out-and-out brainless. The once-independent Himalayan kingdom had been conquered by the PLA in 1950 and was entirely closed to outsiders. Nonetheless, we both had dreams of hitchhiking into the faraway region. I picked a route through Yunnan Province that would take us to Tibet's southeastern border. Foreigners were getting turned back along the more commonly used entry points. To avoid detection, we traveled separately three hundred miles south to Guilin, a city famous for its great stone outcroppings along the banks of the Li River.

We met at the railway station. Fay's eyes again picked me out of the crowd. From there, we took a boat down the Li River to the little town of Yangshuo, nestled among the mountains and surrounded by rice paddies and fishponds. Skeletal peaks festooned with gnarled pine trees loomed above the boat. Mist floated in the valleys. A fisherman with a conical hat maneuvered his sampan down the middle of the river; a cormorant, a rope around its neck to prevent it from swallowing the fish it caught, perched on the bow. A tourist from Hong Kong burst onto the deck with a boombox, cranked up a Cantonese disco tune, and began dancing.

We arrived at the Yangshuo Hotel, the sole establishment in town,

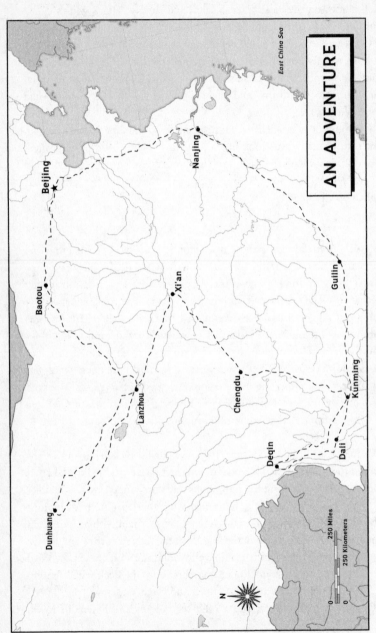

AN ADVENTURE

East China Sea

Pomfret, and his then-girlfriend Fay, took a 55-day trip through China, in the summer of 1981. They left Nanjing in the direction of Guilin, and traveled by railroad and bus; though they had planned to reach Tibet, they were turned back at Deqin where we were told that there was only one room available, even though it was clear that the place was half empty. "You'll have to stay together," the manager informed us sternly. Financial interest had trumped the law banning unmarried men and women from sharing a room. Under rules established by the Ministry of Education, foreign students had to pay only six *yuan* (less than two dollars) for a hotel room, while foreign tourists paid fifty times as much. So hoteliers had no financial interest in allowing foreign students to fill more rooms than necessary.

That evening Fay and I ate an early dinner and returned to our room at dusk. It was on the first floor, facing a small courtyard, with two small single beds draped in mosquito netting. The thin cotton mattresses rested on lumpy rope lattices. We shut the tattered curtains as best we could and hid behind the mosquito netting. Fay and I had never been alone inside a room. I took off her Mao jacket, sweater, polyester blouse, T-shirt, and long underwear to discover a contraption that looked more like body armor than a bra. I struggled with the snaps, first with one hand, then with both. She helped me. Her skin was smooth, and it glowed in the approaching darkness. I touched her legs, moving my hands upward.

"My auntie is here," she cooed into my ear. "Your who?" I whispered back, undaunted. "My big auntie," she insisted, guiding my hand away. "My number three, my regular interval, my unlucky number. . . . You don't understand?" And then she laughed. I looked down and saw a piece of paper poking out from under her flesh-colored underwear, more girdle than briefs. Fay had stuffed her panties with wads of sandpaper-rough toilet paper; she was having her period.

After Yangshuo, we headed by train southwest to Kunming, the capital of Yunnan. We bought our tickets on board and stood for forty-eight hours straight, wedged between a band of coal miners and a group of old ladies. At several points in the journey, fights erupted between travelers over seats and choice standing places away from the putrid bathroom. China is the only country in the world to acknowledge as a psychiatric condition the effects of traveling in overcrowded trains. They call it *lutu jingshenbing*, or travel psychosis, the symptoms include insomnia, dehydration, hallucinations, and violent outbursts. People who commit crimes while suffering travel psychosis, are spared the death penalty. I didn't kill anyone on that trip, though I was pretty pissed off when I opened my travel bag to find that the train's coal dust had blackened all my clothes.

In Kunming, we switched to buses, bouncing west into the foothills of the Himalayas toward the Tibetan border. In the town of Dali, we stayed at a 150-year-old shingled inn, where we were given adjoining rooms. The inn creaked so much—the beds, the floorboards, the chairs, the doors—that every move made a ruckus. Chinese, used to living cheek to jowl, often three generations sharing a room, had mastered lovemaking in close quarters. I was a newbie, petrified that our squeaking would get Fay into trouble.

Each morning we drank tea and ate steamed buns on a balcony overlooking the gate to the small city. And each morning a man would walk through the gate backward, yelling revolutionary chants at the top of his lungs. Once, passing under our balcony, he tilted his head, saw me, and saluted. "Hey, Joe, where you go?" he cried in English. He had been a schoolteacher before the Cultural Revolution, a shopkeeper told us. His father, a mechanic for the U.S. Air Force during World War II when American military supply planes flew over the Burma hump into Yunnan, had taught his son pidgin English. After the 1949 revolution, his father had been executed by the Communists for cooperating with the Americans. During the Cultural Revolution, the son was beaten for his father's sins and imprisoned in a small underground hovel. Eventually, he had gone mad.

As we approached the Tibetan border, the landscape turned even more rugged. Our rickety bus bumped over gravel and dirt roads on the edge of precipitous canyons of granite and basalt. Down below, whitewater rushed over car-sized boulders and the carcasses of real trucks and buses that had lost their footing on the treacherous road. As we ascended, the air thinned, but the crowd on the bus did not. Fay held my hand tighter and complained of trouble breathing.

China as I knew it disappeared. Above ten thousand feet, houses of brick and cement gave way to dwellings of wood and mud. Roof tiles gave way to thatch. In the lowlands, the majority of people were Han Chinese; but up here, it was stately Tibetans, their hair and clothes festooned with turquoise ornaments. Monks, in crimson robes with bare arms worked into iron, did push-up prostrations in plain sight of passersby. Tibetan children would appear at the truck stops barefoot and in rags, their faces streaked with snot.

Deqin, the last town before the Tibetan border, was, as I suspected, closed to foreigners. What I didn't know was that it was also a military district. When our bus arrived at the checkpoint, we were told to disembark and present our documents to a soldier standing guard. Fay got off first, and I was last. I was dressed in Chinese garb—green army pants and a blue Mao jacket. I presented the guard with my student's card. He didn't look at my face; he just waved me through.

We checked into a small guesthouse near the truck stop. We'd heard that Han Chinese drivers refused to travel this road because of widespread opposition among Tibetans to China's rule. Our plan was to hitchhike into Tibet on a truck driven by a Tibetan.

On the street, we watched Tibetan men sporting cowboy hats and bejeweled knives saunter by, leading horses. Others hurried past clutching live chickens. Muslim fur traders loaded animal pelts into East Wind army trucks. Late in the afternoon, after a meal of noodles at a small Muslim place, we returned to the hotel to find the police waiting for Fay. They bundled her into a jeep and directed me to move on.

Night was falling so it took me a while to find the right police station. Fay had been in custody for two hours. I feared the worst—beating, torture. The fact that she was caught with a foreigner only served to heighten my concern.

"You can leave," said a fat officer at the station as he picked his teeth with a toothpick. "Go on to Tibet. We'll find you a seat on a truck."

"What about my friend?"

"Leave her here. We will make sure she gets back to Nanjing."

The officer told me that Fay's identity card was suspicious. Indeed, it was a fake. Military families had different ID cards and Fay did not want to bring her real ID, worried that, if discovered, her trip with a foreigner would hurt her father's position. A fake ID was a serious crime, the officer explained. They had to investigate. I argued that I could not leave my friend in Deqin. Like the Chinese, I said, we Americans value our friendships. It's just not in our nature to walk out when someone's in trouble. By this time another officer had joined us. They both nodded but didn't seem ready to budge.

I had in my wallet a business card from the bureau chief of the *New York Times* in Beijing. I pulled it out and passed it to the officers. If you keep her, I threatened, I will call this reporter and say you have detained an American. I will call my embassy as well. My bluff gave the officers pause. They told me to wait outside. I walked out of the station house to an open area where a group of young Tibetan men and women had gathered. A few had begun a traditional Tibetan dance. One of the men approached me.

"What happened in there?" he asked.

"They've arrested my friend."

"They've arrested a lot of our friends, too. We hate them."

This was a comparatively easy time for Tibetans living under Chinese rule. China's Communist Party boss, Hu Yaobang, had traveled to the region in 1980 and apologized for the excesses of the Communist occupation: the destruction of temples, the beatings, the imprisonment and execution of Buddhist nuns and monks. Nonetheless, mistrust of China remained high.

About an hour later, Fay was released. She came down the steps to the square where I was waiting. Her face was pale. They hadn't beaten her, but they'd scared her. We touched hands but did not embrace. The police had ordered us to leave Deqin the next day. Banned from entering Tibet, we made our way back into China.

As we traveled away from Yunnan, I worried constantly that Fay would be arrested again. A week or so later, we were on a train heading north to Xi'an, the site of the famed tomb of the Chinese emperor who first united the country in 221 BC. I had used my white face to gain entrance to the dining car to escape the packed "hard seat" section. A railway police officer took an interest in us and sat down at our table. My hands started shaking as he peppered Fay and me with questions, and I dropped bite after bite of chicken on the table and the floor. Luckily, Chinese expected foreigners to be clumsy with chopsticks. We both quietly rejoiced when he finished his meal and walked away.

By the time we got to Xi'an I was doubled over with stomach cramps and vomiting. I felt so sick that I checked into the hospital, where I was diagnosed with an ulcer and given six packets of mysterious pills that seemed to do the trick. My hospital stay blew the last of our money. We were forced to panhandle from Western tourists to buy train fare to Beijing. Those few dollars got us standing-room tickets; we spent two days stuck on the tiny platform between two railway cars. In Beijing, we spent the night on top of a brick wall outside the train station, surrounded by scores of other travelers, some with hair so matted they must not have bathed in weeks. My weight had dropped from 185 to 165 in a month. Fay herself was so frightened of being apprehended by the police that she developed her own version of *lutu jingshenbing*. To this day, she has a fear of traveling.

It was time to go back to Nanjing.

As my time in China drew to a close, I became even more worried that Fay would meet a nasty end after I left. The campaign that had begun with "Civilization and Courtesy Month" had morphed into a witchhunt for people of loose morals and freethinking views. The government was shutting down liberal newspapers and periodicals. In Nanjing, police heightened their surveillance of foreigners. Fay stoked my concerns, partly because she was legitimately frightened, but also because she believed that scaring me would push me to help her leave China.

Much as my classmates had taught me how to look at Chinese women through their baggy clothes, I found myself unconsciously adopting their standards for women. I sought the advice of several trusted classmates, among them Ying Haikang, who was born and bred in Nanjing and who, through his father, had good connections in the Nanjing police force. I wanted to know what would happen to Fay once I'd left. Should I marry her to protect her against a police charge of hooliganism and a trip to the labor camp? Old Ying, as I called him, answered me with questions of his own.

Was she a virgin when we met? I did not know. Did she smoke cigarettes? Sometimes. Do you know where she goes when she leaves you? No. Old Ying's face scrunched up as if he was in pain. "Little Pan," he said, dropping his voice several octaves for ominous emphasis, "she's not a good girl. Who knows, she might have another boyfriend. And she for sure has a past."

I asked Old Ying to use his father's connections to see if the police planned to arrest Fay after I left China. He reported back a few days later. "They say she is badly behaved, but they don't plan on doing anything to her," he said. Her father's position in the military protected her. Old Ying's views seeded my doubts about Fay. I would go to bed at night imagining her trysts with other lovers, worried that I was getting bamboozled.

The logistics of our relationship also conspired to stoke my paranoia.

Tracking Fay down was next to impossible, though she always knew how to find me. When we met, I would ask her where had she been; she'd respond by telling me that I was "turning Chinese," a legitimate point.

After we returned from traveling together, we started meeting at her family's apartment, located on the top floor of a building that had once housed diplomats, back when Nanjing was the capital of China. Fay and her sister shared one room, their parents another. Relations between the two generations were so strained that the parents never ventured into their daughters' room, which now allowed Fay and me to be together, playing cards or making love, without fear of intrusions.

One evening in early 1982, Fay asked me what my intentions were. Did I plan to leave her alone in China? I dodged the question, but she persisted. Did I know what was going to happen to her if I left her? she asked. "They will arrest me for sure," she said. "And it will be all because of you."

"I'm twenty-two," I said. "I can't get married. I'm too young."

"You're leaving China without me?" she shrieked. "I want to go with you to America." She sobbed. "I want to go." Tears streamed down her face. I got up and left. She pulled at my arm. I pulled away. She ran to me and hugged me. I moved toward the door, opened it, and walked out. "Don't go," she said. She followed me to the stairwell. I could hear her sobbing as I mounted my bike. "I want to go to America."

We didn't stop seeing each other. We hatched a plan; I would begin raising cash to bring her to the United States, where she would study. When my parents declined my entreaties to pay for her to be enrolled in an American university, Fay and I decided that I should smuggle antiques out of China and sell them in the West. Through her friends and mine, I amassed a duffel bag's worth of vases, bowls, and plates.

We said what I thought was good-bye on a rainy day in Nanjing in early February 1982. I would be taking the Trans-Siberian Railroad across the Soviet Union to France, where I had been accepted in a program to study French. We went to Nanjing's Sichuan Restaurant for a farewell meal and sat in silence at a corner table, picking at pork in garlic sauce and stir-fried vegetables. Patrons from all over the restaurant, sometimes standing up from their seats to get a better view, provided a running commentary on our every move.

Leaving Nanjing, I went to Shanghai for a few days. On the final night, as I trudged back to the fleabag hotel where I would sleep in a room with thirty other men, there was Fay, walking toward me in the middle of the street, like a vision out of a dream. How she found me I will never know. "We are fated to bump into each other for the rest of our lives," she said. "I found you in a city of ten million people."

From Shanghai, I took the slow train up to Beijing. The border crossing from China into Mongolia went smoothly. Chinese customs agents did not check my bag; antique smuggling had not yet become endemic. I arrived in Paris seven days later, at night. After close to two years in the land of gray, I felt like I had just dropped in from another planet. I had not drunk wine since I had left the United States. I had seen a woman wearing a short skirt only once—in Shanghai, from afar. And rarely, if ever, had I seen so many streetlights. It seemed as if Paris was on fire. The next day, I found a reputable Chinese antiques dealer and brought my duffel bag to his shop. My stash, he informed me, was worth a hundred dollars—less than we had paid for it. With that ended my halfhearted efforts to bring Fay to America.

10

NEW STREET CROSSING

At Nanda, everyone was always hungry—not just for love. The food offered in the campus dining hall was lousy and, what's worse, there wasn't enough of it. With a dull thud, the kitchen matrons would slap a ball of rice in our tin lunch boxes and slosh the dish of the day on top. I knew what rice was supposed to look and taste like, and what we were served did not qualify: square, sawed-off grains that tasted like wood shavings and smelled like a swimming pool because of the chlorine used to kill the manifold vermin thriving in the rice bales. Tiny pebbles lurked among the low-grade chaff, waiting to pop out a dental filling with one bite, shooting reverberations to your toes. Staples like meat and bean curd were still rationed. (In 1979 there was no meat for seven months in Nanjing and sugar shortages were routine.) When there was meat, it was all fat. The only vegetables were soggy cabbage leaves or greasy garlic shoots, both fart-inducing, a bad thing when you're bunking with seven other guys. And never could you eat without first examining your food for fragments of the local daily. Most people used newspaper, not pricey toilet paper, to wipe themselves. Since the contents of pit toilets were used to fertilize crops, it was common to find scraps of newspaper that survived the wok.

On holidays, such as National Day on October 1, we would get more food than usual. This prompted my classmates to take the basins they used to wash their feet into the dining hall to load up on whatever starch and scant vegetables or meat might be available. Along with white metal teacups and clunky thermoses, these basins—decorated with red Communist stripes and a peony, China's national flower—were the first useful consumer goods offered to the Chinese in decades. Everyone had exactly one.

On one such holiday, a roommate named Liu Jintian returned to our dorm with a mountain of rice, easily five pounds of it, crowned with a minuscule summit of stringy cabbage. I watched in amazement as the barely five-foot-five Liu inhaled the whole thing in twenty minutes flat. He rinsed out his mouth noisily with a mouthful of tepid tea and then spat contentedly on the floor.

The dining hall did not provide seats for students until the middle of their sophomore year, so they stood around small, knotted wooden tables. In those days the standard Chinese meal included three dishes and soup; the dining hall usually served two dishes and no soup. After months of student complaints, the cooks, grizzled former PLA veterans whose proximity to the food was evident by their paunches, started throwing together a few bones, boiling water, and a little cabbage. Soup.

One day I saw a roommate, the wet-dreaming Old Ma, hanging around the soup pot, ogling a meaty bone. In a scene out of *Oliver Twist,* Ma snatched the bone from the boiling vat and scampered out of the dining hall with his prize jutting from his mouth. Behind him, screaming bloody murder, came a portly cook, his apron flapping in the breeze.

Still, I seemed to be the only one who griped about the food. So many of my classmates had come from poor villages, they considered it a luxury to be served regular meals that they didn't have to procure themselves. My friend Book Idiot Zhou was particularly happy. Compared to the meager fare he was used to eating at the Shen Kitchen Commune, he was of the opinion that Nanda's dining hall served up a thrice-daily feast.

A freshman at twenty-three, Zhou was the average age of students in my class, a group composed of teenagers as well as people pushing forty. Even though Nanda was 250 miles from his village, he stayed closely tied to the land. At planting time and then at harvest, Zhou would return home to help his father.

Starting in 1978, twenty years after the formation of the communes and the ensuing famine, farmers across China demanded that collective land be returned to the control of individual families. They had learned that the state could not be relied on to feed them during hard times. Under a new system adopted nationwide, the collectives would continue to own the land, but those who sowed it could reap the benefits in the open market. But the dismantling of the commune system also meant the end of government-sponsored services such as irrigation work and road repair. Zhou's father now had more land than ever before, but he needed his son's brute strength to make it work.

As a poor peasant, Zhou qualified for a monthly scholarship of 18.7 *yuan,* the equivalent of a few American dollars. He sent most of the money home to his parents, who were struggling to put his younger sister through high school. Nonetheless, he succeeded in saving some money for himself and one day walked to Nanjing's commercial center—called New Street Crossing—to buy shoes. Though he tried to spruce himself up, there was only so much he could do to his tattered Mao jacket. Zhou returned about an hour later, demoralized, after having spent thirty minutes trying to get a shopkeeper's attention. Farmers routinely flocked into stores to gawk at wash basins, thermoses, and radios—the ne plus ultra of Chinese consumer goods—without buying a thing. Clerks learned to ignore anyone who looked poor.

Without his Nanjing University ID to prove that he was a student and not a farmer, Zhou wasn't going to get better treatment. Returning to the dorm, he dug the badge out from under the roll of clothes he used as a pillow, pinned it above the left pocket of his Mao jacket, and stomped back to New Street Crossing. Within seconds of arriving at the shoe counter, he got served.

My classmates at Nanda and other universities were the darlings of the country. There were 1 billion people in China, and only 860,000 were students. To many women, university students were considered the best matches with the brightest futures. University attendance had the power to transform the desirability of men like Zhou overnight. One day they were peasants, no-hopers destined to a life of hard labor; the next they were intellectuals, facing a future of near-endless potential. But like thousands of newly minted university students, Zhou was already spoken for.

During summer vacation after freshman year, Zhou avoided his fiancée, Lin Fei, meeting her only several times. He had an excuse; his father needed him to help work the fields. When Zhou returned to Nanjing the next year, he fired off a letter, asking Lin Fei to agree to a breakup. "We are not a good match," he wrote bluntly. "This marriage is incompatible with the feelings of my heart." Her reply was pure emotional blackmail: seven words in black ink on rice paper. "If we break up, I will die."

Her illiterate parents followed up on their daughter's threat by paying the village scribe to write a letter threatening to hire a gang to demolish the house Zhou had built for his family if he ended the engagement. Zhou's sister wrote to her brother, telling him she could not stand to see their parents cry because of Zhou's change of heart. His old friends and colleagues at the high school said they did not like to hear people call him a lout.

Nationwide, the issue of university students casting aside their countryside loves was ballooning into a serious social problem. Several of my classmates lived in constant dread that women from home would show up at school—their peasant heads wrapped in barnyard scarves, their cheeks reddened by the sun—and appeal to school authorities to force their men back into a relationship. One classmate moved from the first floor to the third floor of our dormitory after his ex-girlfriend showed up outside his window, banging on the glass and wailing.

There was a name for the men who were dumping their village girlfriends: "Chen Shimei," the villain of a Song Dynasty tale of love, treachery, and revenge. Chen was a poor scholar whose dutiful wife supported him during his studies for the examination to become a senior official. He passed the test and entered the imperial court. Concealing his marital status from the emperor, Chen married a princess and dispatched an assassin to kill his wife and their children. The plot failed, and Chen was executed.

In the end, social pressure forced Zhou to marry Lin Fei. Writing about it later, he observed: "After I graduated, we married. The poetry of praise gushed cheaply in my general direction: 'This boy has a good conscience, a good nature, upright thoughts and lofty morals.' When I heard this, I would rejoice secretly. Luckily I didn't take the other route, otherwise, I would have been a Chen Shimei, a disloyal fiancé. That type of social opprobrium makes a man tremble with fear." For a while, Zhou was satisfied with his decision because it resonated with long-standing Chinese values, but Zhou's views on a slew of issues, including Chinese traditions, were changing. He was beginning to see his life and that of those around him as connected, part of a bigger story, of a tragically sad and powerfully impatient country.

Of all the social sciences, the teaching of history was the most strictly controlled and politicized. Mao himself had studied history as a youth and understood that by monopolizing the historical narrative, he could further his control of the state. The Communists imposed a crude and monolithic interpretation on China's three-thousand-year written history, retelling it as a Marxist fairy tale of endless class struggle and imperialist aggression. There was no room for free-thinking Chinese history majors. Indeed, the study of history was really just the memorization of an elaborate system of collective thought-control. Criticism of the regime, when it happened, took the form of allegory, hints, and whispers.

One day in class we heard a lecture on Sima Qian, China's first great historian. In 99 BC, Sima Qian incurred the anger of the emperor for defending a general who had lost a battle. For the crime of contradicting the emperor, Sima Qian was given a painful choice: castration or suicide. He chose castration and wrote an essay arguing that humiliation is sometimes worthwhile. He vowed to press on to complete his life's work, the *Records of the Grand Historian,* the Chinese equivalent of Herodotus's histories of ancient Greece.

"A man has only one death. That death may be as weighty as Mount T'ai, or it may be as light as a goose feather," our teacher read aloud, quoting from the essay. Then he stopped, raised his head, and looked at the ceiling. There were tears in his eyes.

"In the past," he said, his voice shaking, "the worst thing we did was to abuse people." Branded a "rightist" in the mid-1950s, the professor had been forced to work as a street sweeper during the Cultural Revolution and was only allowed to marry in 1978 after the Gang of Four had been arrested and he was in his late forties. Still petrified of the authorities, the only way he felt free to express his hurt was through an allegory two thousand years old.

Zhou opened his heart to several close friends. This country and this system are rotten, he would say, receiving nods of agreement. During one meeting of the history department's Communist Party members and prospective applicants, he let his frustration surface. The secretary opened the meeting, saying the party wanted China's elite to join. One by one the students chirped in, telling him how eager they were to join, too. Then it came time for Zhou to speak. An excellent student, Zhou had been identified early on as a good party candidate.

"I used to worship party members," Zhou said in his clear reedy voice. "But during the Cultural Revolution, I noticed that the people entering the party were all relatives of important people. I stopped worshipping them. I stopped wanting to enter the party." Silence descended on the room.

The party secretary spoke up and, with perfectly twisted reasoning, offered the students a lesson laced with evasion and threats. "It's natural to have doubts," he began, "but this doesn't necessarily have to shake our belief in Marxism."

The secretary's argument was as simple as it was warped. Look at what the Communist Party has done to China: killing 30 million people during the Great Leap Forward, ruining the lives of millions during the Cultural Revolution. Despite these disastrous failures, he said, it remains in power. That's proof of the party's superiority.

"I first realized the superiority of the socialist system during the Great Leap Forward," he said, according to notes of the meeting. "Then we had the Cultural Revolution. The country did not fall apart. This proves the superiority of our system. A capitalist government would not have been able to survive these disasters, but the Communist Party did. Now, there's talk of some so-called democracy proponents running the country. But they could never survive."

Zhou would always remember this argument. No matter what the party would do to China, no matter how many lives it crushed, it remained unaccountable and always strong enough to rout any challenger. The Communist Party will stay in power because the party will do anything to stay in power. That's an argument that Zhou and many others still believe today.

11

A HANDFUL OF BRAN

At dawn on February 14, 1978, Little Guan boarded the first bus she had ever taken in her life to travel 130 miles—over seven hours—south to Nanjing University. She was traveling alone. She had never been more than thirty miles outside of Hai'an County. She had never seen a mountain, crossed a big bridge, watched TV, rode in an elevator. She was twenty-three.

Little Guan was petrified. She was one of a handful of women in her class majoring in history, and none of them were like her, a child of the countryside. Two were professors' daughters, one was the daughter of a top army officer, and another the daughter of a writer. They all hailed from the city and spoke Mandarin without the hick accent that seasoned Little Guan's speech. Little Guan feared they would treat her like an outsider, a member of a lower class. At the White Pasture Commune, Little Guan was the sophisticated one. But at Nanda she felt rusticated and crude. Within weeks of arriving at college, Little Guan saw her first television. "How strange," she told her classmates. "You can see Tiananmen Square through this box. What a wonderful, magical box." Everyone laughed.

The girls shared a room on the top floor of a four-story dormitory that housed boys on the bottom three floors. Despite the apparent proximity, an invisible Bamboo Curtain divided the boys from the girls. If a guy so much as ascended to the girls' floor by mistake, the class would titter about the incident for weeks. A teacher carried Little Guan's wooden trunk to Room 409, a dark space facing north, crowded with four bunk beds. The other girls had arrived earlier, so the best bunks—near the window—were occupied. Little Guan took the bottom bunk by the door, glad that she didn't have to sleep on top because she feared falling out of bed.

As she looked around the room, searching her new roommates for a friendly face, Little Guan noticed that their skin was whiter than hers, their hands were callus-free, their clothes were better. "How can I compare with them?" she thought. "How am I going to make it here?"

Several weeks into their first semester, the history students were given a spot quiz in their world history class. The subject was Friedrich Engels's turgid essay "The Origins of the Family, Private Property and the State," in which Engels argues that under communism, government would eventually wither away, leaving a classless society. It was a ludicrous essay to be reading just as China was emerging from a period of radical and catastrophic communism to undertake capitalist-style reforms destined to bring back social classes and a widening gap between rich and poor. But political dogma, so much a part of the history major, often bore no resemblance to reality.

The multiple-choice and fill-in-the-blank questions constituted a caricature of Communist thought. "True or false?" one question asked. "Smashing the Gang of Four was a turning point of great significance for our party?" True. "Yes or no?" went another. "Does the fact that the party has corrected the mistaken slogan 'Continuous revolution under the dictatorship of the proletariat' mean that the revolution is over?" No.

When Little Guan got her test back, she took one peek at her score and shoved the paper inside her desk: 75. A failure, she thought. She had never received such a low mark. Then the teacher announced that only four students in the class got a 70 or above, and only one had received a 75. Little Guan had scored the best in the class. With that jolt of self-confidence, she began to amass the courage to explore the world outside her dorm room.

Little Guan had never been in such a big city. In 1978, the tallest building in Hai'an was three stories. Ten stories qualified for skyscraper status in Nanjing. When she first arrived, Little Guan was afraid to cross the street alone—so many buses, trucks, and bicycles! She needed a classmate's hand to guide her. She would not bike the six blocks to the shopping area at New Street Crossing unless a friend came along.

Competition at Nanda was intense and the workload was heavy. The students followed the Maoist exhortation to study hard: "Good, good study! Day, day up!" Some students cramming late in the bathroom or hallway fainted because of the pressure; others lost weight or developed nervous tics. But some, like Little Guan, blossomed. Her goal was to be named a "Three Good" student: good studies, good politics, and good fitness. But years of bad nutrition had affected her health. Her wind sprints were just too slow, and she failed the fitness test. Nonetheless, by the end of her first semester, she was asked to join the party. Little Guan declined again. The memory of the lecherous official at White Pasture Commune was indelible.

At the beginning of her second semester, school authorities approached Little Guan and told her they wanted her to live with a foreign student. Little Guan demurred. She said she did not think she was good enough, that her Mandarin was heavily accented, and that she spoke no English. "This shows the school's trust in you," the campus official insisted.

Little Guan left her cramped dorm to share a room on the foreigners' side with a cherubic brunette from northeastern Canada named Mary Boyd. Canadians, like Italians and other Western Europeans, had been coming to China to study since the early 1970s. These students were on scholarships from their home countries and were randomly dispatched— by their embassies or by the Chinese Ministry of Education—to universities throughout China.

Little Guan's worries about living with a foreigner didn't go away immediately. Her view of non-Chinese was the standard one: they had big noses, pink skin, and curvy bodies, which stank. Foreigners showered in the morning, not at night, and after lunch, they did not nap, a necessity for most Chinese. But Little Guan discovered that foreigners, like college tests and city life, just took getting used to. In six months, she had grown accustomed to the hustle and bustle of Nanjing. She had shed her rural habits (including hocking thunderously and spitting on the floor) and realized that she was not any "lower," as she put it, than urban folk. She soon discovered she could also adjust to sharing her room with a woman from the West.

Like Daybreak Song, our class Romeo, Little Guan was a hit among the foreign students. Whereas many Chinese would be on their guard for fear of being criticized as too friendly, Little Guan acted naturally. She told stories of her life in the countryside. Her bossy side would surface, and she would order the men around and poke fun at their tone-deaf Chinese.

For Western guys who were desperate for any kind of normal contact with a Chinese woman, her innocent flirtation was warmly received. Five feet tall with pigtails and small but sparkling eyes, Little Guan made up for in spunk what she lacked in beauty. Despite her small stature, her personality dominated a room.

Mary and the others found Little Guan—like other Chinese women—to be more mature than Chinese men. Perhaps because they were universally spoiled by their parents, the boys grew up more slowly. The women knew how to do chores. And they were more flexible when it came to facing down hardship.

Mary Boyd's friendship with Little Guan taught Mary about the wide gap between Chinese myths and reality. Despite the stereotype of the collectivist Oriental, for example, Mary discovered that Chinese were often more individualistic than foreigners. Forced into groups all their lives, Chinese actually hated them. Chinese were, on the whole, poor team players. Having had socialist solidarity shoved down their throats for so many years, the idea of team spirit was anathema.

Mary and Little Guan had a cozy relationship in their capacious room in Building 10 of the foreign students' dormitory. Every few months, sometimes every few weeks, they rearranged the furniture, coercing their male classmates into moving their desks and their beds draped with mosquito netting. They shared a daily afternoon coffee, the beans purchased at the Friendship Store or sent via care package from Canada. Little Guan had never tried coffee before, but she was hooked. She drinks it to this day.

The women were just a few months apart in age. Mary was born on May 16, 1955, and Little Guan on July 15, so Little Guan took to calling Mary "elder sister." In the spring of 1979, Mary had an eye operation at a Nanjing hospital, and Little Guan went to see her. Little Guan figured it was the least she could do since Mary was far from her family. She also was curious to see how much better the Chinese doctors would treat a foreigner. Mary had her own room and round-the-clock nursing care. As a way of thanking her for this small kindness, Mary threw Little Guan a surprise birthday party in their room.

When Little Guan arrived that evening, she stood gaping at the cake and the presents and all the people. She immediately remembered a Communist

Party order requiring Chinese students to report any special events held by foreigners and realized her birthday party was just that. Little Guan announced that she had forgotten a book at the library and bolted off to the Foreign Affairs department to inform officials that her roommate was throwing her a birthday party and make sure it was permissible to attend. But the officials had long since gone home for the night. Having failed to snitch on herself, Little Guan returned to her room, where Chinese classmates and foreign students from Nanda and other institutes around Nanjing ate and danced past midnight. "Happy Birthday" was sung in several languages and Little Guan blew out the candles on her cake. "It was my happiest party ever," Little Guan recalled years later. "It also was the first time someone ever kissed my hand."

The next morning, as she was returning from breakfast, Little Guan was chased down by a Foreign Affairs functionary and ordered to the office. One of her classmates, indeed one of the Chinese guests, had ratted her out.

"How can you let a foreigner know your birthday?" the official shrieked.

Little Guan ignored the question.

"I tried to report this to you, but you had all gone home," she maintained.

"Why did you tell her your birthday?" the official persisted. "You told her that so she'd give you a party!"

"No, I told her that because we were born in the same year, and we wanted to see who was older."

"Well, in the future," the official warned her ominously, "you had better watch it when you speak to foreigners."

Just as Little Guan turned to leave, she stopped at the door and addressed the official. "Why don't you go tell the foreigners your birthday and see if they throw you a party?" Little Guan's "mistake" would have lasting consequences at Nanda. For years afterward, Chinese students were instructed not to "easily let the foreigners give you a birthday party."

By her junior year, Little Guan was lagging behind her classmates in the search for a husband. Nanda's regulations explicitly banned anyone from having a boyfriend or a girlfriend. But there was not a lot the university authorities could do to stop a generation that had repressed its desires—for everything, including sex—for so long. Some were bold; others took measures bordering on the bizarre. One classmate refused to walk on the same side of the street as her boyfriend. Instead they would stroll on opposite sidewalks, matching each other's pace.

In a country where by the age of twenty most women were engaged if not married, the stress of finding a mate was intense, especially for women over twenty-five, like Little Guan. Men demanded that their brides be virgins, but many of the women had exchanged their chastity for a ticket out of the fields, sleeping with the local party boss or his son.

For the women who nationwide made up roughly one quarter of university students (at Nanda and other top universities, they comprised just 12 percent), finding a mate was more difficult than it was for men. Chinese men favored women with some, but not too much, education. This predilection was amplified by questions of pride or what the Chinese called *mianzi* (face). If a woman outshone her man, he would lose face among his friends and associates. *Boshijie* (PhD Elder Sister) was another way of saying "old maid" in Chinese.

Still, Little Guan wasn't about to take just anyone. She had set specific conditions for her ideal mate. First, he had to be from her class at Nanda because Little Guan believed that their experience as one of the first classes to enter college after the Cultural Revolution was so unique that only someone who had struggled as she had would make a fitting match. Second, he had to have lived in the countryside so he would understand her. His parents had to have been educated, and the family could not have a daughter so they would treasure her as if she was theirs.

One spring evening, she accepted an invitation to dinner at the house of the son of a provincial party leader along Beijing West Road. The street was lined with parasol trees with their massive leaves, thick trunks, and mottled bark. Whereas most Chinese lived in rabbit warrens, this neighborhood had been constructed before the revolution for officials from the Nationalist government and the houses were palatial, with grassy backyards, wood-paneled living rooms, telephones, refrigerators, and fans.

When Little Guan came to the door, she was let in by a maid. She had never seen a maid before. As she entered the room, she saw European chandeliers and colorful carpets. She also realized, gaping at the biggest dining room table she'd ever seen, that she was not the only one who was going to dine with the family.

That night after dinner, the official's son sat with her in the quiet of the backyard. A spring breeze rustled through a small grove of bamboo; a fountain tinkled. Little Guan was terrified. She turned to her suitor and blurted out: "I can't fall in love with someone who is too perfect. I can't do that."

He looked at her with his big eyes, completely amazed. How could she refuse this opportunity? But Little Guan was looking for love and understanding, not a life of comfort. That evening was followed by another failed introduction, this time to the son of a chemistry professor. He was struck off Little Guan's list for being, of all things, too short.

Little Guan divided men into two categories: the rational and the romantic. The rational were those you could grow old with. The romantic were ones with whom you could study calligraphy. "Of course, I wish my future husband would be able to play the violin and make me giddy, but that is impossible because I am not that kind of person either," she wrote in her diary.

During her junior year, a classmate told Little Guan that Ding Bangjun, a broad-shouldered boy, also from Hai'an, wanted to be her boyfriend. The use of a third party to convey love messages was routine. Students would also bring a friend along on the first date. Ding was one of the quieter boys in the history department; even so Little Guan had noticed him because she always had an eye for handsome men. Ding fulfilled another one of Little Guan's conditions, inspired by the death of her little brother, Yonglong; he was younger than Little Guan. Chances were he wouldn't leave her alone.

Little Guan told her classmate that Ding should deliver his message himself. Even though she had no special feeling for him, she wanted to give him some face. If Little Guan had rejected him outright, it would have been bad for his reputation.

Little Guan and Ding started spending time together as friends. One day, she went with him to the post office as he sent money home. Because he qualified as a poor student, Ding received a monthly government allowance of eight *yuan* ($1.25)—barely enough to live on. Yet there was Ding, taking half of his stipend and sending it to an orphaned high school classmate. "This moved me," Little Guan later recalled. "I thought, 'Well, if he's that good to a classmate, he'd be very good to his wife.'"

Sometime into her last semester, Little Guan's father and Ding's father met in Hai'an to discuss the possibility of their children's romance. Both teachers, they knew each other. They agreed that marriage might be a good thing. In his next letter, Little Guan's father suggested she spend more time with the young man from Hai'an. Ding's father did the same. Little Guan liked the idea. The fortune-teller predicted this, she said to herself. Ding's village was situated to the south of White Pasture Commune.

One day, Little Guan walked over to Ding's room and asked if he had received his father's letter. While it was still rare for a girl to enter the boys' dorm, it was no longer cause for general panic. Ding walked outside with her, looking like a deer caught in the headlights.

"Really, I'm no match for you," he mumbled nervously as they strolled together. "I am going to write a letter to my father to tell him that I am not the one for you. You're too good for me." Little Guan was touched.

"You never said bad things about me like the other boys did, and besides it's not clear to me that I'm too good for you," she countered. "We can give it a try."

They had stopped walking and stood standing side by side. Neither could look at the other one. "You are my top choice, and I am your last choice," Ding blurted out. "If you want to spend time with me that's great, but you can always still look for others." Little Guan thought, "Wow, this guy is so smooth." But she was moved.

That simple conversation set their relationship rolling. The more Little Guan saw Old Ding, as she called him despite the fact that he was younger, the more she liked him. "It is not a love for all time," Guan told her diary, "but it is what I want. We fight sometimes, but that is normal. And I don't treat him like a guest."

Little Guan had recognized that she needed a man different from her beloved father. A man like her father, she wrote, would always have a hard time. "He was too honest," she later wrote. "In this eunuch culture where cunning, selfishness, toadying and scheming are considered intelligent, he was like a child who had lost his way, completely unaware."

What Little Guan wanted, she wrote, was a man who could cope with the twists and turns of life. Someone who could "swim in dirty water but himself stay clean." Old Ding was that man. He attracted her and made her feel so safe that she could doze off while she rode on the back of his bicycle.

▪ ▪ ▪

At the end of December 1981, Nanjing University announced the students' job assignments—the biggest day of their college careers. The *fenpei,* or allocation system, was part of the state plan for the economy. Bureaucrats, not the market, assigned every job, just as they determined which machine tool would produce which widget.

Most students accepted their job assignments meekly. China's system did not countenance opposition unless you had powerful relatives. As *fenpei* approached, my classmates became extra vigilant about what they said in public and how they acted. Any misstep, political or otherwise, could tip the balance.

Inevitably, some were shattered by their assignments. One girl from another department hanged herself in her dorm room after receiving the news that she would be working in a dirt-poor region of western China, the equivalent of Siberia. Qian Yu, the disco dancer, took the bizarre step of entering a Buddhist monastery after he had failed to win a job in his hometown, Shanghai. His decision to dabble in religion had its desired effect; authorities at Nanda summoned him from the monastery and, in exchange for him agreeing to drop Buddhism, pledged to help him return to Shanghai.

Little Guan won a plum assignment, close to the best in her class, a position in Beijing. After "Long live Chairman Mao," the second sentence a student learned at elementary school was "Beijing is the capital of China." Chinese of Little Guan's generation were taught to revere the capital as much as they were taught to love China, the Communist Party, and Chairman Mao. In the early 1980s, living standards in Beijing were higher than any other place in China, food was more plentiful, and the schools were better.

Little Guan had never been there. She was assigned a position in a big publishing house. She would become an editor. Again, the fortune-teller's predictions rang true. He said she would have an easy time making it in the capital. Little Guan won the job assignment not because of her connections or party affiliation; she possessed neither. She won it because of great grades and her true-grit smarts. If anyone could make it in Beijing, a professor told her, she could.

Old Ding, by contrast, had been given a job as an archaeologist at a museum in Hefei, the capital of Anhui Province to the west of Jiangsu and a twenty-four-hour train trip from Beijing. Anhui is where Pearl Buck's 1931 Pulitzer Prize–winning bestseller, *The Good Earth,* is set. The novel is about a rural family facing famine. Since the Communist Revolution, life had not improved. Anhui was so poor that foreigners were prohibited from visiting long after other parts of China were opened to Western visitors.

Little Guan told Old Ding that she did not want to go to Beijing because the temptations of the capital—notably its large pool of eligible bachelors—would be too great for her. "Within two months, I would end my relationship with you," she said. He remained quiet.

Even though they had never kissed and had barely held hands, Little Guan had decided she wanted to marry Old Ding. She did not care too much about using a man to climb a ladder of success, nor did she care about money. "I wanted someone who would love me and whom I could love," she said. "I always hated girlish men. I wanted a real man, and Ding was a real man."

Little Guan worked the system. First, she lobbied for Ding to get a transfer to Beijing, but no one at Nanda would help her. The party official who had criticized Little Guan about her birthday party opposed the relationship. "He's too good for you," she told Little Guan when she went to plead Ding's case. "You haven't even written an application to enter the party, and Ding is already a member. He should be with a party member, not someone with free thoughts like you." Little Guan tried to wrangle a job assignment in Nanjing, four hours by bus from Hefei, but the university official blocked her there as well. So Little Guan did what no one else in her class—and few across China—had done. She rejected the chance to go to Beijing and turned down the job. "If worse comes to worse, I will sell pot stickers," Little Guan told a group of her roommates, who, amazed by her decision, surrounded her in her dorm room. "I just want to be with my man, to marry and have a home and a family."

Little Guan's father used to tell her that she was easily satisfied, like an old hen happy with a handful of bran. She just wanted a warm nest for herself and her husband. She was not going to get it.

12

SPIRITUAL POLLUTION

After the arrest of the Gang of Four, the Nanjing city government made a token payment of a thousand dollars to Old Wu and his siblings as compensation for their parents' murders. His father's book on ancient scholars, which had been used as proof of his wayward views, was republished, albeit in a censored form.

Old Wu graduated from Nanjing University in 1982. Already a party member, he could have easily leveraged his status as the son of a wrongfully killed party bigwig into a cushy government or party job. Instead he accepted a position teaching history at Nanjing Normal University, where his parents had taught and died. My classmates praised Old Wu's lack of political ambition and his disinclination to parlay his family's suffering into power and perks. I, however, was completely baffled.

It seemed to me that Old Wu was choosing to do things the hard way. How could he have agreed to live literally in the shadows of his parents' deaths, lecturing in the same hall where they once taught, walking past his parents' murder scene every day? I asked him whether he didn't need some type of psychological asylum from the past, but he looked at me as if I were nuts. "Nanjing is my home," he said. "I was known at Nanjing Normal. I was protected there." Old Wu's status as the son of a victim gave him cachet at the university; it guaranteed him an easier life.

The men and women who killed Wu's parents were never prosecuted, although police know who they are. Two Chinese journalists were present at the beatings on August 3, 1966, and the photographs and written report that they filed that day remain in the archives of the Jiangsu Province department of public security. The reason they were not brought to justice is that their families were powerful and they themselves have since risen to prominence in the Jiangsu provincial government.

If my parents had been murdered by the state, I would have devoted my life to vengeance, to political activity, or at least to unearthing the evidence stashed in the provincial cop shop. Why wouldn't Old Wu do the same? Where was his sense of justice? Why did so many stories in China always seem to end with the bad guys getting away, literally, with murder?

Just because the guilty weren't punished does not mean that no one served time. In 1978, party officials in Nanjing settled on a man named Tang Daming, who was sentenced to eighteen years for masterminding the murders. Tang was an easy target. He was a minor participant in the killings and was not politically well connected.

Tang, who served five years before being released, now works in the library of Nanjing Normal University, where he and Old Wu cross paths every week.

While Old Wu and Little Guan dreamed of a simple life, Daybreak Song was making his more complicated. No sooner had Antonella left Nanjing than Song took up with another Italian, Maria Luisa Giorgio, a brunette with limpid eyes. Song was courting a girl back home in Yancheng at the same time.

Song seemed to view his love affairs with Antonella and Maria Luisa as one kind of love—passionate, intimate, and dangerous—and his relationship with the Chinese girl back home as virginal and safe.

Song approached his studies as he approached romance; he was half-hearted, but the results were excellent. Along with six other students, he won a coveted scholarship to the university's graduate history program. A position as a grad student conferred high social status; the stipend and perks were certainly far above those of China's businessmen, restaurateurs, and small-shop owners. Most Chinese had yet to embrace Deng Xiaoping's contention that to "get rich is glorious." Many continued to hold a Maoist-era view about business, believing that money was "dirty" and so were the people who handled it.

Becoming a grad student allowed Song to put off the painful process of entering the job market. Freethinkers and nonparty members like Song would often wind up getting dispatched to teach at a small institute in far-away provinces with no hope of professional success.

Having failed to stop nose picking and other social ills with its feeble "Civilization and Courtesy Month," hard-liners in the party decided to up the ante. In 1983, the party launched a campaign against "spiritual pollution," which began as a crusade against writers who argued that the party's refusal to take responsibility for China's bloody past made for a twisted society. It would soon expand to include such vague targets as "individualism," "reactionary and vulgar" art, "loose behavior," and unconstitutional speech.

The campaign ensnared one of our classmates, Zhang Aibing. Zhang was among the youngest students in our class, a bright boy and the son of two hospital workers from Anhui Province. Graced with an infectious laugh, a solid physique, and bullish self-confidence, he attracted women. After graduating in 1982, he, like Song, won a slot as a graduate student in Nanda's history department. The pair moved to a better room, sharing their digs with two other history grad students.

One day in the fall of 1983, Zhang's girlfriend, a singer in a government song-and-dance troupe, came to his dorm room. It was locked. She heard rustling inside. The girlfriend learned from a student down the hall that Zhang was in his room with another woman, girlfriend number two, a math major. The singer fled the dorm in tears and headed to the Nanjing Bridge, which, since its completion in 1968, had been a favorite suicide venue—four hundred feet above the chocolate swirl of the Yangtze River. A police officer stopped her as she tottered along the walkway. Her brother-in-law, also a police officer, came to the scene and took her home, where she churned out a ten-page report about the two-timing Zhang which she submitted to the party.

The party secretary in the history department launched an investigation. Zhang, it was discovered, had snapped nude photos of his lovers and had also forged permission slips allowing him to spend several nights in hotels with them. After six long months, he was expelled, banished to a dead-end job in Anhui as a teacher at a vocational college. In a lone act of protest, Zhang changed the characters, but not the pronunciation, of his given name. Aibing, Lover of the Military, now meant Lover of Ice.

Zhang's expulsion was a wake-up call to players such as Daybreak

Song: it was time for him to get out of China. Song had intended to write his dissertation about Tibet, but he was not able to gain access to any official files; the government had banned research into anything involving ethnic groups, borders, and foreign affairs. Song hoped to do real research and not the stuff undertaken in institutes where scholars regurgitated the party line, plagiarizing one another to avoid the risk of having a dangerously original thought. So he parlayed his relationships with Maria Luisa and Antonella into an introduction to an official at the Italian embassy in Beijing. Though he spoke not a word of Italian, he was awarded a scholarship to study in Florence for a year. Two months later, in October 1988, at the age of twenty-nine, Song boarded a plane for the first time and flew for sixteen hours from Beijing to Dubai to Rome, becoming the first member of his class to realize another dream of their generation: going abroad.

13

PETRIFIED MARRIAGE

In his last year at Nanda, Book Idiot Zhou finally entered the Communist Party, swallowing his antiparty pride in the hope that it would result in a better job assignment. It didn't. He was told he was going to be sent to Dongtai, just a few miles away from Shen Kitchen Commune. Unlike Little Guan, Zhou didn't have someone like Old Ding on whom he could rely. After graduation, he'd returned home and married Lin Fei, who, with her rural resident's permit, was even more helpless than he was.

So Zhou took the only route available to him to leave the countryside. He enlisted in the People's Liberation Army. The decision appealed to his father. Ever since Zhou had been rejected from the armed forces during the Cultural Revolution, his dad had harbored the dream that someday his boy would have the right stuff. Zhou graduated from Nanda in July 1982 and a month later entered the PLA as a lieutenant.

Zhou was assigned to the Bengbu Tank Institute in southern Anhui Province. In Bengbu, a grimy little industrial center on the banks of the Huai River, Zhou was billeted in a one-room apartment with a common shower and toilet down the hall. He awoke on his second day realizing he had made a mistake. "This is going to be a tragedy," he wrote in his diary. "I have to begin my struggle to leave." Lin Fei was not allowed to live with him; Zhou's officers told him that they could only change her resident's permit after Zhou completed fifteen years of service.

The PLA was a conservative, bloated bureaucracy that was far better at crushing dissent than defending China. In February 1979, the PLA invaded Vietnam as part of Deng Xiaoping's plan to punish China's former ally for overrunning Cambodia and cozying up to the Soviet Union. The PLA performed horribly, losing an estimated 20,000 men.

Deng used the debacle to discard dead wood—and potential political rivals—from the military brass, leaving senior officers even more careful than before. In the wake of these events, Zhou was assigned to teach modern history to recruits at the tank institute and ordered to stick closely to the party line.

Because the PLA demanded a zombielike adherence, Zhou was obligated to attend each and every meeting his superiors held. The officers would drone endlessly, so Zhou carried a pin to prick his palms when he felt drowsy. Those who did doze off were punished severely: forced to sit through endless criticism sessions, locked up, and denied food. At meals, Zhou's superiors ordered him to drink *baijiu*, a fiery grain alcohol with an airplane fuel stench. Zhou ended many evenings vomiting into a plastic bucket.

The history taught at the Bengbu Tank Institute was even more dogmatic than the pabulum served up at Nanjing University. Nanda's professors merely brushed over the truth; at Bengbu, they lied, rendering history into a Communist cartoon show. All the villains were landlords and capitalists; the heroes, dirt-poor peasants. Hong Xiuquan, the lunatic leader of the Taiping Rebellion, an uprising that left millions dead in the mid-nineteenth century, was hailed as a revolutionary martyr, his manic barbarity and very un-communist conviction that he was Jesus's younger brother airbrushed out of the narrative. The United States remained the source of the world's evil, even as in real life Chinese leaders were conspiring with the U.S. against the Soviet Union's occupation of Afghanistan and establishing a joint eavesdropping facility in northwest China to monitor Russian nuclear tests.

Zhou was allowed to return home once a year, and his wife could come to Bengbu twice. On one of these conjugal visits, Lin Fei became pregnant and in January 1984 gave birth to twin girls. Their daughters were born one year after the government embraced the idea that it needed to more tightly control the growth of China's population. A recent census, the first in more than twenty years, confirmed that the population had surpassed 1 billion, a jump of more than 300 million people. The government responded by promulgating a revised marriage law that increased the marriage age from eighteen to twenty for women and from twenty to twenty-two for men. Officials redoubled their efforts to enforce China's one-child policy that had been on the books since the 1970s. Women with more than one child were ordered to get IUDs. Compulsory sterilization programs for both men and women became common, as did forced abortions. In the countryside, land contracts for peasants were linked to a secondary contract, mandating that couples have just one child. Authorities regularly bulldozed the houses of farmers breaking the one-child rule. The policy was even more strictly enforced in the cities, with those who flouted the law losing their jobs and benefits. Twins were therefore seen as a blessing. But in Zhou's case, the blessing was mixed. One daughter was healthy; the other had Down syndrome.

In China, a handicapped child was traditionally considered a punishment for sins in this life or a previous one. Whenever the family left the house, Zhou's daughter invariably would be surrounded by onlookers who gaped at her, mimicking her slack mouth and jumpy walk. Handicapped children were looked on as wasted lives consuming precious resources and were often sterilized once they reached puberty. Many more were killed in the delivery room.

The birth of their handicapped child pushed Zhou and Lin Fei further apart. Her understanding of genetics was primitive. She believed that men's sperm determined everything about a baby. The twins' birth was a sign, she said, that Zhou was a bad man and a failure. "From that moment on, I was on an unhappy merry-go-round between my work in Anhui and my home in Jiangsu, two hundred miles away," Zhou later would write. He was also on a merry-go-round regarding his obligation to support his family, which he took seriously, and his increasingly troubled relationship with his wife. On top of all this, he was stuck in the PLA.

China's armed forces held on tightly to their educated officers. Permission was required for anyone in China to switch jobs. The same held true for the military, which was the toughest organization to leave because of its political clout. Zhou's political commissar rejected his request to resign. Zhou countered that he hated teaching at the institute because it amounted to deceiving young people. In his classes, he had stopped going by the book and begun criticizing the party and lambasting Mao. "We talk about how beautiful everything is, but then these kids enter real society and don't know how to function," Zhou said. The commissar laughed and replied, "What do you want me to do about it? I still won't let you leave our school."

Zhou then plotted to get himself kicked out of the military, feigning illness and finding a friendly doctor who gave him a medical release. The commissar laughed when he saw it. "Little Zhou, I will support you as a sick soldier forever," he said, "but I will never let you leave."

This type of unyielding obstruction was routine. The Chinese called it "red-eye disease," a jealousy so powerful and endemic that it compelled peers to plot against each other and allowed superiors to toy with their underlings. During my time at Nanda, when Chinese would ask me what I thought was the biggest difference between my country and theirs, I would reply that, in the United States, competition generally inspired people to achieve, but in China it drove them to wreck each others' lives.

For Zhou, neither honesty nor deception worked, so he tried the last avenue available to him. He determined who among the senior officers had the most liberal reputation, and then told him of his disenchantment. The official, who had been persecuted during the Cultural Revolution, was receptive. After six months of lobbying, the institute agreed to let him go. He left the PLA in February 1986.

According to government regulations, Zhou was supposed to return home to his village on the Jiangsu coast, a prospect he loathed. Having spent his adult life trying to leave the countryside, he was damned if he was going back there now. Bengbu, though a tiny city for China (just four hundred thousand people), was still a better bet. Zhou landed a job there as a teacher at the Anhui Institute of Finance and Trade.

Zhou's scheming, conniving, and plotting were routine for people coping with a rapidly changing country. In the countryside, the communes had been dismantled. In the cities, former political prisoners, small-time crooks, and people with bad political backgrounds, recently freed from the gulag, had opened restaurants and shops, brightening China's previously colorless streets. These outcasts were the first entrepreneurs; everyone else belonged to work units which, like the military, would not let their employees go. Just a few years before, many of these fledgling business-men and a few women would have been thrown in jail as "capitalist road-ers." Now they were on the street, hustling for a better life. The key was working the system: finagling supplies, finding someone willing to rent out space, hiring your relatives, scraping together a loan from friends. Those with the creativity to pull it off in these early years had once been the rene-gades and malcontents of Communist China.

The mid-1980s saw a lot of firsts in China. The Changhong TV factory began producing color television sets. The first Chinese fashion models trav-eled overseas to parade down Western catwalks. The so-called "Patriotic Capitalists"—members of the pre-1949 business elite who elected to stay on in revolutionary China but were repaid for their loyalty by being jailed and tortured during the Cultural Revolution—were placed back in positions of authority at the central bank and other government advisory posts.

In response to the need for foreign capital and technology, Deng Xiaop-ing had established four economic zones in the south of the country where investors were offered incentives, including a corporate tax rate half that of the rest of China and an exemption from import duties on raw mate-rials. Unlike their counterparts elsewhere in China, executives in the eco-nomic zones were given the freedom to pay piecework wages, to hire and fire employees, and to negotiate their own contracts. The power of labor unions was weakened and that of managers increased. By the end of 1983, the four zones, Shenzhen, Hainan, Xiamen, and Zhuhai, had lured $2.8 billion in foreign investment, nearly half the national total.

With money comes leisure. When I crossed the border into Shenzhen from Hong Kong in 1980, it was barely more than a frontier village. By 1984, officials and workers on holiday cavorted at Shenzhen's "Honey Lake Country Club"—complete with a two-thousand-seat theater and an amusement center where shaggy-haired youths cruised in bumper cars and played electronic five-card stud. To seal the rest of China off from Shen-zhen's "decadent" influences, the authorities erected an internal border: a fifty-mile-long barrier with spotlights, barbed wire, and land and sea checkpoints.

Zhou was anxious to take part in the creation of this new, wealthier, and more relaxed society, but family responsibilities weighed heavily. He felt trapped between two worlds, the old one of the countryside and the new one being created in China's cities. Zhou penned an essay, "I Regret Not Being a Chen Shimei," which was published in one of the new semi-independent weeklies. Appearing in 1984 under a pen name, Zhou's essay tracked the path of his disenchantment with his marriage. It struck a chord among the men—and women—of his generation trapped in loveless unions that might have made sense during the Cultural Revolution but which appeared increasingly ludicrous now.

When Mao dispatched 18 million city-dwelling youths from various social backgrounds to the countryside to "learn from the peasants," desire, loneliness, or resignation propelled hundreds of thousands of them into the arms of one another or rural boys or girls. Those who married were trapped in the countryside. If they left the countryside, they would have to leave alone because China's system generally banned the spouse from leaving, too. If they tried to get a divorce, their career and social reputation would be finished. But staying in these dead-end relationships, what the Chinese called "petrified marriages," consigned them to a life of loneliness and frustration.

Zhou's essay told the story of his courtship of Lin Fei, his entrance into university, his attempt to break off the relationship, Lin Fei's threats, and the condemnation of his peers for his attempts to extricate himself. "Each day was uneasy, and each day I was continually on the run," Zhou wrote. Earmarked for the support of his aging parents (his mother had contracted leukemia) and his own family, Zhou's salary "basically was a big zero," forcing him to borrow whatever cash old friends could scrape together. "But the worst torture was a crisis in our emotions," he wrote of his marriage. "There was a large gap between us. We had lost a common language."

One day he asked her, "Are you happy?" Unexpectedly, Lin Fei said she regretted marrying him, too, admitting that she wished she had married a peasant. "Heavens," he wrote, "look at what we've become."

Of course, Zhou wrote, he had thought about divorce. But when he read reports in the papers about divorce cases that languished for decades, awaiting party approval, he said he lost interest. Zhou concluded with some questions: "Can we really say we have advanced historically when we force two people who do not want to be together to get married and have children? . . . What is it about Chinese Communist culture that belittles the search for love?"

Articles like Zhou's, offering pointed social criticism, were appearing with increasing frequency as writers and thinkers pushed the limits of what was acceptable. Liberal factions within the party hierarchy protected them from the censor's knife. Then, conservatives would gain the upper hand, muzzle gutsy periodicals, and jail prominent thinkers. Cultural politics was a schizophrenic affair with spasms on the left and the right as party factions battled over the pace of reforms. One year it was a fight against "spiritual pollution," the next it would be "leftist excesses," and then "bourgeois liberalization." The average person was bombarded by a dizzying array of slogans spanning the political spectrum. Magazine editors would commission an article one week and kill it the next because the party had changed its line.

Separated from his family, Zhou taught and read. In the classroom, Zhou regurgitated propaganda. But at home, as he devoured history books smuggled in from Taiwan and Hong Kong, his views evolved. Mainland Chinese writers had also started publishing harrowing tales of what happened to people who had dared to criticize Chairman Mao. The result for Zhou was a complete rejection of everything Mao had accomplished. And as for Mao's lieutenant, Zhou Enlai, generally beloved by most intellectuals, "I thought that he was worse than Mao. Mao at least was a man. Zhou Enlai was so rotten that people thought he was good. He duped people into thinking he had a conscience. He didn't."

Zhou followed his piece on married life with a powerful criticism of China's criminal justice system that focused on something the state had dubbed its Strike Hard campaign against crime. China under Mao had low levels of crime—criminality being the exclusive province of the state. But street crime was now on the rise as a result of the increasing gap between rich and poor, the newfound mobility of the Chinese, and the collapse of group-think. One of the proposed punishments for criminals was to annul their city resident permits and force them to live in the countryside. Zhou found this absolutely amazing. "Is it really party policy to exile criminals to the countryside?" Zhou asked in an article titled "Let's Talk about the Unequal Status of Peasants," which is still cited in Chinese academic journals today. "What does this say about what it means to be a farmer in China?" Zhou had picked up on an early signal: the party was abandoning its rural roots and transforming itself into an organization of city-based bureaucrats. Concerned about the sensitivity of the topic, a magazine in Shanghai waited two years, until 1988, before publishing the essay.

That year, Zhou returned to his village and did something both unusual and courageous. He undertook a survey of the devastation wrought by his Red Guard team on his home village of 2,500 people. According to his research, his team burned two tons of books, ransacked five Buddhist temples and four Taoist shrines, and chopped hundreds of old carvings— dragons, phoenixes, gremlins, and birds—from the eaves of ancient court-yard houses. Dozens of his victims had been seriously hurt. Ten people committed suicide following beatings.

Zhou ran into one man he and his comrades had crippled. They had strung the man up by his thumbs because a neighbor had claimed, falsely, that he was using a secret radio transmitter to contact Taiwan. The man was now selling cups of tea by the side of the road. His hands were man-gled beyond use, and he served the drink by clasping the mug with his wrists and offering it, like a prayer, to his patrons. Zhou stopped to buy a cup to get a closer look at his horrible handiwork, said nothing, and moved on.

Zhou's research was unusual because it underscored his willingness to explore the personal consequences of what he had done in the name of Chairman Mao. Instead of hiding behind history, he confronted it. By 1988, Deng Xiaoping's campaigns to criticize Mao and the excesses of the Cultural Revolution had ended. Zhou, typically, would not go along.

Many in China, including some of my classmates, believed that not looking back was good for the country. It allowed China to move for-ward, they said. The destruction of traditional culture during the Cultural Revolution had so weakened family ties, for example, that once the state loosened its policies on travel, millions of people hit the road in search of a better life. These people manned the factories that were remaking China and the world. But others, like Zhou, believed that the Communist Party's unwillingness to allow a clear look at the past fostered a world devoid of beliefs and concerned primarily with one thing: the pursuit of material possessions. More broadly, China was a country where shame, not guilt, was the primary force restraining people's behavior. If someone could get away with something without being discovered, he or she often did so, free of the pangs of conscience. Zhou's conscience was not so easily numbed.

14

YIN FINDS YANG

On January 12, 1982, Little Guan was awarded her diploma from Nanjing University. Two days later, she and Old Ding went to the marriage bureau and registered. That night, he took her to dinner. Too poor to afford a ring, Old Ding bought her an ersatz gold necklace engraved with the English word "Love" from a Nanjing department store. She put it on, and with that they were husband and wife. One of the last to find a boyfriend in her class, Little Guan was the first to marry.

The couple didn't have money for even the simplest of weddings, so they told their parents that they had the ceremony in Nanjing and told their Nanda classmates that they had married back in Hai'an. After a month at home in Hai'an, the couple returned to Nanjing, spent a day packing up their worldly possessions—ten boxes of books, two wooden trunks, and an envelope containing one hundred *yuan* (sixteen dollars) in borrowed money—and boarded the train to Hefei, the capital of Anhui.

Little Guan was heading into the unknown with her new husband, her status uncertain in the new China. Because she had refused her job assignment, she was effectively a nonperson, belonging to no work unit, technically without the right to reside in Hefei. She could not obtain ration tickets to buy rice, cotton, meat, and other necessities of life. With his job at the museum, Ding had only enough for one person.

The couple purchased the cheapest seats available for the eight-hour train from Nanjing to Hefei. They found no place to sit in the packed railcar. Six people squeezed on seats built for three. Travelers—toothless old men, young recruits in uniform, workers in proletarian blue, farmers with their cotton jackets leaking padding—crammed the aisles. Boxes and trunks, coops stuffed with clucking chickens, and vats dripping soy sauce lined the luggage rack overhead. Around them billowed a haze of rancid smoke from home-grown tobacco and the coal that powered the locomotive. Among those standing were old ladies and pregnant women; people no longer gave up their seats to each other, although they did stand up for foreigners.

About halfway into the journey, Little Guan slipped into a seat just as its occupant got off the train. Opposite her was an older man. He bent over and asked her where she was going. "To Hefei, to start a family," Little Guan answered.

"What are you going to do?" he asked.

"Probably sell pot stickers," she replied.

Little Guan told him that she had just graduated from Nanjing University but that she had refused her assigned job. When the train arrived at Hefei, the older man—in an unusual act of kindness—scribbled his number on a piece of paper and told Little Guan to call him if she had any trouble.

Little Guan and Old Ding moved into their new home: a fifty-four-square-foot room with no toilet and no running water in a museum dormitory for single men. Old Ding had to stand guard when Little Guan went to the toilet at the end of the hall. She could shower once a week. Other classmates had it just as bad. The educational system had nearly buckled under the weight of an entering class of 272,970 freshmen in 1978. Four years later, employers across the country reeled from the challenge of finding housing for the new graduates. Not only had no new housing been built in decades, but the worst housing available was assigned to recent graduates by bureaucrats who feared that the newcomers would soon replace them. One classmate, assigned to an archaeological institute in Hunan Province, was quartered in a bathroom for six months while he waited for a room. Several classmates moved back in with their parents. Though many young men and women married soon after graduation, most of them still could not live together because work units lacked housing for married workers.

Work units were responsible for providing everything for their employees. You worked, lived, dined, saw the doctor, schooled your children, grew old, and died within the gates of your "work unit." It was one of the promises of socialism: cradle-to-grave treatment that pinned its members in the all-encompassing embrace of the party-state. The work unit gave you security, while also infantilizing you. It facilitated a thoroughgoing process of thought control. The work unit administered the party's various political campaigns—from the one-child policy to attacks against fancy clothes and lavish weddings. Everyone in your work unit was a colleague. Your colleagues knew all your secrets; when you fought with your spouse; when you bought a new fan; when you had dinner guests and who they were.

Not long after their arrival, Little Guan went to the province's personnel department to find a job. The bureaucrat in the office was unwelcoming. Every university graduate had a work unit. How was it that Little Guan had none? What was her problem? He didn't believe her explanation—that she had refused a posting in Beijing to start a family. "You rejected your job assignment for your husband?" he scoffed at her. "For love?"

"The only thing we have for you is a high school teacher's job," he muttered as he leafed through her file.

Little Guan had already spent years as a high school teacher. She had not crawled her way out of the commune to Nanjing University only to return to her old profession. But the bureaucrat was having none of it. "If you want to work, you will have to take this job," he said. He tossed her some documents. The job was at a high school 150 miles and ten hours by bus from Hefei. It seemed as far away as Beijing.

Little Guan called the man she met on the train, who turned out to be a mid-level party official. He arranged an interview for Little Guan at the local gazette, Anhui's edition of the monthly periodical of new laws and regulations promulgated by each of China's provincial governments. Within three days she was offered a job as an editor. She returned to the province's personnel department and informed the bureaucrat, who told her that he wouldn't allow it. "Your file has already been sent to the high school," he said. "You belong to them now." The only way to obtain approval to work at the gazette, he said, was to go to the school and persuade a school official to hand back her file. Little Guan contacted the school. No one there had ever heard of her; the bureaucrat was lying.

Months had passed since Little Guan and Old Ding had moved to

Hefei. Though Ding had been sharing his rations with Little Guan, the couple rarely ate their fill. Faced with the prospect of more hunger and no hope, Little Guan returned to the bureaucrat's office to retrieve her file, without which she couldn't take the editor's job. "I'd rather die of starvation in your office than die at home," she said. "I have nothing to eat. Give me my file, or I will die in your office.

"Open that drawer and give me my file," she demanded. The standoff continued for a while. Finally, the official handed over Little Guan's documents.

Like Book Idiot Zhou, Little Guan was no stranger to "red-eye disease." In White Pasture Commune, her principal had tried to derail her plans to go to college. But she thought a backwater like Hefei would welcome a young college graduate. After all, less than two percent of the 15 million people who entered the workforce that year had a college degree. Like many of her classmates, however, Little Guan had an expectation of life after graduation that outpaced the changes slowly being made throughout China. At Nanda, they were told they were the saviors of the motherland. But outside the university's gates, society was still totally bureaucratized. In the hard sciences, aged researchers monopolized grant money because seniority carried more weight than brains or talent. In the social sciences, few dared to challenge the party line. Upon graduation, my classmates invariably met with disappointment. They would have to wait a few more years to unleash their true potential.

In June 1982, Little Guan and Old Ding moved into a larger apartment, albeit one shared with another woman. The couple finally had enough room for a double bed—a flimsy contraption fashioned from bamboo. For chairs, they used piles of books lashed with rope. To make a dinner table, they balanced a wooden plank on top of the tub. And despite their housemate, Little Guan and Ding, both of whom were virgins when they were married, had discovered the joys of sex. "I'm a lusty woman," Little Guan said later on. "I married him because he was attractive. I probably could have found someone more successful. But I wanted a man who attracted me, and Ding did. He had broad shoulders and a tapered waist, and I wanted that. He would leave for work and say, 'I want to shrink you and put you in my pocket.'"

For decades China's Communist leaders had discouraged people from enjoying sex. While Mao and others in the party leadership took mistresses and fathered children out of wedlock, the rest of the population was instructed to view intercourse as a necessary evil. This was in marked contrast to ancient Chinese society, which was relatively open-minded about sex. Early philosophers, such as Confucius and Mencius, looked on sexual desire as natural. Confucian philosophy emphasized personal and governmental morality, justice, and social correctness, but it did not condemn sex. Taoists divided the world into the feminine *yin,* and the masculine *yang,* and believed that a robust sex life helped keep the balance between the two forces. Taoists also held that total control over one's ejaculation was the key to immortality. Painters depicted Taoist monks with enlarged heads filled, they believed, with warehoused semen.

The height of China's self-confidence both politically and sexually came during the Tang Dynasty (AD 618–907). The Tang aristocracy was of mixed blood, combining Caucasians, Central Asians, and Han Chinese. Virginity was not required for marriage into the elite, and widows regularly remarried. Communist China's prudishness had its roots in the Song Dynasty, which began in AD 960, when China found itself besieged from the north, east, and west, eventually losing the sixteen northern provinces within the Great Wall to nomadic invaders. Beijing was occupied. A crisis of confidence, of Chinese identity, ensued.

In response, scholars called for a moral revival. The movement, called neo-Confucianism, resembled a fundamentalist religious revival, a search for a new belief system to make China great again. These neo-Confucian scholars were a strange bunch. They wore outmoded clothes and walked with slow and ponderous steps, their hands clasped in front of them—open right hand over closed left fist—to emphasize their seriousness of purpose. They were seen initially as freaks and ridiculed. But with each defeat on the battlefield, and as foreign forces chipped away at the remains of the Chinese empire, their message gained adherents. The neo-Confucianists called for their followers to overcome their passions and devote themselves to China, duty, and virtue. Virginity became an obsession, as did the chastity of widows. Neo-Confucianists popularized the custom of binding girls' feet, breaking the bones in the arches by tightly wrapping the feet with long strips of cloth. This deformed the bone structure, creating what the Chinese called "three-inch lilies." In the ideal world of neo-Confucianism, husbands and wives treated each other with the formality of houseguests, never so much as undressing in front of each other.

The neo-Confucianists also encouraged a puritanical and strictly authoritarian form of government, including state censorship and thought control. For the next ten centuries, the pendulum of social mores swung between the strict neo-Confucian views of the besieged Song Dynasty and the comparatively freewheeling views of the confident Tang. Neo-Confucian influence played a critical role in the historical mystery of why what was once the most advanced society in the world, whose ships had reached the shores of Africa hundreds of years before Spanish and Portuguese galleons, fell stagnant for so long.

The neo-Confucianists' authoritarianism and prudery fit snugly with Communist Chinese ideology. The party worshiped virginity and told its women to be chaste. "Our concept of chastity is an expression of the spirit of communist civilization in the realm of love and marriage," went one Communist publication printed in the 1980s. "Unmarried women must preserve their purity." Indeed, the first divorce among my male classmates, in 1985, was triggered because he couldn't deal with the fact that his wife was not a virgin when they were married. The issue almost drove him mad.

"I spent months trying to discover whether it was or wasn't consensual," he told me. "The more I loved her, the more this wound cut me deeply. I became like a detective in my relationship with her. Was it rape? What exactly were the circumstances? Did she enjoy it? She said she was barely awake. But was she? Did she love him? It destroyed our relationship."

With the advent of economic reforms, the stultifying prudishness of the Cultural Revolution was left behind. In 1980, the government issued its first handbook on sex since 1957. The first printing of 2.5 million copies sold out immediately, with copies reselling at twice the original price on the black market. Over the next four years, more than ten other sex booklets would be published.

Though these were not the Kinsey Reports, Chinese sex ed constituted a breakthrough of its own. The one-child policy meant that young people would have to be given information essential to using contraception. A lot of the advice involved simple how-to diagrams. Even though nude photographs were not allowed, the fingerprints of China's censors were evident on every page. Masturbation was frowned upon because "it would sap energy away from completing the four modernizations." Couples were encouraged to limit their lovemaking, again because it would deplete the oomph necessary to build a new China.

Starting in the mid-1980s, travelers from Hong Kong and abroad smuggled in pornographic videotapes. Old Ding got a few copies, borrowed a TV and VCR, and he and Little Guan excitedly settled in for a few nights of titillation. Instead, she was disappointed. "We'd done it all," she quipped.

Little Guan started acting as a couples therapist to her friends. She helped arrange some new marriages and patched together some old ones. One older friend complained that she had never had an orgasm, nor did she know of a single female who had. In fact, modern Chinese doesn't even have a singular word for orgasm. The technical term—*xing gaochao* (sexual high tide)—is of such recent vintage that many people still don't know what the expression means.

Little Guan found herself on a one-woman crusade to improve the marriages of her friends and acquaintances. The husband of one colleague was in the habit of playing board games in a bar at night, returning home after midnight when his wife was asleep. If he had won, he would disrobe her and, while she was still half asleep, have sex with her. By the time Little Guan's friend was awake, her husband was finished. Little Guan told her that the next time her husband did this, to fight him off unless he spent sufficient time with foreplay, guidance the friend followed. "Nine out of ten Chinese men don't know what they're doing when it comes to sex," Little Guan would say. "I tell them to tell their husbands, 'A woman is like a gold mine and a man is like a miner. His job is to extract the gold.'"

On June 17, 1982, six months after graduation, Little Guan was on a business trip when she vomited in the car. Having lost her appetite, she suddenly found it again when, upon spying a man selling peaches by the side of the road, she bought a bag and proceeded to eat every one. A female colleague tapped her on the shoulder and said, "Little Guan, I think you've got one."

"What?" Little Guan asked.

"You've got one," she repeated, patting Little Guan's tummy.

It was a rocky pregnancy. Little Guan's chronic anemia worsened, and the family's financial straits meant that she remained undernourished. The birth, which came a few weeks early in the middle of the Chinese New Year holidays, was difficult, too. While in labor, Little Guan's blood pressure plummeted. At one point, doctors came to Little Guan's mother with a document, asking her to decide who was more important, the mother or the fetus. She refused to sign the form. Old Ding yanked it from her hands: "Save the mother," he wrote. The doctors scrambled, and in the end both mother and baby survived. It was a boy. They named him Ding Xing— Star Ding.

With a new mouth to feed, Little Guan's family went into debt. They ate meat or fish only twice a month. They made do with a few vegetables, noodles, rice, and gruel cooked with a ham hock or chicken bones. Little Guan continued to lose weight but nonetheless breast-fed her baby.

Together Little Guan and Old Ding made 120 *yuan* a month, about twenty-four dollars. The same year Ding Xing (pronounced *shing*) was born, they managed to buy on credit their first television—a fourteen-inch black-and-white. The TV, their only electronic item other than a battery-powered radio, cost one-quarter the family's annual income. The purchase was a small sign that China was, indeed, making a creaky transition from a command to a consumer economy.

Nevertheless, Old Ding's career was taking off. He spent half of the first year of his son's life on the road at archaeological dig sites. For decades China had neglected its archaeological heritage and, during the Cultural Revolution, the party had actively encouraged the Red Guard to destroy it. Now the government realized that traditional culture was worth preserving and, more important, that money could be made from it. As the country developed, and the government constructed buildings, paved new roads, dredged canals, and dug tunnels, engineers unearthed more and more archaeological finds. Some of the artifacts would find their way into museums in China. The most valuable were often smuggled to Hong Kong and sold to Western or Japanese collectors. Old Ding was also dispatched to Japan on a short-term exchange program. Like all Chinese traveling abroad, he pinched his pennies so that he could afford to buy gifts. In his luggage home, he packed an electronic keyboard and a VCR.

With Old Ding often away, Little Guan became caught up in the fever to go abroad for further studies. China's door had been closed to foreign travel since the mid-1950s when the party dispatched engineers, physicists, and other technicians by the thousands to the Soviet bloc to learn from their Communist comrades. Even though the Chinese and Russians fell out in the 1960s, Russian still remained the primary foreign language taught in China until the onset of economic reforms in the 1980s, when studying English became the norm. Little Guan dove into the study of English and prepared to take the TOEFL, the Test of English as a Foreign Language.

With a busy job of her own and and an exam to prepare for, Little Guan sent Ding Xing to Hai'an to be cared for by her mother. Little Guan felt comfortable with the idea of her son being raised by his grandparents. After all, her grandfather had raised her for the first six years of her life. But when she journeyed home to Hai'an to visit her boy a few months later, she found him with his face full of snot, wearing a filthy romper. She appealed to her parents to pay more attention. Finally, when she discovered that he had gained only three pounds in two years, she took him home and put her TOEFL preparation kit away.

"Even if the United States does have a gold mountain," she said, using the old Chinese name for San Francisco, coined in the nineteenth century when Chinese coolies built U.S. railroads, "I don't want it. If the boy had been better cared for, I would have been in the United States, but I don't regret it. If you gave me the choice between my son and the opportunity to live in America, I'd choose my son. Would I be willing to become a successful professor in America and have a midget for a son? No, thank you."

Once she buried the idea of going abroad, Little Guan's focus was on being a good mother and a wife. Her job came last. If she had to go on a reporting trip for the gazette, she would make meals ahead of time. At home, Old Ding would wash the dishes and slaughter a chicken, if they had bought one. She would do the rest.

Little Guan would often remember her father's saying that she was like an old hen, easily satisfied with a cozy house and a happy family life. She still agreed. She had a good husband who loved her and a fine son. The family had financial difficulties, but so did their friends. She felt blessed.

Hefei, while an impoverished backwater, was one of the centers of the intellectual ferment in China. The atmosphere in Beijing was not friendly to reform, so leading liberals went south to Shanghai, Hefei, and other areas to give speeches and advocate change. Men and women like Fang

Lizhi, a noted astrophysicist and the vice dean of the University of Science and Technology in Hefei, and Liu Binyan, a crusading journalist, concluded that only political reform could break the roadblocks to real change. Both men became prominent dissidents and ended up as political refugees in the United States.

In the fall of 1986, the government held an election for representatives to the local People's Congress at the University of Science and Technology in Hefei. The People's Congress, in theory, was the top law-making body in the government, yet for years it had been a rubber stamp for party decisions made behind closed doors. This time, students and teachers voted for candidates who had not been approved by the party. The candidates registered a win, but the party tossed out the results.

Students began demonstrating in Hefei, spurred on by a speech by Fang in which he argued that democracy is "not granted but won." Protests spread to nearby Shanghai, and by early December students from sixty universities were marching. On December 26, the central government banned demonstrations. The weather had turned cold, and riot police came out even as the marches fizzled; no one was arrested. In Beijing, party hard-liners teamed up to purge the general secretary, Hu Yaobang, for going easy on the protesters. Fang was fired from his job as vice dean and expelled from the party.

Little Guan and Old Ding were moved by the calls for freedom and democracy but also scared. Little Guan's experience during the Cultural Revolution colored her worldview. She understood that her whole life could be taken away in a flash on some official's whim. So, while in her heart she hoped for a freer country, she kept her own counsel.

As the years passed, things continued to look up for Little Guan, Old Ding, and their son. In 1988, Old Ding was promoted to the post of chief of the Anhui Provincial Museum's archaeology department. That same year, Little Guan also switched jobs. Urban economic reforms were beginning to take hold. In Anhui, banks and insurance companies, once merged in huge government conglomerates, were separating. When the Anhui Province Insurance Company was uncoupled from the Anhui Province People's Bank, Little Guan joined the insurance firm as an editor on its newspaper. The job offered better hours and an apartment, a two-room, three-hundred-square-foot space with its own plumbing. Running water and a toilet, Little Guan thought, how extravagant!

PART III

1989

15

CROSSED PATHS

While I was spared the dead-end job assignments that faced my classmates in China, the responsibility of having to pick my own career path weighed heavily on me. I had no idea what I wanted to do. After a few months in France, working as a bartender and travel guide, I returned to the United States in the fall of 1982. I'd decided to go back to Stanford and get a master's in East Asian studies. Following that, when the opportunity arose for a one-year Fulbright scholarship in Singapore, I took it.

I hated the weather in Singapore, and I couldn't find friends. At a Christmas party in 1983, I met a Reuters reporter and told him I was thinking of journalism, an ironic twist considering the energy I had expended trying to differentiate myself from my father. He asked my age. Twenty-four. "That's too old to start, mate," he declared. A few months later, having finished my master's thesis on the ongoing war between Vietnam and Cambodian guerrillas, I made a plan to escape to Japan.

Fay, meanwhile, had achieved her dream of leaving China. Six months after I left Nanda, she married an Australian and had moved with him to a beachside community outside Perth. But Fay, always footloose, was easily distracted. She found out I was in Singapore and decided to surprise me, figuring that the odds of unearthing me among Singapore's 2.5 million people were even better than those in Shanghai.

But the meeting was not to be. On the same day she flew in to Singapore, I flew out, bound for Tokyo. Fay's voyage would prove fateful anyway. After failing to find me, she returned to Nanjing to see her parents. There she learned that it was lucky that she had left China. During the 1983 campaign against "spiritual pollution," the police in her neighborhood had been given arrest quotas for women of "loose morals" and had come to her parents' house looking for her.

Fay then went to Hong Kong, where she met an American traveler. She returned to the United States with him. In Las Vegas, she divorced her Australian husband, married the American, and decamped with him to Southern California, where she bore him three children—two girls and a boy.

Moving to Japan improved my spirits. I practiced judo, immersed myself in the study of Japanese, made friends. I supported myself by teaching English and working as a copy editor at a Japanese newspaper's English-language news service. Compared to China, Japan, with its dexterously sliced sushi, its effervescent neon, the cacophonous din of Pachinko parlors, was erotic and electric. Every night, the subway platforms were mined with the vomit of intoxicated salarymen. At sake bars, my Japanese friends listened agape to my stories about life in China. They had a visceral fear of China well before that apprehension was fashionable in the West. China is a threat, they argued; its rise will shake the world.

In early November 1984, as I was hitchhiking to the northern island of Hokkaido, it began to drizzle. The drizzle turned into a downpour. When one car screamed by and swamped me in a wave of water, something clicked. "It's time to go home," I said to the road in front of me and crossed to the other side of the highway. By the end of the day, I was back in Tokyo. By the end of the month, I was pounding the pavement in the United States.

I found a position with a small newspaper in southern California, covering cops and crooks. A year later I joined the Associated Press in New York, working the graveyard shift. In the summer of 1988, the AP dispatched me to Beijing.

If China had just been waking up in the early 1980s, by the late 1980s it was fully caffeinated. Beijing pulsated with an intellectual fervor not seen since before the revolution. Not a week went by without something memorable occurring: a guerrilla art exhibition, a market-oriented reform, demonstrations big and small, a party, a play, the pointed lyrics of a new song. At universities, Nietzsche, Sartre, and Milton Friedman were trumping Marx and Mao. The air was filled with the romantic buzz of China's infinite possibilities. Changes were sweeping the Communist world from Beijing to Budapest, and freedom was considered within everyone's grasp. China's intellectuals looked at the United States and saw a model for their country. Mikhail Gorbachev's Soviet Union and Lech Walesa's Poland showed the way to get there.

On college campuses, students met to discuss the big issues of the day: political reform, economic restructuring, inflation, corruption, and the remarkable changes that Gorbachev was bringing to the Soviet Union. By January 1989, leading intellectuals had launched a letter-writing campaign for the release of political prisoners. "It's not that I don't understand," ran the lyrics of a popular rock-and-roll song, "it's just that the world is changing too fast."

The gross domestic product had more than doubled since 1980, yet it was a system in transition, moving cautiously away from central planning, gradually adopting the institutions and mechanisms of a market economy. It was a complex transition. Relaxing restrictions on economic activity quickly alleviated some of China's most pressing economic difficulties, but it created a new set of headaches. Inflation became a problem for the first time since the early 1950s, as did growing inequality and corruption. In May 1988, spurred by price increases and the increasing wealth of its people, China's mint printed its first fifty- and one-hundred-*yuan* notes; previously the highest denomination had been ten.

I moved into a small two-room apartment in one of the diplomatic compounds where foreign journalists were confined. Although my quarters were cramped, it felt marvelous to be back in China. The three-person bureau was always busy, and days and nights blurred together.

In the late autumn of 1988, a Chinese friend told me he knew an actress who wanted to meet a foreigner. The prospect interested me. She worked for the People's Liberation Army, which, in addition to fighting wars and bullying China's citizenry, also operated a wide array of businesses, including pharmacies, machine-tool plants, and movie studios. I was single, and China seemed a lot looser than when I had lived there in the early 1980s.

We met at a small Western-style restaurant. Nana, the actress, smiled and made eyes at me, praising my Chinese. When we parted that afternoon, she gave me her phone number. "It's my own number," she said. Phone ownership had jumped 500 percent since 1980. For the first time, friends could call friends.

Nana was recently divorced, unusual in those days, and had just emerged from a troubled love affair. As she later explained it, she and a cameraman had slept together several times during a movie shoot. He had fallen in love and had pleaded with her to marry him. The only problem was that he was married, too. She refused, and the man killed himself. His wife, in an unprecedented move in a country with barely any legal system, sued Nana for damages. While the case never made it to trial, it finished Nana's career as an actress; no production company would hire a woman with her complicated past. Nana had decided to move to Canada. When I met her, she was waiting for an acceptance letter from a language school in Toronto.

A day after our first meeting, I called her, and she invited me over to her apartment, a one-room studio inside a PLA compound on the city's west side. She met me at the gate. I was dressed in my Chinese overcoat, once again with a surgical mask to cover my Western nose, and PLA-issue sneakers. Threading her arm through mine, she spirited me into the compound, past a sentry, and up the back stairs to her room. It was my first visit to a Chinese military installation.

A dim yellow light illuminated Nana's room. Against one wall was a large armoire with a mirror on the door. Next to that was a small coffee table with a chair. But the main piece of furniture was a king-sized bed in an old wooden frame with a cracked headboard. Nana said that the bed dated from before the revolution.

The phone rang. From her body language I could tell it was a suitor. "What are you wearing?" I heard him asking through the receiver. Nana blushed. She couldn't leave the room; the phone cord was barely a foot long. She couldn't ask me to step outside either; I was a foreigner in a Chinese army barracks. And yet Nana seemed to enjoy being romanced on the phone by one man while a second sat on her bed. She reached out her hand to me, and I stroked it. She squeezed my hand tightly and pulled me toward her. She bit my lip and giggled into the phone. I took it a step further, rolling up her sleeves and biting her arms. She gasped and finally hung up. We fell on each other. "Do anything you want with me!" she panted into my ear. "Anything." I said something to the effect that this was a decision we should make together; she wasn't interested. "Anything you want . . ."

What a change this was from my furtive attempts to avoid making the floorboards creak with Fay. Nana didn't care what the neighbors thought and didn't fear the police. In fact, now that her movie career was shot and she was decamping for Canada, she reveled in notoriety. "I want my neighbor to hear me," she blurted out one evening. "I want her to be jealous of my sex." Nana's impetuous passion mirrored the society around her, single-mindedly focused on sating various appetites. She approached the world with ferocious hunger; befuddling at times and awesome at others.

In December 1988, the Central Museum of Fine Arts, a massive, blue-gray Stalinist-style building in central Beijing whose only sop to traditional culture was a soaring tiled roof, held its first exhibition of nude paintings. More than twenty thousand people flocked to the show on the first day, paying the equivalent of twenty-seven cents—five times the normal price of admission. Packs of men gaped and giggled at paintings of women with Chinese faces and Playboy Bunny bodies. Bookish students pondered abstract mounds. A small man in a wheelchair arrived with a coterie of aides and nurses. He was Ai Qing, China's most famous living poet. Ai had been banished during the Cultural Revolution to China's northern desert, where he cleaned outhouses for more than two decades, forbidden to read and write and forced to live in an earthen dugout. "Underneath, everyone is naked and everyone knows their nakedness," the seventy-nine-year-old poet remarked, his gnarled hands trembling. "Why then, when we want to paint our bodies, do so many of us think it's strange? I think it is good."

Nana and I attended the exhibition together. "Of course it should be banned," she tittered, her beautiful mouth wrapped in a pink scarf and her eyes laughing at me. "Seeing all these nudes makes me want to do it. It makes all of us want to do it. That's our problem. We've been waiting for too long." She rushed me out of the museum and back to her room.

Later that month, I had the opportunity to return to Nanjing for the first time in six years. The streets of the city were churning with young men carrying banners and chanting slogans. Unlike the student-led demonstrations in 1985 and 1986, powered by idealistic calls for the government to respect the results of elections, these marches revealed another side of China.

On Christmas Eve 1988, two African students invited two Chinese women to a dance at Hehai University in Nanjing. As the self-styled leader of the Third World, China played host to thousands of African students in the name of solidarity with the former Western colonies which had recently won their independence. The university had recently promulgated a regulation aimed at preventing Africans from taking Chinese women to their rooms. Women were now required to register if they wanted to visit an African friend. Afterward, police would seek out the woman and order her not to see the African again. On that evening, two Africans refused to register their guests. A security guard insisted, and a brawl erupted that lasted until morning, leaving eleven Chinese students and two Africans injured.

The next day, three hundred Chinese students, goaded by bogus rumors that a Chinese man had been killed in the rumble, ransacked the Africans' dormitories at Hehai. The African students fled to the railway station, hoping to hop trains to Beijing to find safety in their countries' embassies. The police stopped them. By this time, thousands of students from universities all over the city were marching against the Africans.

The protest quickly morphed from a racist rant against black men mixing with local women to broader appeals for human rights and political reforms. Complaints about everything—from the food in university mess halls, to the stale Communist curriculum, to the outmoded job allocation system—were pasted onto banners and carried to the Drum Tower intersection near Nanda. Chants of "Kill the black devils" vied with "Give us human rights!" The demonstrations were declared illegal, and riot police were mobilized from surrounding provinces to pacify the crowds. The government would eventually expel three of the Africans for fighting; no Chinese was punished.

The Nanjing protests helped mark the end of China's self-appointed leadership of the Third World. If the motto of China's Communists in the 1950s and '60s was "Workers of the world unite," by the 1980s it had mutated into Deng Xiaoping's exhortation, "To get rich is glorious." Chinese by this time had shed any Communist pretensions to liking their darker brothers and had returned to imperial China's racial stereotyping that linked dark skin with poverty and backwardness. I was once on a bus with Luru, a student from Zaire whom I had met at the Beijing Languages Institute, when we were approached by a dowdy middle-aged woman. She licked her fingers, rubbed them up and down Luru's forearm, and shook her head in dismay. "So dirty," she pronounced. No one on the bus appeared the slightest bit dismayed.

The Nanjing protests, with their convoluted theme of racism, nationalism, and democracy, were the precursor to the nationwide demonstrations that would rock the government months later. At the time, I did not understand that the students' mixed message was, in fact, the message. I viewed the Nanjing protests as a bad thing and would later embrace the Tiananmen Square protests as a good thing. In reality, the sexual politics, racism, nationalism, and yearning for more freedom were all parts of a muddled whole.

In February 1989, Nana's acceptance letter arrived from a language school in Toronto. She acknowledged to me that she had continued to sleep with her ex-husband. Nana explained that without her, he would be unable to find anyone with whom to have sex. I continued to see her. She referred to herself as a *huli jing* (a "fox spirit")—a demon who inhabits the body of a beguiling woman, seduces a virgin male, and on their wedding night eats his heart. I wasn't a virgin, but I got her point.

Nana also thought I was sleeping with other women, an assumption about Westerners that was commonplace among Chinese. Nana believed that all Westerners slept around and had little affection for their families. From Nana's perspective, I lived in a world without obligations, devoted solely to the satisfaction of my impulses. In a way, her views about me represented a fantasy world for an attractive Chinese woman caught up in a society with crumbling familial obligations and a fraying social straitjacket. Nana abhorred compromise, viewing freedom as an all-or-nothing affair, not as a complex trade-off of benefits and sacrifices. "That's not freedom," she would say dismissively. "I don't like it." Nana's attitude ran through her generation and the next—China's restive students—like a refrain. In the end, their absolutism would help precipitate a calamity.

16

SHOW ME THE MONEY

Book Idiot Zhou could only dream of a world without obligations. By the mid-1980s, Zhou had succeeded in moving his family from the Jiangsu countryside to Bengbu to join him at the Anhui Institute of Finance and Trade. The family was still desperately poor; every effort they made to improve their lot seemed to be stymied by a hardhearted bureaucracy. When his wife opened a small store specializing in knitting sweaters for students, the authorities shut it down because she lacked the necessary permit. She started a laundry service, washing students' clothes, but it, too, was shuttered.

"For several years my dinky salary had to support my parents and my family," Zhou later would write. "One child needed medicine and nourishment. Other than amassing a mountain of debt from my friends, there was no other way."

Zhou began to think the unthinkable: going into business. Raised with the conventional view of merchants, which ranked them below government officials and scholars, Zhou had also absorbed Communist propaganda describing business owners as "capitalist bloodsuckers." But not only was party strongman Deng Xiaoping changing the economy, he was changing minds.

In just a few years, China had ditched the we're-all-poor-together egalitarianism upon which communism was based and had rejected thousands of years of prejudice against merchants. Society was now catalyzed by a quest for cash. Hucksters and hustlers morphed the party's politically correct new slogan, *wang qian kan,* or "Look to the future," into a sound-alike *wang qian kan,* or "Show me the money."

Deng devised a new way to describe China's economy, calling it "socialism with Chinese characteristics." From then on, every capitalist-style reform was justified as falling within this deliberately vague, catch-all category. Policymakers were now free to jettison the lunacies of Stalinist central planning, so long as they didn't discard the one thing the party held dear: its continued domination of society and political life.

Deng was pushing on an open door. For more than thirty years, the Communists had managed to do the near-impossible: suppress the entrepreneurial genius of the Chinese people, so evident in Hong Kong, Taiwan, Singapore, Thailand, the United States, and elsewhere. Maoism was a catastrophic experiment at forcing the Chinese to live under an entirely alien creed. Finally, it had been buried.

Zhou's colleagues and friends were buzzing with talk about new possibilities. Several Nanda classmates had already "jumped into the sea," as the Chinese called going into business. Zhang Aibing, the grad student who had been tossed out of Nanda for having too many girlfriends, opened a coffee shop; another bought and sold iron ore; another raised mushrooms in the basement of his apartment building.

In 1987, a high school classmate from Dongtai contacted Zhou with a proposition. The classmate knew of a pharmaceutical factory in Guangzhou that wanted to buy enzymes found in, of all places, human urine. What he needed was a source. Zhou's friend had heard that Nanjing University had the technology to isolate the enzymes and that the chemistry professor in charge of the process was also from Dongtai. He asked Zhou to contact the man and work out a deal. The professor agreed to share the technology. Zhou, his classmate in Dongtai, and a third man then formed a three-way partnership to open plants to extract these enzymes. Zhou was the only one without capital, so he agreed to establish and manage the facilities in exchange for a piece of the profits. "It was pretty fitting," Zhou said with a laugh. "I'd made a few pennies collecting turds as a boy. Here I was doing pretty much the same thing."

Within months, Zhou and his partner, Sheng Hongyuan, had secured contracts to collect urine in Bengbu and other cities. For a fee, local sanitation departments allowed them access to the public toilets. Zhou and Sheng would then organize a platoon of laborers to pedal three-wheeled bicycles mounted with huge vats to collect the goods each day. Because of the stench produced by large quantities of urine, they based their extraction plants on the outskirts of cities, renting workshops from moribund state-owned firms.

The extraction process involved funneling raw urine through a series of columns where it was washed by reagents and the appropriate enzymes separated out. For every ton of urine, they would extract sixty grams of a raw material that the pharmaceutical company used to make an anticlotting heart medicine called Urokinase and one hundred grams of a raw material for a medicine called Ulinastatin that helped dissolve gallstones. Zhou transported the enzymes once a month by bus to Guangzhou. And with that, Book Idiot Zhou jumped into the sea—of urine.

Toilets have provided foreigners with some of their most indelible memories of China. They are generally squatters, meaning seatless, often little more than a hole in the floor over an open cesspool. The Achilles tendon of the average Westerner is much less flexible than that of the average Chinese, making the experience of crouching over a large shit pit (often with keys, a mobile phone, loose change, and a wallet in your pocket) a risky affair.

Men's rest rooms are designed with a long trough for urination along one wall and squatter cubicles along another. In the 1960s, the government removed the doors from the cubicles as part of an Orwellian decision to deny privacy everywhere.

I have seen many memorable things in Chinese bathrooms: a toilet poised over a pigpen, pink snouts poking up in ravenous anticipation; prodigious piles of shit deposited in and around the pit and up the wall to a height of more than three feet, indicating a blast radius of unthinkable ferocity; toilets with excrement on the ceiling, hanging like stalactites over my head.

Zhou, true to his "book idiot" roots, found the business compelling and the more urine he amassed, the more he became interested in the relationship between the Chinese and their bodily wastes. On the side, he researched a history of the Chinese toilet.

The Chinese, according to Zhou's research, have been pondering human excrement for centuries. He noted that Lao Tzu, the great sixth-century BC Taoist philosopher, gave the subject some serious thought. "When the Tao is present in the universe, horses haul manure," Lao Tzu mused in his famous treatise *Tao Te Ch'ing*. "When the Tao is absent, war horses are bred outside the city." Shit, according to Lao Tzu, symbolized peace.

In the ensuing 2,600 years, collecting night soil for fertilizer became a lucrative business, with medieval entrepreneurs and later gangland dons battling for access to the chamber pots and outhouses of the Chinese. In 1933 a "night soil war" erupted in Beijing, when the new mayor, Yuan Liang, vowed to break the back of the gangs who monopolized the city's collection routes. The mayor put night soil collection under city administration; the manure barons responded by ordering their men to stop emptying the citizenry's chamber pots and public toilets. The citywide stench was atrocious and the climax came when eight thousand shit shovelers, wielding vats full of crap, massed at city hall. The mayor commanded the police to clear them out but the officers balked at getting their hands and everything else dirty. Night soil collection stayed a private business.

In the early days following China's Communist Revolution, the lack of chemical fertilizers made night soil worth its weight in gold, leading state authorities to strictly regulate its collection. By the Cultural Revolution, urban youths who had been "sent down" to the countryside would routinely lead bands of peasants into cities to raid public toilets.

By the 1980s, Zhou wrote in his history of the Chinese toilet published in 2005, chemical fertilizers were replacing night soil, and the Chinese were turning their attention to piss. In the early 1960s, scientists began dumping extracts from the urine of post-menopausal women into fish-breeding ponds to induce carp to have more fry. In the 1970s, Nanda's chemistry department built a small production plant to extract enzymes from urine to make medicines. With the advent of economic reforms later that decade, Nanda started a company to sell its enzymes to Chinese pharmaceutical firms. Overnight, the streets around the Drum Tower District near the university were dotted with men on three-wheeled bicycles hauling enormous chamber pots to the small chemical plant inside the university gates.

In the beginning, urine processing was done by local governments and institutions. But with a growing economy and a boom in health-care spending, demand for urine by-products soared and state-run firms were too slow to respond. As was happening in other areas of the economy, pharmaceutical manufacturers looked to private players, like Book Idiot Zhou, to take the lead.

With his job at the institute in Bengbu, Zhou kept one foot in socialism. Teaching provided him with a safety net of sorts: an apartment and medical care. Zhou's other foot was in the rough-and-tumble world of Chinese capitalism. Several days a week, he taught Marxism, Leninism, and Maoist thought and railed against exploitation by the capitalist class. The rest of the time he spent as a budding entrepreneur, employing dozens at rock-bottom wages, working the system to enrich himself, his partners, and his family. "I was inhabiting two worlds," he said.

17

TO THE BARRICADES

China itself had become two worlds, and they were about to collide. On Saturday, April 15, 1989, Hu Yaobang, the seventy-three-year-old Communist Party chief who was purged for being too soft on student-led demonstrations in 1986, died of a heart attack after a politburo meeting. Throughout the weekend, dozens of posters went up at universities around Beijing commemorating Hu's death. Students placed wreaths at the Monument to the Revolutionary Heroes in the center of Tiananmen Square, something that hadn't been done since the last major protest there, in 1976, to commemorate the passing of Zhou Enlai.

Hu's death was the spark China's students and reform-minded elite had been waiting for. For months, pro-democracy activists had been meeting on university campuses to debate political reform. In early April, Beijing University, which since the early twentieth century had stood at the center of China's political movements, banned a "Democracy Salon" that had been gathering on campus. On April 5, students defied the ban and met in the open air, bundled up against the early spring chill. I was there. Perhaps it was my New Yorker's skepticism, but I sensed a lot of despair lurking behind the defiance. After student leaders and a dissident spoke, the crowd remained silent. Then a bespectacled young man in a worn Mao suit spoke up. "It's not so much fear that I feel," he said. "It's just hopelessness. Our leaders don't listen to the people. They never will."

At Tiananmen Square, posters praised Hu and called for his remains to lie in the mausoleum of legendary leader Mao Zedong on the square.

"Sincere men have died while hypocrites live on," declared one. The Monday following Hu's death, demonstrations began in Beijing and Shanghai with hundreds of students marching. By Tuesday their ranks had grown to thousands and by Thursday, tens of thousands. Students were marching in more than six cities, calling for political reform and the establishment of an independent student union outside the control of the Communist Party.

Following a memorial service for Hu on Friday, April 21, the head of the Communist Party, Zhao Ziyang, left for a scheduled trip to North Korea. Conservatives within the party seized upon Zhao's absence to convene a politburo meeting and denounce the demonstrations. Their fulminations appeared in an April 26 editorial in the *People's Daily,* the official paper of the Communist Party. The editorial labeled the demonstrators, more than two-hundred-thousand in Beijing alone, "antiparty and antisocialist" and accused the demonstration organizers of "flaunting the banner of democracy" to "sow dissension among the people, plunge the whole country into chaos, and sabotage the political situation of stability and unity."

In years past, such a clear statement of the state's intent to hammer dissent, made on the front page of the party's flagship newspaper, would have cowed all but the most foolhardy Chinese. But unlike my classmates, this younger generation had no firsthand experience of the ruthlessness of the Chinese state. No one had been arrested during the last two spates of student unrest—in the mid-1980s in Shanghai and during the anti-African marches in Nanjing in 1988.

The editorial sparked popular outrage. Hundreds of thousands of ordinary citizens, angered by growing corruption and worried about high inflation, defied the government's ban on protests. And when Zhao Ziyang returned to Beijing, he publicly distanced himself from the conservative position. On April 27, protesters streamed through the gates of Beijing University in the northwest corner of Beijing, gaining marchers as they streamed south into the city. Just outside of the gates of People's University, about three miles from Beijing University, the marchers confronted a police cordon.

Covering the march for the AP, I was near the front of the crowd as it rocked against the police barricades. People were blowing whistles and banging pots and pans. It was a parade, circus, and protest combined into one. The protesters were elated to be out on a beautiful April day, elated to be Chinese, elated to be righteous. The rocking became more frenzied, and with one climactic push and an enormous roar, the crowd barreled through the police lines.

Thousands of people leaned out windows and cheered as we surged by. Kindergarten children stood at the gate of their school and applauded. Patients in nightgowns emerged from a hospital to accept pamphlets handed out by students. Students with arms linked sang the national anthem and shouted "Long live democracy" and "Down with bureaucracy, down with corruption."

By the time we reached Tiananmen Square, more than four hours later, thousands of ordinary people had joined in. The soldiers who had been guarding the square faded out of sight. I had never been in a crowd of that size before, and it was intoxicating. It was by no means a mob. Indeed, people even said "excuse me" when they stepped on your toes. I was swept away in the emotion of the day, marching with people who were peaceful and who wanted what was right and good.

The demonstrations quickly spread to dozens of cities, including Shanghai, Chengdu, and Nanjing. A clearly sympathetic media reported on the marches, marking the first time since 1949 that the press had exercised a semblance of freedom. A few days later, the May 1 International Labor Day holidays brought a new surge of demonstrators. Thousands of students from across China took advantage of their school vacation to descend upon Beijing, expanding exponentially the size and scope of the movement. The Consolidated Student Union of Colleges and Universities in Beijing, which had been leading the movement, splintered in two; some members stuck to the students' original demand for the government to recognize an independent student association. Others pushed for a more radical agenda, the overthrow of the Communist Party. On May 12, the protest leaders from both splinter groups announced a hunger strike, vowing that they would fast until senior government officials met with them to consider their demands.

It was an ingenious move. In a country with such recent experience of famine, where "Have you eaten?" was a common greeting, the image of students fasting for their beliefs tugged at the heartstrings of people nationwide. As the days passed, scores of white-gowned medical personnel volunteered for duty in Tiananmen Square, by now a tent city teeming with protesters around the clock. Student leaders, fully aware of the dramatic potential of their weakened constitutions, would faint publicly, often in front of the cameras, before being rushed off to a jerry-rigged hospital tent for intravenous drips. Some of it was a stunt. Three students I knew from the Beijing Normal Teachers College would each fast for eight hours a day so that together they would constitute one fasting demonstrator. They called their eight-hour shifts "being on duty." As the weeks passed, the government looked increasingly hapless. Each day it issued a deadline for students and other protesters to leave the square. Each day the demonstrators' defiance grew. On May 15, another deadline passed, forcing the government to relocate a welcoming ceremony for the visiting Soviet president Mikhail Gorbachev from the Great Hall of the People, which bordered the square, to Beijing's international airport. By mid-May, more than one million demonstrators thronged the streets of Beijing.

The students leading the charge were by and large a happy-go-lucky group of twenty-somethings. Most were born during the Cultural Revolution but had no memory of it. Because they had not seen the worst of the party's handiwork, the ease with which it mangled lives and ate its young, they didn't fear the party the way my classmates did. Those in Tiananmen Square had a greater sense of the possible. As the Chinese say, a newborn calf doesn't fear a tiger.

I was by no means the best journalist among the group of foreign correspondents in Beijing, but I spoke some of the best Chinese and, just a few years earlier, had gone to school with men and women much like the ones now marching. While many Western correspondents viewed a conversation with a group of Chinese students as an impossibly challenging language lesson or a trip to a Chinese dorm room like a journey to another planet, for me hanging out with the students felt like home.

One sunny afternoon, I and another American reporter interviewed a student leader named Wu'er Kaixi in his dorm room at a teachers' college in Beijing. I lounged on Kaixi's oily bedroll, taking in the stench. My American colleague declined an offer to sit on the bed, preferring the less malodorous safety of a stool.

Wu'er Kaixi was a member of a Turkic ethnic group, the Uighurs, who inhabit China's Xinjiang Province in the country's far northwestern corner.

He was an electrically charismatic, roguishly handsome young man of many appetites, food being just one. Several days after the hunger strike began, Wu'er asked me to pick him up at 2:30 a.m. in an alley by Tiananmen Square. "Bring your car," he growled, his voice scratchy from days behind a bullhorn.

Kaixi was waiting under a tree. He directed me to drive him to an outdoor food market. "Get out and get me some food," he commanded, after making me promise to keep the meeting off the record. "I can't get it myself. If anyone sees me, it will hurt the movement." After stir-fried pork with noodles, he moved on to shredded chicken with noodles, bell peppers and ham with noodles, and noodles in soup—all slurped down at full volume next to me.

Covering the protests, I got caught up in the excitement. "This is the most amazing thing I have ever seen in my life," I enthused in a letter to my parents in late May 1989. "I have a sense it's going to end badly but at the same time it is remarkable to behold. Today I saw one million people on the street. One million! And what do they want? Just a chance at a better life."

I avoided the darker side of the student organization. The student union was organized in a way depressingly similar to the Communist Party, configured along Leninist lines with a politburo and Central Committee. Donations flowed in, but there was no way to account for the money. I had a gnawing sense that the students really had no idea what they wanted other than change, any change. Getting interviews with student leaders involved negotiating my way through a phalanx of self-important, self-appointed student guards who maintained order during the demonstrations and made up rules as they went along. I was once riding my bicycle by a group of fasting students along the northern edge of Tiananmen Square when one student guard rushed out and gave me a shove, causing me to crash and rip the skin on my right arm from wrist to elbow. "No bike riding," he barked as I lay there bleeding on the asphalt. No bike riding in the biking capital of the world?

When students and intellectuals in the movement got together, the meetings generally fell into two categories: staged programs where the assembled would fawn over a featured speaker, or gatherings that started as shouting matches and degenerated into fisticuffs. There was no give-and-take between the leader and the led, and no debate, as I was used to in the West.

During one protest, I climbed to the top of a pedestrian overpass at an intersection in western Beijing to survey the crowd. There were thousands upon thousands of people. Banners written in red and black ink, demanding human rights, expressing support for the hunger strikers, calling for democracy, floated above the crowd. I felt a tug at my elbow. It was a friend who had brought along a man dressed in the green khaki uniform of the People's Liberation Army. "I would like you to meet someone," she said.

He introduced himself as Liu Gang. He was in his late thirties, tall and slender, with a strong jaw and, unusual in a country where people had bowed for centuries, a firm handshake. Liu Gang was both a People's Liberation Army officer and a musical composer. He had been marching with an army cultural troop to express support for the hunger-striking students. He invited me to dinner that night. As a river of protesters flowed below us, we went our separate ways.

Liu Gang and I became fast friends. We would meet often, in grungy noodle shops and out-of-the-way eateries. Beijing now boasted a slew of good but tiny private restaurants, where I would squeeze myself between a half-foot-high stool and a foot-high table and shovel down the deliciously greasy fare. Liu and I shared an interest in jazz—I passed him tapes from 1950s jazz greats. He would call me at the AP office with the latest rumor about the protests and the machinations within the party.

On May 18, Premier Li Peng, the government's leading hard-liner, finally met with several student leaders in Beijing. The meeting was broadcast on national television at 11 a.m. that day. Li blamed traffic congestion for arriving five minutes late. (Actually, the party had deliberately withdrawn traffic police during the demonstrations to enhance the impression of mass havoc in the capital.) Student leader Wu'er Kaixi, who attended the meeting in a hospital gown, interrupted, pointing out that the premier was not five minutes late but a month late. Furthermore, he added, shaking his finger at Li Peng, it would be the students, not the government, who would set the agenda. Wu'er Kaixi's performance made for good TV but lousy politics. That night, the party's politburo decided to enact martial law beginning at midnight May 19.

At the poliburo meeting, Deng Xiaoping accused the party chief, Zhao Ziyang, of splitting the party and suggested that Zhao be relieved of his duties. In the predawn darkness of May 19, Zhao went to the square to visit the students on hunger strike. With tears in his eyes, Zhao stood in one of the buses that had been turned into dorm rooms and apologized. "I have come too late," he said, requesting that the students who had fasted end their hunger strike. They complied.

That afternoon, Liu Gang called me and told me to meet him later that day. I drove over with a colleague from the Associated Press. Liu got into the passenger's seat of our car. "I've got a secret speech for you," he declared. That got my attention. Liu began reading us a speech given just hours earlier by Li Ximing, secretary of the Beijing Municipal Party Committee. I sat in the back, exhausted. I had been working close to twenty hours a day, catnapping in the square, biking around the city from the university district in the city's northwest corner to Tiananmen Square, meeting with students and ordinary people, trying to gauge their mood.

As he read the speech, I groggily realized it was the draft of the announcement that the military was entering Beijing to restore order by force of arms. The proclamation would be made on radio and TV later that evening. Handed the biggest scoop of my career, the declaration of martial law in China's capital, I dozed off, and didn't write a thing.

By declaring martial law, the government banned marches, strikes, class boycotts, distribution of pamphlets, spreading rumors, attacks on leaders and media outlets, and "any other destructive actions." It said PLA troops had been authorized to take any measures necessary to maintain order in the city of 10 million. Foreign reporters were also prohibited from "inciting or instigating Chinese to march" and banned from conducting interviews.

Soldiers were deployed around the city in several directions. At each point, a phalanx of citizen protesters surrounded their vehicles. Intersections were blocked with trucks, buses, and lane dividers; marchers formed human barricades. People engaged in a lively debate with soldiers in their open-air troop trucks, cigarette smoke corkscrewing under the streetlights.

With soldiers bearing down on Beijing, I found myself stepping out of my journalistic shell, pleading with my contacts in the student movement to obey martial law and lead the students from the square. One afternoon, I spent several hours waiting for an audience with Feng Congde, another leader of the movement, and the husband of Chai Ling, a diminutive woman protest leader with a radical flair. Feng finally saw me, ushering me into a white tarpaulin tent on Tiananmen Square that stank of old socks and soybean milk turned bad.

"Why don't you declare victory and go home?" I asked. "Clean up the square and return to school?" Feng admitted that he, too, wanted the students to leave but contended that events were out of his control. None of their goals had been achieved, he said, the party had not budged, even on the simplest demand—to allow the creation of a student union independent of party control. In addition, the vast majority of the students on the square were from out of town, having journeyed days by bus and rail to get to Beijing. The new arrivals were no more politically motivated than many spectators at, say, Woodstock. The Sun Yat-sen Park, just north of the square, had morphed into a love motel, with couples rustling in the bushes and sprawling on park benches. There was little chance anyone would be able to prevail on them to leave Beijing, much less the square, he said. For them the antiparty party had just started.

By this point, I began bumping into matronly middle-aged women on the square who stepped gingerly over bedrolls and frantically peeled back tent flaps to peer inside. When I asked them what they were doing, I always got the same reply: "Looking for my child." Students from Beijing were abandoning the square, convinced by their parents that a crackdown was nigh. Student leaders were also slinking off. The last time I saw Wu'er Kaixi was on the night of May 30 when I picked him up from an alley near his university and drove to the home of a Scandinavian diplomat, escorting him past the Chinese guards. Wu'er Kaixi spent the evening inquiring about political asylum: What would happen if he sneaked into an embassy? Could a diplomatic pouch hold one man? The diplomat smiled, well, diplomatically at Kaixi's naïveté without providing him much hope. We left together, and as I drove him to a dark intersection, Kaixi looked at me, his young, handsome face pinched with worry. "Where am I going to go?" he asked me. "I'm too young to go to jail."

Four days later, on the evening of Saturday, June 3, I had just finished dinner at the house of a friend who lived on the western end of Chang'an Boulevard, which bisected Beijing and led to Tiananmen Square. We had gone downstairs to take a stroll in the evening cool. Because of the daily demonstrations, cars had not moved along Beijing's main east-west artery in weeks, transforming it into one of the world's longest pedestrian promenades.

Starting that afternoon, Beijing TV had been broadcasting, in the name of the martial law authorities, an "urgent announcement" stating that whoever went outside of their home would bear responsibility for the consequences. By the evening, units from an estimated thirteen army corps were deployed around the city, a total of 350,000 soldiers dispatched to Beijing. The urgent announcement did not stop the people in my friend's neighborhood of Muxidi from thronging the street. We walked toward a small bridge. Protesters had placed two buses there to block the army from entering the city. A lively debate animated the crowd. "They are the people's army!" shouted one man. "They wouldn't dare kill the people."

As darkness fell, my friend went upstairs to check on her aging father. The crowd thinned. I stayed outside. Shortly after 8 p.m., an army unit appeared on the far side of the bridge and attempted to move the buses. Scores of protesters swarmed over the bridge, blocking the soldiers' way. Unlike in the past weeks, the soldiers didn't back down; they swung their truncheons and beat the demonstrators, some of whom began throwing rocks. The crowd around me sensed something. Alarmed looks were exchanged; many hurried home. The battle between soldiers and demonstrators lasted for more than an hour. In a last-ditch effort, demonstrators hauled burning rugs onto the buses, illuminating the sky.

The soldiers began to fire live ammunition low into the crowd, hitting people in the stomach and legs. The night, balmy with a calm breeze, crackled with automatic gunfire. People fled in all directions. Some returned, rocks in hand. Armored personnel carriers rolled onto the bridge and began butting the buses aside, cutting a path into the inner city.

I was petrified. Because I had never heard live gunfire before, it took me a few minutes to realize that I, too, could get shot. I was standing about one hundred feet north of the intersection. A crowd surrounded me and began yelling: "They are shooting us! They are shooting us! They are shooting the people!" I saw in their eyes a wild insistence. "You must report this to the world," yelled one man. Then the bullets zinged in our direction. I found what I took to be relative safety by lying flat on the asphalt, pinned up against a curb. Others ran. I remember thinking they must be crazy. As I lay on the ground with my cheek against the roadbed, I saw several demonstrators fall. The armored personnel carriers had done their work, ramming a channel through the burning buses. Then came the troop trucks, fifty of them rolling through the crumpled roadblock. Random gunfire killed a housekeeper on the fourteenth floor of one building. Another woman was wounded as she looked out of an eighth-floor balcony onto the scene.

I sprinted north, away from the intersection to where I'd locked my bicycle. I couldn't quite grasp what I had just witnessed. With the first fusillade of gunfire, the party had shown its true colors. The two-month-long standoff had ended. I focused on one goal: beating the army to Tiananmen Square. Too green to worry about security and too pumped up on adrenaline to grieve, I got on my bike and rode the roads and alleys parallel to Chang'an Boulevard, toward the square.

For the next several hours, I made my way slowly to the square, heading down alleyways to watch the bloody progress of the army as it moved from west to east along Chang'an Boulevard. Days before the declaration of martial law, my bureau had rented mobile phones from a telecommunications company. I phoned the AP office in Beijing, where bureau chief Jim Abrams was taking calls from four reporters on the street. At the intersection of Xidan and Chang'an Boulevard, the site of the Democracy Wall in the late 1970s, I saw about one hundred students waving the flags of the Beijing Aerospace and Aviation University and the Nanjing Chinese Medicine College. They faced the army, shouting that they were ready to "die for the motherland." The soldiers approached and, after shooting to the sky, leveled their weapons and shot several demonstrators. The students fled.

As I crept toward Chang'an Boulevard to see the action, I was not alone. A collection of onlookers—a crew of teenagers, a rail-thin old lady, a middle-aged man in an undershirt and shorts—had sneaked down the street, taking shelter in the vestibules of buildings and behind signs. Shots sent us scurrying. Some soldiers were beaten by demonstrators, some were disemboweled, and some escaped. Wounded demonstrators, sprawled on the back of three-wheeled pedicabs, were pushed groaning up side streets, where they were deposited at hospitals already reeling from the enormity of the bloodshed. At the front door of Beijing's main maternity hospital, the mouth of one doctor was red with blood from mouth-to-mouth resuscitations. As I rode west to east, parallel to Chang'an Boulevard, sometimes alone in alleyways, I was barely one-quarter mile from the bloodshed. On those skinny streets, lined with the blackened brick walls of courtyard houses, the gunfire seemed a world away.

I reached Tiananmen Square ahead of the army shortly before midnight, entering from the east after biking around the northern edge of the Forbidden City and through one of Beijing's oldest neighborhoods, Beichizi. Smoke floated through the floodlights illuminating the square. A motley crew of men and women faced off against the army's vanguard along Chang'an Boulevard. The "urgent announcement," ordering people off the streets, droned through loudspeakers.

Tanks began rolling across the northern edge of the square; more tanks waited at the southern entrance. Hundreds of PLA troops, their weaponry and helmets glinting in the floodlights, massed on the steps of the Great Hall of the People and the Museum of Revolutionary History—along the west and east flanks of the square. They had arrived there by way of a secret military tunnel system under Beijing and announced their presence with a unified whoop. Student leaders, screeching through bullhorns, called on the remaining five hundred or so demonstrators to gather around the Monument to the Revolutionary Heroes at the heart of the square.

I made it to the monument. Being closer to other people made me feel safer. Cycling alone in the alleyways, I had been scared, the darkness and tranquillity somehow more foreboding than here in the center of the storm. But it wasn't just the students who were naive. I was a newborn calf, too. We were trapped.

At about 2 a.m., a squad of soldiers entered the northwestern corner of Tiananmen Square and demolished a command headquarters that had belonged to the "Beijing Autonomous Workers' Union," ending the two-month-old existence of the first and only labor union independent of party control since 1949. The tanks flattened the fifteen-foot-tall Goddess of Democracy, a plaster-of-paris knockoff of the Statue of Liberty erected by art students directly opposite the portrait of Mao.

I climbed the steps of the martyr's monument to get a better view, phoning in the events as I saw them. Around me, students continued to chant, "Down with corruption! Long live democracy!" At 4:25 a.m., the lights in the square were extinguished. In the darkness, the students huddled at the foot of the statue and began singing the "Internationale," the anthem of the Paris Commune, the failed Communist takeover of the French capital in 1848. It sounded pathetic.

In its last moments, the student movement became hostage to the romantic disorderliness that was its most attractive feature. As the army closed in, nerves frayed even more, and leaders who hadn't already disappeared now fled. A young woman next to me sobbed unconsolably in the arms of her boyfriend. He tried to comfort her, but he looked at least as scared.

Unbeknownst to many students, Hou Dejian, a well-known Taiwanese singer who had joined the demonstrations in late May with his own hunger strike, had started negotiations with military officials for a peaceful withdrawal from the square. The military agreed, and Hou returned with the news, which was put up to a voice vote by the students. Though the "stay" votes were clearly louder, Feng Congde, the one remaining leader, snatched a bullhorn and announced, "The go votes have won!"

Picking up banners and scattered clothes, several hundred demonstrators and a half-dozen foreign holdouts like myself began moving across the square, past the mausoleum that stored Chairman Mao's body, to the southwest corner along a route predetermined by the military. The sky was beginning to lighten. Once we left the square, no soldiers lined our route; a few officers with walkie-talkies peered at us from alleyways, monitoring our progress. After several blocks, the students let their banners sag and either junked them or dragged them from behind. I separated from the group at the Xidan intersection and walked over to the Minorities Hotel to file a final bulletin. My mobile phone had run out of juice. There was no food at the hotel, but the concierge opened a small store and slid me a bag of peanut M&Ms.

In the chaos, I had lost my bike. I arranged for someone from the AP bureau to pick me up a few blocks north of Chang'an Boulevard, now closed by the military. I got in the car and rode in silence. Though I wasn't surprised by the crackdown, the crazed violence of it all had shocked me. I sank into the passenger seat, emotionally and physically drained.

On June 7, I called Liu Gang, my composer friend in the People's Liberation Army. His wife answered the phone. "Tell him to be careful," I said.

Though she didn't reveal it, agents from the Ministry of State Security and the People's Liberation Army had arrested him the previous day. They interrogated him about his relationship with me. Weeks earlier, while Liu Gang read us the party speech in the car, Chinese security agents were parked behind us in a white van equipped with a directional listening device and a telephoto lens.

On June 9, Deng Xiaoping made his first appearance since the crackdown, emerging to greet a group of officers representing the various army corps that had entered Beijing. What had happened, Deng told the smiling soldiers, was inevitable. "It was just a matter of time and scale," he continued. "It is more to our advantage that this happened today. What is most advantageous to us is that we have a large group of veteran comrades who are still alive. They have experienced many storms and they know what is at stake. They support the use of resolute action to counter the rebellion."

Two days later, the government issued a most-wanted arrest list of twenty-one student leaders. Several were already on their way out of the country, smuggled out via an "underground railroad" funded by Hong Kong movie stars, and aided by the muscle—and speedboats—of organized crime.

On June 14, the U.S. embassy reopened after having been shuttered for weeks due to security concerns. China and the United States had become engaged in a war of words after China's leading dissident, the astrophysicist Fang Lizhi, and his wife had taken refuge inside the embassy on June 5. A crowd had gathered around the building—harried students and academics, including those who had participated in the demonstrations, government officials and businessmen—desperate for visas to flee China.

I returned to the AP bureau and banged out a piece on the embassy's opening. It was my 107th story since the demonstrations began two months before, and it would turn out to be my last. Sun streamed through the bureau's windows. It was a beautiful day. The phone rang, and I answered it. As the speaker talked, my eyes turned toward the motes of dust spinning in the sunbeams.

"This is the police in charge of resident foreigners in China," the voice said. "Are you Pan Aiwen?"

"Yes."

"You are ordered to appear at our bureau immediately," he said and hung up.

At the police station, located in an old courtyard house near Tiananmen Square, I was ushered into a large room and told to sit down. A few minutes later, two small, fine-featured men walked out from behind a screen, one of them clutching a blue file. I wondered if they were from the police or state security. They did not identify themselves or shake my hand.

"How long have you been in China?" one of them asked.

"Not yet a year this time."

"But you've lived here before," another said.

"So you know," his partner added, "that this is not just an ordinary chat."

"Yes," I replied. My legs had begun to shake.

"We want to clarify some things that you were involved with," one of them said. "After the martial law order was issued, you broke the law."

"There are some situations about which we hope you will speak with us clearly," his partner continued. "That will allow us to clarify the situation. Do you understand?"

"Yes," I said.

"We have arrested your friend Liu Gang," he said. "Do you know him?"

I denied knowing him. Both men became enraged and began screaming at me. Up to this point, I had been conversing in Chinese, but I realized that they must know English so, to put myself on safer ground, I switched.

"We have photographs of you together," one said, continuing in Chinese. "Don't try to deny your relationship. We know everything."

"This situation is already clear," his partner added, again in Chinese. "We hope you can make it clearer."

I was befuddled by the logic, which must have been the intent. I wondered if they would hit me. I wondered if it would hurt. I felt extremely uncomfortable and suddenly very small, although I would have towered over both of them had I stood up. We went around and around like this for three hours. After they brought out a photograph of Liu Gang and me eating together, I acknowledged knowing him.

"Oh, him," I said. "We just talked about jazz and girls. He is a composer."

As if on cue, the pair blew up again.

"You must seek truth from facts!" one of them yelled at me. "If we had no proof, we would not bring you here. You Americans must be clear about this."

I repeated that Liu and I spent our time discussing jazz and girls. They accused me of receiving documents from him. I denied it. They accused me again. I denied it again.

"If you don't admit things, it won't be good for you," one said. "It won't have a good effect on your situation in China."

"This thing—music and girls—is not enough," the other added. "It's too far from the real situation."

"Are you seeking truth from facts? Or are you avoiding the issue? Explain yourself clearly!" his partner shouted.

"Your friend has already admitted everything," one said. "He admitted you met five times. He admitted everything about you two. We want you to speak about the facts."

I demurred again. I'd been in the room for nearly four hours, and I was exhausted. After I refused again to detail my relationship with Liu Gang, they got up and left. A few minutes later, at exactly 5 p.m., they returned. One of them opened the blue clipboard, looked at me, and said, "Your attitude has been both uncooperative and unfriendly." He then read me an order expelling me from China. My crimes, the order read, were "violating martial law regulations and stealing state secrets." I was given three days to leave.

That night in a room in a military installation in the northwest section of the city, state security agents allowed Liu Gang to watch the national news that led with my expulsion and that of a correspondent from Voice of America. "What do you think of that?" an interrogator asked him. "Pan Aiwen told us everything. You're finished."

Liu Gang was moved out of the barracks and into the custody of the Ministry of State Security. For the next decade, I carried the weight of knowing that my involvement with a Chinese person resulted in his imprisonment. It changed the way I looked at the country. In the past, I had understood that the system routinely crushed lives—often for no reason. I had worried about Fay getting arrested because of our relationship. But I had been blithe, naive, and careless because underneath I never thought it would happen to someone close to me. Liu's imprisonment was an important lesson, which came at a great price; what was worse, the price was not paid by me.

That night I returned to my small apartment, where I watched a rebroadcast of the state-run national news report. I left China two days later, on June 17, the same day a court sentenced eight men to death for beating soldiers and setting fire to vehicles during the crackdown. Several days later, Zhao Ziyang was formally removed from his post as party chief and placed under house arrest in a courtyard home down a quiet alley in Beijing. It was there, save for an occasional round of golf and a daily walk, that Zhao would stay for the next fifteen years until his death in January 2005.

Deng chose Jiang Zemin, an owlish former employee of a Shanghai ice cream factory, as China's new party chief. Jiang, the party boss in Shanghai, had squashed protests there more peacefully. Catapulted to power partially because he did not have blood on his hands, Jiang's appointment served the party's purpose of minimizing the emotional impact of the killings. Jiang was the third leader Deng had chosen to run China. He had gotten rid of the other two. Jiang's prospects looked no better.

A few months after the crackdown, the Ministry of Propaganda organized an exhibition called *The Truth about the Beijing Turmoil*. Held in the vast confines of the Military Museum, near where I had witnessed the PLA open fire, the exhibition was filled with photographs of the demonstrations, student leaders, and the slain bodies of soldiers. Not a single memorial to civilians was included. In the back of the exhibition hung a life-size photograph of me standing behind Wang Dan, the thoughtful student leader who had subsequently been arrested and who would serve two stints in prison before being exiled to the United States in 1998.

The caption read: "In violation of Chinese laws and relevant regulations during the martial law period in certain parts of Beijing, Pan Aiwen, an Associated Press correspondent, kept frequent contacts with ringleaders of illegal organizations, passing on information, providing asylum, and obtaining top state secrets by unlawful means."

18

ASYLUM

When the Chinese government declared martial law in Beijing on May 20, Daybreak Song led a delegation of Chinese students from Florence to the embassy in Rome. Throughout the world, expatriate Chinese congregated near their embassies to express their support for the students.

For Song and other Chinese living abroad, the June 4 crackdown was all the more shocking because it was carried live on TV. Three days after the violence, Song led another protest—this one a forty-eight-hour hunger strike in front of the Chinese embassy. The fast was joined by a Who's Who of Italian luminaries—political party chiefs, actors, singers, even chefs. After the demonstration ended, officials at the embassy sent out a meal for everyone.

Once Deng Xiaoping emerged to back the crackdown, Chinese embassies around the world snapped into line. They warned Chinese students that any subsequent protests would be considered anti-Chinese and that demonstrators would be reported to security services back in China. Song was not cowed. On August 1, the sixty-eighth anniversary of the founding of the People's Liberation Army, he led a third demonstration at the embassy's gates in Rome to show support for the thousands of students and workers who had been caught in the nationwide dragnet to arrest leaders and participants of the marches. Again, dozens of Italian politicians joined in.

After that demonstration, Song, who had been elected head of the

Italian branch of the Independent Federation of Chinese Students, met with an official from the embassy. Song wanted to renew his passport, which would expire at the end of 1989, and stay in Italy. A few weeks later, Song was summoned back to the embassy and told that permission to do so had been denied by what the official called "the relevant authorities," which invariably meant the secret police, because Song was breaking Chinese law by leading demonstrations. With an expiring passport, Song now risked deportation.

Song had continued his relationship with his second Italian girlfriend from Nanda, Maria Luisa Giorgio. Having returned to Italy in 1986 to be with him, by 1988, she had landed a job at the Fiat truck plant in Nanjing. Before the crackdown, Maria Luisa had asked Song if he intended to stay in Italy, in which case she would not take the job. No, Song replied, he planned on returning to Nanjing to complete his PhD.

Several months after the crackdown, in the fall of 1989, two exiled senior leaders of the democracy movement came to Italy. Having found out about Song's interest in Tibet, they asked to meet him. The dissidents wanted to contact the Dalai Lama, the exiled spiritual leader of the Tibetan people, whom they had heard was the inside favorite to win that year's Nobel Peace Prize. (They were right.) Song, by virtue of his interest in Tibet, became not only the leader of the independent union of Chinese students in Italy but also the democracy movement's representative to the exiled government of Tibet.

The democracy movement's goal was to create a web of relations between exile groups devoted to changing China, led by those who had been smuggled out of the country, and the thousands of Chinese students and scholars overseas who were outraged at the bloodshed in Tiananmen Square. Add to the mix independence activists from Taiwan and Tibet, and it is easy to see how these exiles thought they had the raw material to become a potent force in Chinese politics. In December 1989, the Dalai Lama and Chinese exiles met in Paris and issued a joint document calling for democracy in China and genuine autonomy for Tibet. Song was there.

Song was as awed by the Dalai Lama's charisma as he was dumbfounded by the ignorance of the Chinese exiles, many of whom had held high-ranking positions in the Chinese government. None of them knew whether Tibet had, in fact, been independent of China throughout much of the past thousand years. If democracy activists could be this ignorant, Song thought, imagine how the rest of China's bureaucracy was. Song vowed that if he returned to China, he would work to improve its policy on Tibet.

True to government tactics, each embassy in the West had been ordered to identify one dissident ringleader. In Italy, it was Song. Chinese embassy officials ordered students to avoid Song and threatened those who met him with unspecified consequences once they returned to China. Song's only option other than returning home was to request political asylum in Italy. He pleaded with Maria Luisa, still in Nanjing, to return to Italy to help him. The decision was a tough one for her. She knew that if she left Nanjing, she would not be able to return to China for a long time; yet with Song pushing, she agreed. Song applied for political asylum in late December 1989. After a year's wait, Italy provided him with a refugee travel document, though not with full citizenship. With no steady source of income, the couple faced the future with dread.

Maria Luisa went back to school for a doctorate in art history, which afforded her a small stipend. They lived for free in an apartment in Rome owned by her parents. She pushed Song to get a job, but he refused. While his old colleagues and classmates in China faced interrogations, expulsions from the party, jail time, and betrayals, Song was slipping into the unique despair of the exile.

Song would start books but never finish reading them. He would sleep all day and refuse to bathe. He began painting the apartment but then stopped halfway, littering rooms with paint cans and paintbrushes. He was not interested in meeting Italians. Maria Luisa would go to a movie with friends and ask Song along, but he would decline. He did not want to go to the seaside. He refused to travel. He just wanted to pore over books he'd never finish.

For centuries, exile had been the worst punishment, short of death, meted out by the Chinese state to its intellectuals. Exile was a particularly painful penalty because in China the highest ideal for an intellectual, even for a freethinker like Song, is to serve the state. Now Song was cast aside, an enemy who could not return.

In the spring of 1991, Maria Luisa came down with chicken pox. For four days she sweated in bed with a high fever, and Song did nothing for her. It seemed to Maria Luisa that Song did not care whether she lived or died.

"I told myself that in the future, if you ever believe he has feelings for you, remember today," she told me. "Remember today."

The Tiananmen Square crackdown had destroyed more than hopes for democracy; it also marked an end of innocence, shutting the door on pro-Western idealism and the country's romance with the Western world. In response to the massacre, international sanctions were slapped on Beijing, and naive Westerners removed the rose-colored spectacles through which, despite all the evidence, they'd insisted on viewing China—and were horrified to discover how gullible they'd been. Book Idiot Zhou had it right. Nonetheless, sanctions along with other actions such as the U.S. congressional decision to block China from winning its bid to host the 2000 summer Olympics, gave the party an opportunity to convince Chinese that, once again, the world was ganging up on them.

The reality of life in post-Tiananmen China forced many of my classmates to change their lives. Several of them were booted out of the Communist Party and fired from their jobs. College professors who had been active in the demonstrations were hounded out of academia. The snitch society returned as citizens were rewarded for ratting out their friends and colleagues.

Relationships imploded as well. One classmate, an active participant in the protests, was placed under house arrest following the crackdown, ending what had been a promising academic career. Within a year, his wife had run away with another man to the United States. My classmate wound up going into the real estate business in Hainan Island, a tropical, sun-drenched smugglers' paradise just off the northern coast of Vietnam. As hard-liners rolled back market reforms and plotted to return China to the Dark Ages, Hainan was one of the few bright spots of economic freedom.

"Before June 4, we were so idealistic and pure, but after June 4 things changed," he observed years later. "I became tactful, slick, and diplomatic. I didn't care about people like I used to. Now I'm looking out for number one."

19

FISHY HANDSHAKES

Book Idiot Zhou documented the demonstrations in Bengbu with the precision of an accountant, keeping a running diary of protests and the local government's response. He went to every demonstration, carefully snapping thousands of photographs with a borrowed camera because he was still too poor to afford his own. When Zhou got the film developed, all of it came out blank. The film developer, following party orders, had purposely exposed the film.

Convinced that the party would smash the student movement, Zhou marched anyway. In May 1989, when the hunger strike on Tiananmen Square began, the institute's teachers walked off their jobs to support the students. Before making their decision, several all-day bull sessions were held in which the teachers mulled over the future of China and the necessity of democratic political reform. As usual, Zhou spoke his mind publicly. But when asked to organize a team to support the demonstrating students, he refused.

When Chinese authorities declared martial law in Beijing on May 20, Zhou knew it was only a question of time before the party would send in the army to quell the demonstrations. In Bengbu, when the crackdown came, there was no violence. Police were deployed across town and at the gates of his school; the students stayed in their dorms.

The crackdown marked China's return to paranoid Maoism. Zhou wrote a "self-criticism," as all party members, teachers, and students throughout the country were ordered to do, documenting his involvement in the protests. He was compelled to attend meetings and political study sessions. Zhou watched colleagues who had marched together for democracy turn on each other in the party study sessions. A competition broke out to see who was the most patriotic and who loved China more. At one meeting, a colleague went so far as to claim that no one in Eastern Europe, a region that had recently buried communism, had ever seen color photographs. "So, gosh," the man enthused, "we can see how advanced China is becoming. We have color photographs. We've even surpassed Eastern Europe."

Alienation from the institute pushed Zhou to focus more intensely on his career, supervising the collection and processing of tons of urine a day. Still, the peasant-turned-history-teacher-turned-capitalist faced a steep learning curve. In 1991, Zhou was accepted in a program at Beijing University designed to keep history and politics professors up on the latest trends in teaching Marxism. Zhou spent most of his time setting up a urine extraction plant.

Zhou landed two contracts with the Beijing municipal government to buy urine collected at public toilets. Over the course of the next months, he got to know each public toilet intimately (one thousand in all) while pedaling his bicycle through Beijing neighborhoods, showing his workers where the collection sites were.

None of his laborers had ever been in Beijing before. Zhou couldn't find urbanites willing to do the dirty work. His crew constituted the first of a wave of migrant rural workers who would transform China's cities. Over the next few years, hundreds of millions of people would leave their villages for a new life in sweatshops or at jobs that locals no longer wanted: collecting trash, waiting tables, sweeping streets, and collecting urine.

Although the internal passport system had not been dropped, meaning it was still technically illegal for rural men and women to work in cities, the demands of China's economy for cheap labor forced local police departments to stop rounding up migrants and to look the other way. By not reforming the residential permit system, the party actually served the interests of China's new capitalists, who could treat their workers badly and even refuse to pay them because, technically, the workers were breaking the law by having traveled to the city in the first place.

Zhou found most of his crew in his hometown of Dongtai and a few in Bengbu. Other laborers hailed from Shandong, Henan, Sichuan, and Hebei—farm boys with strong bodies and a willingness to do anything to get out of the fields. Zhou saw himself in these workers. It seemed like only yesterday when he, too, had been desperate to flee the Shen Kitchen Commune.

Zhou managed a stable of eighteen three-wheeled pedicabs. Each pedicab was outfitted with a small flatbed fashioned from bamboo slats. Each flatbed carried a maximum of thirty-six barrels; each barrel held more than forty pounds for a full load of fifteen hundred pounds. Zhou's processing plant—a bankrupt state-owned factory that he had rented from a local party secretary—was south of Beijing's downtown, three and a half miles from the nearest toilet. The workers made as many as nine trips a day, seven days a week, earning the equivalent of fifty dollars a month.

One day in January 1992, Zhou discovered that the plant's drainage system was blocked, leaving him with no place to dump several vats of effluent. Zhou had been told that the runoff, mostly ammonia, would harm neither people nor animals, so he discharged the stuff into the ponds of a local fish farm. The proprietors had stocked the pools with carp they planned to sell during the upcoming Chinese New Year's festival. Chinese traditionally eat fish during the New Year's festivities because the word for fish, *yu,* sounds similar to the word for "plenty." Because of China's capitalist reforms, it was now fashionable to eat carp, because its name, *li,* sounds like the word for "profit."

Zhou spent the Spring Festival holidays dredging thousands of dead fish out of the fishponds, leaving a stench on his hands and clothes for months. He reimbursed the owners the equivalent of two thousand dollars for the loss—a small fortune in those days. The locals, it would turn out, were actually sympathetic to Zhou's plight. Here was a bumbling, gap-toothed college professor trying his hand at business. No matter how hard he tried, Zhou was still very much a book idiot.

By early 1992, five years into his business and one year into his stay in Beijing, Zhou had so little money that his platoon of eighteen pedicabs had dwindled to a squad of five. His business was failing, although the market for enzymes was good. One day a Nanda classmate spotted him at the Guangzhou airport, pushing boxes of his product on a luggage cart.

"He was all sweaty and looked totally harried," the classmate recalled. "It wasn't a pretty sight."

Zhou periodically would ask his partner in Dongtai for a share of the firm's profits. Each time the partner would refuse, saying the business was facing difficulties. Then on another trip to Guangzhou, Zhou asked a representative of the Guangzhou pharmaceutical company how he thought the business was doing. "Not bad," he replied. "We must have made several hundred thousand together." Other than the occasional pittance to cover expenses, Zhou had not seen any money from his Dongtai partner in more than six years.

His experience was typical for many Chinese entrepreneurs. So new to the business of business, the Chinese ripped each other off with mind-boggling regularity. The country's lack of a moral compass only made things worse. Zhou once stored 120 pounds of enzyme at a friend's refrigerated warehouse. The friend sold it and refused to give him any money. Zhou hadn't asked for a contract because to do so would have amounted to an insult. Business was all done on a handshake, yet in China, handshakes were worthless.

Zhou was also facing a personal crisis; the strain of supporting his family had begun to overwhelm him. The needs of his handicapped daughter, the tension between the management of his business and the Marxism he taught at the institute, and his loveless union with his wife made Zhou feel as if his life was fracturing. Zhou finally asked Lin Fei for a divorce. Surprisingly, she agreed, on the condition that he meet two demands: a cash advance for herself and child support for their two daughters. Zhou then went home and asked his parents. They, too, assented.

Zhou also needed to get approval from the Anhui Institute of Finance and Trade. Divorces were viewed as bad for the party's image, so officials tried to reconcile the pair. One of Zhou's superiors at the institute came to his office uninvited and sat down. "Divorce is not good for social stability," the man lectured. "It is not a patriotic thing to do. I suggest you wait five years. Then perhaps you won't be interested in such a move."

In just a few years, urban China had turned from a conservative world stressing self-denial and sacrifice to a libertine's dream of frenzied searches for money, pleasure, and individual gratification. In the 1980s, a hit song, sung by a saccharine siren from Hong Kong, whimpered, "I've fallen in love with a man who won't come home, I am standing by a locked door."

The song reflected the tenor of the times; love was waiting, love was sacrifice, and all love stories ended in tragedy. By the mid-1990s, Wang Fei, a slinky rocker from Beijing, released a pointed rejoinder in her hit "Bored." "Who says falling in love with a man who won't come home means that you have to wait forever?" she purred. "Isn't there another way to end this story? . . . I don't want to sacrifice myself. I don't want to be peaceful and composed."

Porn shops, massage parlors, and other staples of the sex industry exploded throughout the country. The businesses were owned by police departments and military units that transformed precinct houses and army installations into karaoke halls, whorehouses, gambling dens, and discos. A tacit social contract had been hammered out between the party and the people. While the party maintained its rigid ban on political activity, it widened substantially the space for personal freedom and self-realization. As long as people accepted Communist Party rule, the new deal went, they would be allowed to do almost anything—from amassing riches to supporting concubines to bungee jumping to collecting cars.

Divorce rates skyrocketed. In the past, a key impediment to divorce was a lack of housing. Couples who had legally split were often forced to continue to live together in rabbit-warren apartments, with one sleeping in the bed and the other on the floor. But in the early 1990s, the government launched a housing reform program designed to end the old system in which work units were required to provide housing for employees. The reform program was part of a broader policy aimed at getting work units, let's say, steel mills and car manufacturers, out of the real estate, child and geriatric care, education, and restaurant businesses in order to force them to focus on making steel and cars. The government encouraged, even mandated, that urban residents buy their own homes. It began to give local governments the right to auction off large tracts of land to developers. By 2005, the newly minted real estate industry had built 250 billion dollars' worth of new homes and buildings. Apartments abounded, creating for the first time in Communist history a market for rental units. Young lovers moved in together without marrying. Estranged husbands and wives had someplace to go besides the couch. Zhou himself owned three apartments at the institute—one he used as an office, one where he lived with his family, and one he rented out. Zhou moved to his office and, after months of bureaucratic inertia, the institute agreed to the divorce.

During this time, Zhou had met another woman, also unhappily married, who leaned on Zhou to help her. If he could give her three thousand dollars, she would be able to buy custody of her child from her husband and persuade him to divorce her. Divorce settlements in China were as contentious as in the United States, even though no attorneys were involved. Once again, Zhou asked his business partner for his share of the profits, this time so he could secure his divorce and help his girlfriend out of her marriage. Again, the man refused.

Zhou went to Dongtai and confronted his partner, demanding that he give Zhou the Beijing portion of the business. He relented. Zhou found himself at the end of 1994 a single man and the sole owner of his own urine-extraction business in the capital.

PART IV

INTO THE SEA

20

FAKE FOREIGN DEVILS

After I was expelled from China, I felt, like Daybreak Song, that I had been exiled from my homeland. I had gained my first sense of personal independence in China—learning a language and living on my own. China taught me to swim with the crowd. On buses, my sharp New Yorker's elbows had been worn down by a relentless sea of Chinese. I did not flinch when old ladies grabbed onto my coattails to hoist themselves on board. In the summer, I would roll up my pants legs and slap my calves arrhythmically, like a Chinese man. I loved the practicality of the Chinese for bringing their rattan cots onto the streets in the summer to sleep and their weirdness for walking backward in the park for exercise. In the winter, I guzzled bitter herbal concoctions that promised to beat chest colds, and I avoided ice water for fear it could damage my intestines. My Chinese friends insisted that in a previous life I must have been a Chinese. Perhaps a hog farmer in Manchuria, one friend suggested, a play on the fact that I was born in 1959—the year of the pig. The life I had constructed, centered on China, was now over. I had moved to Hong Kong, where the alien dialect and its very proximity to a border that I could not cross only served to make me miss China more.

I became a fireman in the AP system, traveling from my base in Hong Kong to New Delhi, Kabul, Kandahar, Kuwait, Islamabad, Sri Lanka, the Saudi desert, Saigon, Sarajevo—anywhere a body was needed, which increasingly meant war zones. I'd return to Hong Kong from my stints in those dismal locales and resume contact, through phone calls and letters, with Chinese friends across the border. From afar I had been trying to romance a woman in Beijing. I knew it was over when in 1992 she called and suggested an import-export partnership, which would begin with me sending her earrings to sell to China's youth. Whatever cockeyed romantic notions I had entertained about our future together were quashed. But that conversation also signaled something else: China was changing again.

In the years since the Tiananmen crackdown, China had been run by a band of hard-line leftists who saw the crushing of the pro-democracy demonstrations as a way to turn back the clock on economic reforms. These same hard-liners looked out from behind the red walls of the party's headquarters in Beijing and saw a world uniting against them. The Soviet Union and eastern European regimes had collapsed. The United States and western Europe had imposed economic sanctions on China. Many in the party believed that Gorbachev's glasnost and perestroika had caused the disintegration of the Soviet Union, so the enemy became reform. The party's new bogeyman became "peaceful evolution"—the idea that China's Communist system, like those in eastern Europe, would naturally give way to a version of a Western democracy in a process that was as undetectable as it was inevitable. Peaceful evolution, the party feared, would certainly bring an end to its monopoly on state power.

In 1990, the Central Party School organized a series of seminars called the Anti–Peaceful Evolution Class, where questions such as "Who was going to be China's Gorbachev?" were raised to prepare against that possibility. The state-controlled media criticized special economic zones like Shenzhen and Hainan Island, accusing those who accepted foreign investment of turning China into a foreign dependency.

Then, starting on Chinese New Year's Day in 1991, a series of four signed editorials appeared on the front page of the *Liberation Daily,* the party's newspaper in Shanghai. In a break with the spirit of the times, the editorials called for speedier reforms, criticized the party's obsession with keeping capitalism out of China, and blasted party officials for fence-sitting. The editorials were planted by Zhu Rongji, Shanghai's party boss, who had been ordered by Deng Xiaoping to push back against the hard-line tide.

Just three years earlier, Deng had masterminded the June 4 crackdown. Now he was signaling it was time for the crackdown to end. China still needed to build its economy and let its people get rich. To accomplish this, the hard-liners had to stop blocking market reforms. Though the editorials prompted a conservative backlash, it was clear that Deng's position was gaining support among a public that had grown tired of the aging conservatives and their antediluvian vision for China. Communist Party general secretary Jiang Zemin, who had taken a go-slow stance toward economic reform, switched sides and backed the moderates. In a speech commemorating the party's seventieth anniversary on July 1, 1991, Jiang said China should stop worrying about whether a market system was capitalist or not and move on with reforms.

In January 1992, Deng buried Communist economic ideology forever, opening the floodgates for the hypercapitalism of today. He took a month-long journey to Guangdong Province in what would be called his "Southern Tour," a phrase redolent with historic overtones intended to conjure up images of a Chinese emperor leading his entourage on a fact-finding mission across his domain. While in the south, Deng told one official that the hard-liners in Beijing "are just farting." To another: "If we don't reform, we'll face a dead end." He commanded another: "You should topple whoever opposes reform." "You should go faster!" he urged the men and women of China's richest province. Then he coined another slogan, "Economic development above all."

The trip—and Deng's sloganeering—set the foundation for Deng Xiaoping Theory, which remains to this day the guiding light of Chinese communism. Simply put, whatever grows the economy is good—provided that the Communist Party remains in control. Within several years, Deng had appointed Zhu Rongji to the post of premier and chief party official in charge of the economy. Nearly thirty-five years after Deng had overseen the campaign that had purged Zhu as a "rightist," Deng entrusted the same man with the economy.

I had been lobbying Chinese officials in Hong Kong for a chance to return. Their office was in the local headquarters of the Xinhua News Agency, doublespeak for Hong Kong Party Central, located in an almost windowless building looming over that symbol of Hong Kong's capitalist excess: the Happy Valley racetrack. Each time I returned to Hong Kong from a trip to a war zone, I would take the officials to lunch (they always came in pairs) and make my case. The AP bureau chief, Bob Liu, a green-eyed Eurasian with close ties to the Communists, worked his magic, too. In August 1991, the Xinhua News Agency informed me that I would be allowed back for a short reporting trip.

Shortly before Deng's Southern Tour, I returned for a trip through Guangdong and Fujian provinces, the only region where I was allowed to travel. I could not go to Beijing and was obligated to take along a guide from the All-China Journalists Federation, a front for the Ministry of State Security.

I had not been in southern China since 1980. A vast megalopolis had replaced the unbroken string of rice paddies I had gazed at during that first train ride more than a decade earlier. Chockablock with factories, grim Dickensian workers' dormitories, and skyscrapers wrapped in silver, the Pearl River Delta had turned into one vast production plant, cranking out Barbie dolls, microwaves, sweaters, toaster ovens, and mobile telephones at a rate far faster than any place else on the planet. A new country was being built—feverishly and with a reckless abandon.

As market reforms in the rest of China had screeched to a halt, southern China was doing its own thing. Its boomtowns—Shenzhen, Xiamen, Guangzhou, Haikou, Zhuhai—had become meccas for people wanting a new life. Frustrated officials and political dissidents junked their old lives and "jumped into the sea." Jilted lovers found succor in the arms of numerous sexual partners. And no one pried. Those were impersonal places, built on hard work, smarts, greed, corruption, and sleaze. People were drawn there because the boomtowns offered things found nowhere else: personal freedom, opportunity, and a second chance. Those who moved to the boomtowns referred to themselves as immigrants, which made sense; the boomtowns were a new world.

My official minder turned out to be an easygoing guy angling to junk his career as a bureaucrat-spy and immigrate to Canada. We traveled by car from Guangdong to Fujian, careening along a narrow highway that connected the two provinces. We stopped at roadside eateries, dined with young businessmen, sang off-key karaoke, got a flat and hitched a ride on an army truck. After my recent reporting experiences, dodging rockets in Kabul and stumbling into a shoot-out in Sri Lanka's civil war, China seemed almost paradisiacal.

In the few years since the Tiananmen Square crackdown, a calculating, irreverent nihilism had replaced the pro-Western idealism that once gripped China's youth. On the streets of Shenzhen, and in the fast-growing southern cities like Dongguan, Guangzhou, and Xiamen, young men and women from northern China hustled to make a *yuan*. They let their T-shirts speak for their politics. I saw one man wearing a shirt emblazoned with the picture of a begging dog over a slogan that read "Real honest, real frugal, real down-to-earth, really know my place, real obedient, really well-behaved." Another, worn by a young woman, said simply "Tiananmen."

In Dongguan, I met the vice mayor, Yuan Lisong, an oleaginous official with a dead-fish handshake. Yuan handed me two business cards. One introduced him as the city's vice mayor. The other, neatly turned out with a gold leaf logo and pica print, identified him as the managing director of Fook Man Development Co., a Hong Kong–based investment company. Yuan noted that he sat on the board of three other companies based in Hong Kong, was part owner of a five-hundred-room hotel in Los Angeles, and had plans to expand his empire to Singapore and Frankfurt. Thousands of other officials were doing the same thing—holding down a position at home while they opened up businesses abroad. In Dongguan alone, a prefecture of 1.3 million people (tiny by Chinese standards), each of its thirty-three villages had businesses established in Hong Kong. Some had more than ten.

Men like Yuan, a forty-eight-year-old Communist Party apparatchik, stood at the forefront of the creation of a new system: a dog-eat-dog or, in the even more precise Chinese locution, man-eat-man world that was absent the troublesome constraints of Communist ideology or Confucian beliefs. Chinese called people like Yuan "fake foreign devils"—a take-off on the nineteenth-century slur for the "foreign devils" who brought opium, Christianity, and international trade to China. Yuan's firm in Hong Kong was technically a foreign company, although it was owned and operated by Chinese citizens. When Yuan invested back in China, he could profit from a slew of tax breaks and other benefits designed to encourage foreign invest-ment. Yuan's firm also automatically received an export license, thereby opening a conduit to move even more money out of the country. According to the International Monetary Fund, Chinese companies were doing this at the rate of billions of dollars each year. Yuan had named his firm Fook Man; it meant "enrich the people" or, better yet, "rich people."

It was curious, I observed, for a senior party man to use a private firm to skirt Chinese regulations. Yuan laughed, slipped his alligator skin loafers on and off and looked me over with a big grin: "If I didn't travel the world, I would know only how to plant rice."

21

KILLING THE CHICKENS

Big Bluffer Ye didn't wear alligator shoes, but once economic reform was back on track, he also wanted a seat at the table.

Ye had labored as a faceless bureaucrat in the party's Organization Department for more than a decade, marrying in 1986 and having a son three years later. In December 1995, his devotion to the party finally paid off; he was appointed deputy chief of Nanjing's Drum Tower District. It was Nanjing's richest district, the site of the provincial government offices, most of the city's twenty universities, the best schools, and the nicest residential neighborhoods. Deputy district chief was a traditional position for young, promising cadres like Ye. At thirty-seven, Ye was certainly not the youngest official among his peers, but nonetheless he was moving up the party ladder.

In the years that followed his promotion, more than one quarter of the Drum Tower District would be torn down and rebuilt. China's Communists had never liked Nanjing. It was the capital of the old regime that fled to Taiwan in 1949. For decades, the party had kept Nanjing in an enforced state of penury as a way to prove the success of the new China—Mao's China of peasants and proletariat. But by the time Ye entered the Drum Tower District government, the city was making up for lost time. In a few years it would boast a Wal-Mart, a Warner Brothers multiplex theater, Haagen-Dazs ice cream parlors, and Starbucks coffeeshops. Subway lines were being dug, skyscrapers were going up, and more bridges and tunnels were being built to span the Yangtze River. Ye's office would be one of the centers of this furious development. In the district, it granted the permits to demolish buildings and construct new ones.

Everyday, Ye walked along a street called Hunan Road on his way to work. The street was a hodgepodge: bustling food stands serving noodles, steamed buns filled with pork and cabbage, and the pot stickers that Nanjing was famed for. There was a line of cramped mom-and-pop stores selling fruit, vegetables, and odd assortments of hardware and household items, including the ubiquitous party-issue washbasins. Traffic was always heavy on Hunan Road; accidents, thefts, and fisticuffs were commonplace.

Big Bluffer hated the disorderliness of Hunan Road. He hated the farmers who flooded the area to sell goods and in the process blocked traffic. He hated the government's inability to control and manage the street. Most of all, he hated the fact that people were spending money there, but his office didn't get a cent of it because all transactions were done in cash and no one kept receipts. Across town, in another district, city officials were busy turning an old Confucian temple into a massive tourist attraction, with boat rides down the still-fetid Qinhuai River. The plan was to restore the banks of the Qinhuai to their prerevolutionary glory, when singsong girls, courtesans, and royal playboys hobnobbed along the river. The temple project stood as a kind of rebuke to Ye, who wanted to go the party one better with Hunan Road.

One night, Ye had a dream of a classy pedestrian walkway on which lovers and families would stroll, stopping to eat well and spend lavishly. He woke up with an idea. Why not use commerce as a way to transform Hunan Road? His colleagues did not believe he could pull it off. No Chinese city since the revolution had created a new commercial district. Shanghai's main shopping street, Nanjing Road, had been known around the world since the 1930s. Beijing's Wanfujing Street had been bustling for five hundred years. Ye believed that Hunan Road was the party's chance to show that it, too, could create a consumers' paradise.

Ye's first decision was to widen the road, which required transferring textile and electronics factories to another section of town—a controversial move, given the growing international investment in Chinese manufacturing. Ye's directive to local businesses was simple: shopkeepers were welcome, manufacturers were not. The city's People's Congress, which on paper controls the government purse strings, balked at approving money for widening the road and moving the factories. Big Bluffer ignored their concerns. In the first year, he invested four hundred thousand dollars of government money in the area. He also blanketed the streets with tax collectors. Revenues that year hit six hundred thousand dollars.

Ye didn't like the 9 to 5 hours of all of those stores on Hunan Road selling cheap hardware, widgets, shabby second-hand clothes, and plastic jugs. They should stay open later, he thought. Ye got another idea, again from a dream. He invested in streetlights to create a night market. Then he contracted for the construction of a three-story lighted pyramid at the intersection of Hunan and Shanxi roads. Its size and brightness appealed to Ye; it signified modernity. It would act like a magnet, he wagered, drawing people to the district.

The Chinese are great people watchers. *Kan renao* (or "watching a commotion") is a favored pastime. For years there had not been much to do in Nanjing, but people still liked to go out in the evening. When Ye switched on his pyramid of light in September 1996, tens of thousands of people crammed the intersection. The police called Ye and told him to turn off the lights, but he refused. This was Ye's field of dreams. He built it, and they had come.

In less than two years, rents on Hunan Road doubled to fifty dollars a square foot. But Ye was not satisfied. As the pedestrian traffic increased, the very vendors he was trying to put out of business—hundreds of small-time traders, many of whom had been fired from bankrupt state-owned firms—flooded the area. Ye called them vagrants.

"They were all previously inmates of work camps or people from the countryside," Ye told me in 2004, although it was obvious to me that he was exaggerating. "Once they had set up shop, it was hard to get them to leave. We offered them a deal. We set up another night market for them a few blocks away. They could work there as long as they stayed away from Hunan Road. But they didn't accept the offer, so we had to get tough."

On a cool evening in April 1997, Ye ordered a hundred policemen and government workers to Hunan Road in an effort to force out the street vendors. They all fled, but were back the next day, so Ye directed his troops to begin confiscating their goods. Within a few days, they had expropriated hundreds of pounds of fruit, which were then distributed among government employees and kindergartens in the area.

"There were no regulations allowing us to do what we did, but we did it anyway," Ye said with a smirk. "They were in the way of progress."

The battle between Ye and the street sellers went on like this for weeks. One evening, a trader threw hot water on a government worker trying to take his goods; it was the first time a vendor had sought to defend himself against the property seizures. Security personnel took the man into custody. "Should we keep him in jail for a few days?" an underling asked Ye.

"Two years," Ye barked, slapping his hand on his desk. With that one vendor's act of defiance, Ye had been handed the excuse he was waiting for. Within days, the trader, along with several others, were sentenced to two years in a labor camp. Chinese regulations give local government authorities the right to send anyone to a labor camp for three years or less without a trial. Just as important, Ye ensured that cash payments were made quietly to several other traders in exchange for their agreement to leave Hunan Road.

"We were not making any headway, so we decided to get rid of the troublemakers and help out the rest," Ye recalled.

The party was reshaping China, bulldozing or buying off anyone in its way. Ye's technique was typical for an official confronting opposition. Go after the ringleader, jail him, and co-opt his followers. The Chinese call it killing the chicken to scare the monkeys. And the monkeys were scared.

Ye and I were dining together at Hunan Road's swankiest restaurant, a cavernous three-story place where waiters in top hats and tails greeted diners at the door and women in purple hot pants escorted them to their seats. The dining room's central feature was a concrete hill covered in artificial turf, through which flowed a whitewater stream. A pianist in a wedding gown was playing Peter Frampton's "Baby I Love Your Way" on a heart-shaped island in the middle of the raging current.

We were eating in a private room on the third floor. It was opulently furnished in black, gold, and red and had a private bathroom with Italian fixtures. From the ceiling hung a massive chandelier of cut glass set into a black base fashioned in the shape of six breasts with golden nipples; the decor suggested a playroom for a Mandarin Marquis de Sade. Our meal, featuring shark's fin and abalone, was easily worth five hundred dollars, though Ye never paid a bill. As we ate, Ye boasted about his will to succeed—for himself and the party. Then the turtle dish came. "Here, I'll help you," he said, yanking the body out of the shell by the head.

22

WHITE LIKE MOTHER'S MILK

In early 1991, at the age of thirty-six, Little Guan went to the hospital to have her IUD removed. Both Little Guan and her husband, Old Ding, had always wanted a daughter. Ding Xing so clearly took after his father that they thought a girl would take after Little Guan. Old Ding loved the idea of having a daughter like his wife, cute, naughty, but not altogether disagreeable.

Since the early 1980s, the government had harshly enforced its regulations limiting couples to one child. Ethnic minorities, like Tibetans, were the only exception; they could have two. The opposition to this policy was intense, especially in the countryside. By 2003, despite China's ruthless efforts, only one in five children under the age of fourteen were from single-child families. The policy was easier to enforce in the cities, where work units kept closer tabs on its citizens.

Little Guan asked a member of the family-planning bureau what would happen to Old Ding if they were to have another child. She was told that he would be fired and expelled from the Communist Party. By this point, Old Ding was deputy chief of the museum, so he and Little Guan had a lot to lose. But Ding, following the spirit of the times, had been talking about quitting anyway and going into business selling antiques. Since the late 1980s, the market for antiques had blossomed as collectors and cash flooded in from Hong Kong and abroad. For a top archaeologist in Anhui Province, valuable antiques at cut-rate prices were easy to come by. Old

Ding had grown bored at the museum; the higher he rose in the bureaucracy, the less time he spent in the field. Digging was what he loved.

Little Guan then queried her boss about what would happen to her if she had a second child. "I can't fire you because you do all the work," he replied. "But I won't be able to give you a bonus or a promotion for three years." Bonuses usually accounted for half of what office workers like Little Guan made each year. She and Ding did the math one evening in early 1991 as they prepared for bed. "Let's try," Little Guan said. "Our family would be perfect with a little baby girl."

A few months later, she was pregnant. The first two days after learning the news, the pair were probably the happiest couple in the world, Little Guan later recalled. They were exhilarated to be taking their shared fate in their own hands, gaming China's system to achieve their dream. Having rejected her first job assignment in Beijing in favor of having a family with Old Ding, now Little Guan was ready to bet their future to expand it.

But Little Guan's mood changed. When she was pregnant with Ding Xing, all she wanted was spicy and sour food. How was it that during this pregnancy her cravings were the same? Little Guan's morning sickness felt similar as well. Being pregnant with a baby girl should feel different than being pregnant with a baby boy, shouldn't it?

Little Guan worried that perhaps she was going to have another boy. In 1991, ultrasound machines had not yet become popular in China. In a few years, they would be used to such an extent to cull female fetuses that the government would ban doctors from informing couples of their baby's gender. In some provinces, for every 100 girls born, there were 135 boys, a ratio that social scientists ominously predicted would cause serious unrest in years to come. Little Guan went to an herbal doctor who felt her pulse, inspected her tongue, and pronounced that she was carrying a boy. A week later, she had an abortion. The couple tried again the next year. When the same symptoms resurfaced and the same doctor speculated that her fetus was a boy, she aborted again.

Other factors besides the baby's sex weighed on the couple's decision. Did they really want to take on the power of the state? What would happen if Little Guan's boss got a promotion and she had to confront another, less amenable bureaucrat? Deals like the one she'd struck with her boss weren't transferable. What would happen if Old Ding set up an antiques

shop and it went belly up? Little Guan's mother had made a similar decision to abort a child she had desperately wanted twenty-five years before.
Was she fated to repeat this history?

Little Guan told me this story while we strolled along the winding paths
of her gated community in the spring of 2004. It was a warm day and the
playground was full of children, several of them apparently brothers and
sisters. The residents of Little Guan's apartment complex were among the
nouveaux riches, who were also routine violators of the one-child policy.
They had enough money to pay fines, and did not rely on the Communist
Party or the government for their jobs. Little Guan did not really oppose
the one-child policy. "You Americans can sit down to talk and you still
have space to breathe, but it's not like that in China. We really have too
many people," she said. Like other well-off urban Chinese, Little Guan
objected to the inequity of the law. Enforcement was lax in the countryside, allowing for too many of what she called "low quality" births, but
tight in the cities, producing fewer "high quality" kids. "That has consequences for the quality of our nation and race," she observed.

In 1991, before attempting to expand her family, Little Guan was poised
for a promotion to department section chief at the insurance company
where she worked, but she didn't get it. Her boss blamed her steadfast
refusal to join the party. The real reason was more complex. Little Guan
didn't get along with a female superior who was envious of Little Guan's
competence and popularity. For Little Guan, office politics seemed to
reprise the worst parts of her childhood. She had had a mother who did
not like little girls. Now her female boss was jealous, too.

But as compensation for not getting the promotion, Little Guan was able
to wrangle a better apartment, another step in her family's grand march to
a higher standard of living. That April she, Old Ding, and Ding Xing
moved into a 720-square-foot place with two bedrooms, a living room,
and a dining room—a veritable palace. They spent a quarter of their life
savings, four thousand dollars, on renovations and new furniture.

Despite the dead end she faced at work and her thwarted efforts to have
a daughter, Little Guan found herself satisfied with life. She had taken her
first vacation, to the grasslands of Inner Mongolia. Ding Xing was doing
well in seventh grade. Old Ding was a bigwig at the provincial museum.

He had gone back to Japan on an archaeological exchange, bringing home another bundle of gifts: two rings, two necklaces, two pendants, and a calligraphy brush that Little Guan loved. After thirteen years of marriage, Old Ding and Little Guan remained very much in love.

Little Guan and Old Ding would often meet for lunch at home before heading back to work. So it was on Tuesday, May 16, 1995. That night Ding returned home at 10 p.m. from dinner with his colleagues. Several evenings earlier, he had gotten drunk with his buddies, arrived home late, and vomited in the vestibule of their new apartment. Little Guan had gotten mad, so this night he had followed her orders and returned before 11 p.m. When Old Ding entered the house, Little Guan was waiting up for him.

"You're late again," she complained. "I was washing dishes and looking outside, and couples were walking arm in arm. I envied them. You never have time to spend with me."

"Relax," he said. "When we're old and your health is no good, perhaps you'll be in a wheelchair. I'll push you wherever you want to go, into the fresh air, into the sun."

As he took off his shoes, he stopped and sighed. "You know, three-hundred-*yuan* shoes are really better than one-hundred-*yuan* shoes," he declared. Little Guan was overcome with longing. "There he was taking off his shoes, but I never thought he was more beautiful."

Within an hour, it was Little Guan's bedtime. If she was not asleep by 11 p.m, she would be useless the next day. They crawled into bed together and she handed him a magazine. "Read this," Little Guan commanded. She pointed to an article about the travails of women whose husbands were having affairs, a problem bedeviling marriages across China. "Three Things a 40-Year-Old Woman Should Be Afraid Of," went the headline. Old Ding laughed. "In my eyes, you will always be twenty-eight," he said, holding the magazine in one hand while he massaged the back of her neck with the other.

At 1:15 a.m. Little Guan was awoken by a strangled snort. Old Ding did not usually snore. In fact, before they were married Little Guan had warned him that if he snored, their relationship would not work. She hit him and said, "What's up?" She flicked on the lights. His face was red, and his fists were clenched. Four months after they had moved into their new home, the family was still waiting for a phone to be installed, so Little

Guan ran downstairs to a neighbor's apartment to call an ambulance. A doctor arrived about fifteen minutes later.

"Does your husband have a history of heart problems?" the doctor asked as he sat by Ding.

"No."

He had tried CPR and used a defibrillator.

"There's nothing I can do," the doctor said.

Little Guan knelt before him and pleaded. "Please do something," she said. "I'm ready for him to be sick but not to die. We have money. I will sell this house and give it all to you. Please save him."

The paramedics took Old Ding and Little Guan to the hospital. Little Guan returned home to get his clothes, still believing that somehow he was going to make it. Entering his hospital room, she saw his eyes were wide open and had a rush of joy. "He's alive!" she thought.

The nurse walked over and tried to close Ding's eyelids. They wouldn't stay shut. Ding's boss, who'd come to the hospital, tried the same. Finally, Little Guan approached the bed and kissed his eyelids until they closed. He was thirty-nine. Little Guan was a week shy of forty.

Little Guan returned to the apartment. Ding Xing was with neighbors. At 7 a.m. she collected her son and scraped together some leftovers for breakfast. "Is Daddy better?" he asked. "Yes," she replied.

Little Guan could not bear to tell him the truth she could barely accept herself. Though he sensed his mother was lying, Ding Xing couldn't confront her. The 12-year-old boy vomited. As soon as he left for school, Little Guan broke down.

Her parents and in-laws descended on Hefei. Friends and colleagues sent cards and five-foot-tall commemorative wreaths. And still she had not told her son that his father was dead. She'd asked some neighbors to take him in for a few days, but the boy needed to come home for a change of clothes, and flowers were filling up their house. On the phone, Ding Xing kept asking: "Where is my dad? How is he?"

The funeral and cremation were set for May 20. The evening before, Little Guan asked her neighbors to send Ding Xing home. Little Guan sat in a rocking chair, considering what she must do. She had not been able to eat any solid food since her husband died. The hospital had put her on an intravenous drip. A great debate had swirled around who would tell Ding Xing. Ding Xing's grandparents and Little Guan's bosses at work all had their ideas, motivated by their concern that the boy would lose control or perhaps have a breakdown. Little Guan declined their help. Carrying her IV drip, she went downstairs to wait for him at the gate of their compound.

"Ding Xing," she said, "Daddy was not saved. We could not save him. He has died. I know I look horrible, but don't worry. In a few months, you will have a mother who can smile again, laugh again, dance again, and sing again. As long as we work together, we will get back our own life. Do you believe Mama?" Ding Xing was crying. Little Guan wiped his eyes.

"I believe you, Mama," her son replied.

"We can't let people who see us want to give us money," she said. "We must live well, live happily. I would rather people be jealous of me and what we have than pity us."

The Chinese wear white at funerals because it symbolizes mother's milk and therefore hope. White is also considered an intermediary between the two central colors in Chinese culture: red, for happiness, wealth, and fame, and black, which the Chinese associate with feces, backwardness, and bad luck.

The next day, clothed in white, Ding Xing led the funeral procession, carrying a portrait of his father in a black frame. Mother and son brought the ashes home. They wanted Old Ding to tarry a while longer in a house that he had dreamed about for more than ten years.

On the sixth Sunday after Old Ding's death, again dressed in funereal white, the pair made a pilgrimage to Jiuhuashan, the Nine China Mountain, a Buddhist center a few hours from Hefei. During the Tang Dynasty thousands of monks and nuns worshipped there at hundreds of monasteries. By 1995, Communist restrictions on religion had trimmed the number to several hundred aging monks.

Little Guan and Ding Xing were not alone at the mountain retreat. Jiuhuashan had become a magnet for the blessing of the souls of the deceased to ensure them a smooth passage to a new incarnation. Monks read scriptures for Ding's soul. On the boat back, across the Yangtze River, mother and son dropped their funereal vestments into its muddy waters.

Traditional culture's views on widows have shifted wildly in China over the centuries. Widows have been held up as an icon of Confucian chastity

and a raucous symbol of mature female sexuality. Two expressions—
"Gossip besieges a widow's door" and "Like a widow in bed, there's no
one on top to help out"—underscore the mix of wantonness and loneliness that defined a widow's place in society.

During the Han Dynasty (206 BC–AD 200), widows routinely remarried
or took over their dead husbands' jobs. It was not until around AD 1000
and the neo-Confucian revival that court philosophers began demanding
that "a maiden obeys her father, a wife her husband, and a widow her son."
Court scholars venerated characters such as the beautiful Gaoxing, who
cut off her own nose with a knife to ensure that she would go to her grave
a chaste widow.

Echoes of these traditions could be seen in the way Little Guan was
treated by her acquaintances, friends, and colleagues after Old Ding's
death. Some looked at her with pity and tried to give her money. Others
whispered about her alleged sexual adventures. Many old friends simply
disappeared. The museum gave Little Guan a paltry payment each month,
which would cease when Ding Xing graduated from university. The
museum also promised that Little Guan could buy a subsidized apartment
in a new residential building it was constructing. But with time that promise evaporated.

For a while, Little Guan felt that all was lost. She had given up so much;
the opportunity to land a big job in Beijing, the chance to go abroad. Having married a man whom she loved deeply, she found it hard to accept that
he was gone. Slowly, however, she began to feel better. Life having proved
itself so brittle, Little Guan came to cherish it more than ever, and she
accepted fate as she never had before. She read Buddhist texts and the
Bible, which she had received from her husband as a gift. There are
twenty-four hours in a day, she would tell her friends. Whether you spend
them crying or laughing, it's still twenty-four hours. So why not laugh? "I
found out that I'm rich," she told me. "I have a great boy. I have people
who like me."

In 1996, Little Guan took up tai ch'i and progressed quickly. She
stopped taking the heart medication a doctor had prescribed following
Old Ding's death. And she put aside her desire for a big promotion. Her
main goal now was to ensure that Ding Xing got a good education and
was not held back because he had lost his dad.

Two years after Old Ding died, Little Guan awoke in the middle of the night after a strange dream in which her husband came to her, as he routinely did. He said, "I have no home." Little Guan had stored his ashes in an urn in the center of a small altar just off the kitchen. In the dream, Old Ding took her on a journey to his ideal resting place.

She got out of bed and wrote a nine-page letter to Old Ding's parents, describing the dream domicile: a courtyard house, next to a river facing south, with peach and pear trees nearby. Ding's parents found a place that matched the description not far from the village where Old Ding had grown up. They bought it for one thousand dollars from a couple who were leaving rural China to seek their fortune on Hainan Island. A sweet-scented osmanthus tree and tasty peaches grew in the courtyard. One weekend, Little Guan took her husband's ashes off the shelf, boarded a bus to Hai'an with the urn on her lap, and buried it near the trees. Before the burial, while she was tidying her hair, her wooden comb split in two. She saved half and buried the other with him.

23

RICE BOWL CHRISTIANS

Little Guan wasn't really religious in the formal sense. She prayed and flipped coins to find answers to questions about her life. She believed she shared her apartments with ghosts, the ghost of her husband and others who had changed her life. She worshipped fate. Other classmates expressed vague longings for something to believe in. Some said that as they aged they were trying to live according to Buddhist principles. Others acknowledged dabbling in Christianity, going to a few Catholic masses, seeking out a house church, but none of them stuck with it.

But one classmate was a true believer. Lucy Du.

When we were university students, my classmates were distrustful of any faith. They had just emerged from the cultlike madness of the Cultural Revolution. As they grew older, however, and Chinese society lost its moral bearings, the tenor of the conversation changed. My classmates now envied the faithful, especially those like Lucy who believed in a Christian God.

For eight years, the Hudson Christian Church in Newark, New Jersey, stood empty. Built for Presbyterians when the neighborhood along Heller Parkway was predominantly WASP, it had fallen into disuse as Italian Catholics, followed by Cubans and Puerto Ricans, took over the neighborhood. Raccoons infested the church's belfry, leaving their paw prints on the pews. The roof leaked, and the 1930s art deco stained-glass windows were pockmarked with holes.

In 2000, a group of Chinese Christians bought the church, renaming it the Newark Christian Fellowship. The roof was mended, the broken stained glass replaced, and prayers were said to oust the raccoons. Sounds of hymns and fervent sermons, this time in Chinese, echoed again within the arches of Newark's old stone church.

On a brilliant winter morning four years after the church had been renovated, I accompanied Lucy Du, her husband, Tom Zhou, and their two daughters to a service. They lived in Livingston, a sturdy, northern New Jersey suburb of New York, in a simply furnished, three-bedroom house with Mickey Mouse stickers on the light switches, plastic flowers on the kitchen table, and an upright piano in the living room.

The church buzzed with energy. The pews were full of young families. They were first-generation Chinese Americans from Malaysia, Hong Kong, Singapore, and Taiwan. But the majority came from mainland China. Most of the women were housewives, like Lucy. The men worked as computer programmers, doctors, researchers, accountants. Their children scampered through the church's wide hallways and up and down its creaky wooden stairs. Parents greeted each other, punctuating their conversations with, "*Ganxie zhu, Ganxie zhu*" ("Praise the Lord, Praise the Lord"). The smell of the potluck waiting downstairs—pot stickers, pork stew, and vegetables stir-fried in garlic—wafted through the halls.

Two recent immigrants from Beijing herded us deeper into the church. One pulled me aside. "Please don't be upset if you see raccoon footprints," he apologized. "It seems that our prayers have yet to be answered."

The nave was paneled in stained oak from the floor to the vaulted ceiling, fifty feet overhead. Sunlight twinkled through the new stained-glass windows. The Newark Christian Fellowship had no pastor. "Our evangelicalism stresses equality," Tom told me. "Many Chinese churches are like this." The service resembled a Quaker meeting. When someone felt the spirit, he or she either stood and spoke from their pew or walked to the front of the church to address the congregation. We sang from a late-nineteenth-century hymnal with lyrics in English and Chinese.

A man who identified himself as Mr. Wang rose to speak. "Americans look at Christ differently than we do," he said. "Americans haven't suffered for their religion like we did in China." Another man in a seersucker suit with a loud red tie and huge black-framed glasses cleared his throat loudly and spoke in broken English with a heavy Dixie accent. "We are all sinners," he barked. "ALL SINNERS!"

A young visiting pastor from Taiwan, with a velvety voice and a neatly tailored three-piece suit, sauntered to the front and began a sermon about the unity of Christ and the community of the church. God, he said, was present in their fellowship. Tom nodded his head. "Let us sing," said the pastor.

Floods of joy over my soul Like sea billows roll . . .

Lucy Du was the belle of our class, petite, with luminescent skin and a curvy figure. More than twenty years on, she had gained a different notoriety as the only one to publicly acknowledge her religious beliefs. Born Du Mengxi in 1960 in Suzhou, a city in the lower Yangtze River valley famed for its landscaped gardens and beautiful women, she had a childhood that was sadly typical of her generation. When she was six years old, she witnessed her grandmother—the matriarch of a well-off family of businessmen and shopkeepers and the woman who raised her—hauled onto a stage with a dunce cap on her head and a placard hanging off her bent body. Because of a bad class background, her grandmother was viciously criticized for months, often in front of an audience of hundreds. Lucy remembered being ordered to yell insults at her. But she proved incapable of following those orders; in fact, she couldn't stop crying. Lucy's grandmother survived the Cultural Revolution, but an uncle to whom Lucy was also close did not. He committed suicide.

In college, Lucy was pursued by several of our classmates with little success. One, Wang Honglin, a peasant boy from the Jiangsu countryside, who had lost two brothers to starvation during the Great Leap Forward, was so dogged in his protestations of love that our class's party committee got involved, holding a meeting on a relationship that Wang insisted was real but Lucy contended was mere fantasy.

Wang's tenacity was not unusual. Men would often decide on a girl-friend without consulting her and then begin pursuing her with complete disregard for the real feelings of the woman in question. Wang wrote Lucy reams of love notes, which found their way into the hands of our classmates. "I know I look like a rube from the countryside," went one, "but I've got big plans and a big future ahead of me. Give me a chance. I won't let you down."

After leaving college, Lucy was assigned a job back in her hometown, where she met and married Tom Zhou, a delicately featured, studious computer science major also from Suzhou. In 1984 they had a son. Lucy and Tom did not participate in the protests in 1989, but they did pay close attention to the events unfolding around them. Both had come from families with political problems, and both hoped that their country might become more democratic and free. As the demonstrations rocked Beijing and other cities, Tom went ahead with his applications to graduate school in the United States, while Lucy spent her time with their boy. Following the 1989 crackdown, the couple moved to America with their five-year-old son, even though at the time most students made the trip alone. Tom's meager scholarship money would have to feed three mouths instead of one.

In early 1990, Lucy and Tom were invited by an American couple to a Bible study meeting in the northern New Jersey community where they had made their home. Tom had met the American at Rutgers University, where he was pursuing a graduate degree in computer science. Lucy was working in a restaurant. It was there that she took the name Lucy because the Korean proprietor could not say her given name, Mengxi (pronounced *meng-see*).

It took time for the pair's faith to awaken. They had never before been in a church setting. Still, they kept returning to the Bible sessions because they liked the way people treated each other. There was a certain simplicity and straightforwardness in how the participants interacted that appealed to Tom and Lucy. What a change from their own society, which seemed to pride itself on making human relations as complex as possible.

After several months, Lucy and Tom took part in a three-day retreat to study the gospel. At the closing sermon, the preacher gazed out at the assembled worshippers and asked whether they were ready to take Jesus into their hearts. "Then a force, difficult to resist, propelled me to raise my right hand and answer, 'Yes,'" Lucy recalled. Her husband, whom she figured would be warier, also raised his hand. It was a coincidence, Lucy explained, that would spark great wonder in her heart.

Lucy Du and her husband were part of a wave of Chinese immigrants entering the evangelical Christian church. In 1979, the year mainland Chinese began coming to study in the United States in large numbers, there were 366 Chinese Protestant churches. By 2005, there were three times as many, most of the converts being immigrants or students from China. When Lucy and her family moved to New Jersey in 1989, their neighborhood was made up of new immigrants from Taiwan and older Jewish families. Taiwanese comprised 80 percent of the local Christian community. By the time I visited their church in 2004, 80 percent of the worshippers were from China.

Though Lucy Du's conversion took place in New Jersey, it paralleled a similar growth of Christianity in China. In the century before the Communist Revolution of 1949, Western missionaries flooded China, building hospitals, schools, and universities, such as Nanda and Nanjing Normal University. But by 1949, for all their proselytizing, there were barely 10 million Christians—Catholics and Protestants—in China. Christianity floundered in prerevolutionary China because it was too closely associated with imperialism and the carving up of the country by foreign powers. Becoming a Christian was seen as selling out. "One more Christian, one less Chinese," the saying went. Converts were called "rice bowl" Christians—people who praised Jesus in order to finagle material benefits: food, medical attention, education, and a warm place to sleep.

Following the opening of China to the West in 1978 and the collapse of communism as an ideology, millions began looking for something to believe in. Nativist sects like Falun Gong boomed. Buddhist temples hosted the prayerful by the millions. But in the new Chinese marketplace of faith, Christianity, especially evangelical Christianity, was the hands-down winner. Today there are as many Christians in China as there are Communist Party members—60 million.

Christianity's image in China had improved steadily as people realized they could be Chinese and Christian at the same time. Indeed, in the years since 1949, the Communist Party had done a better job of destroying Chinese culture than Christian missionaries had. Ironically, as well, Communism had paved the way for Chinese to accept evangelical Christianity. There is something in the determination of belief required by the evangelical faith that resonates among those who were force-fed an unwavering devotion to Marxism, Leninism, and Maoist thought. Chinese Christians also maintained that there is a causal relationship between Christianity and the power and prestige of the United States. Capitalism and democracy were uniquely Christian phenomena, Lucy and her husband argued, and had reached the apex of their development in America. If China wanted to become powerful and free, they contended, it should embrace the Western faith.

Lucy's faith was the subject of a good deal of envy and respect among our classmates—from well-ensconced party officials, like Big Bluffer Ye, to alienated intellectuals like Daybreak Song. "She has something she believes in; that's good," Ye said one night as we discussed our classmates. "The party has been too rough on people of religion. They are often the best citizens." When Ye visited Lucy's family during a junket to the United States, he spent several days at their New Jersey house peppering Tom with questions about the Bible and religion.

On one of my trips to Livingston, Lucy and Tom brought me to a friend's house in the neighborhood, another three-bedroom house at the end of a quiet cul-de-sac. We removed our shoes at the door, placing them with dozens of other pairs lined up neatly down the hall. Inside, a bustling Chinese brunch was in full swing. In the living room, the hosts had arranged twenty-five folding chairs. A strikingly beautiful elderly woman with a firm handshake and entrancing eyes approached me. She introduced herself as Lina, and said she'd been in the United States for twenty years.

"Do you believe?" she asked me, taking my hand. "Have you accepted Jesus?"

Lina walked to the middle of the room, stood by the piano, and clapped her hands.

"Bible class will begin," she announced.

Lina was the daughter of a prominent Christian banking family in China. Following the Communist Revolution, her family stayed behind, wrongly thinking they would have no problem. The Communists had convinced China's nascent capitalist class that, as long as they were patriotic, nothing would happen to them. But such assurances turned out to be lies. Her family's property was confiscated, and her father was denied medical care and died soon after the revolution. In 1966, when the Cultural Revolution started, Lina was twenty-two. She was exiled from Shanghai to western China to work in a coal mine, where officials hounded her because she was a Christian.

"When night became day and day night, I lost my God and I decided to kill myself," she said.

After painting a white cross on her work clothes, Lina jumped the equivalent of twenty-one stories down a mineshaft. Her body broken and covered in blood, she was nonetheless pulled out alive. Red Guards continued to terrorize her while she was in the hospital, prohibiting nurses from helping her go to the bathroom and coming to her room to yell at her. Still, Lina's failed suicide attempt became a powerful proselytizing tool for the Christians in her coal-mining town. She was the *shuai bu si,* the believer who jumped but would not die.

"It is so lonely loving God on the mainland," she said.

24

YES MAN

Faith gave Lucy Du a place overseas for herself and her family. Daybreak Song, on the other hand, found himself in Italy with no faith, no money, and no place to go. Granted political asylum by the Italian government, Song had turned into a recluse, moping about the house. Unlike many of his generation who longed to leave China or at least become "fake foreign devils," Song kept his heart in China while his body was stuck in Europe. Maria Luisa wanted to break up with him but decided she could not kick him out. She felt responsible. Sometimes she hoped he'd just disappear, but she would not be the one to leave him.

Then, in late 1993, Maria Luisa became pregnant. The couple had not planned on a baby, especially during such a difficult time, but Maria Luisa, who was thirty-seven, would probably not get many more chances to have children. They decided to keep the baby, and Song began treating Maria Luisa better. The realization that he would become a father shook him out of his torpor. He started paying attention to the outside world again. He bathed regularly, slept at night, and actually finished books that he started.

Leila was born on August 24, 1994. Song so threw himself into caring for his daughter that Maria Luisa felt that he was pushing her aside. Song did not speak Chinese with his daughter, even though his Italian, while understandable, was not all that fluent. Maria Luisa believed that Song made a conscious decision to stop his father's words from coming out of his mouth. This son of China who pined for his homeland did not want his daughter to be Chinese, just as Song did not want to turn into a man like his father. Song never beat her, rarely disciplined her, and never came home drunk. Maria Luisa once asked Leila if she wanted a brother. "No, I don't need one," she replied. "I have Papa."

Song's interest in life kept expanding. He took part in scholarly meetings. He traveled to Taiwan to observe an election and bear witness to the only sovereign Chinese territory with a significant measure of democracy. He wrote the occasional essay on Tibet; one was published by a scholarly magazine based at Harvard University. Maria Luisa tried at times to talk with Song about the past, but he was uncomfortable dredging up old sins. "Not only is he a man, but he is a Chinese man," Maria Luisa said. "He avoided his own history. Communication was impossible. We just stopped talking about what had happened. I thought that was very Chinese." Still, when Song asked her to marry him, Maria Luisa agreed. If not the ideal choice for herself, it was best for the baby.

Leila's birth, five years after Tiananmen, coincided with a series of disillusioning developments within the protest movement that only further alienated Song from his comrade exiles. The movement splintered into competing factions as participants accused each other of misusing finds, grandstanding, and secretly cooperating with Chinese state security. Wu'er Kaixi, the charming student leader, had become a party animal in New York, then gotten a job pumping gas in San Francisco before ending up as a radio talk-show host in a small town in Taiwan. Chai Ling, the top-ranked woman in the student organization whose tiny frame belied a commanding voice, had junked politics and gone into marketing in the United States.

With no sign of political reform in China, Song, like many other Chinese, revised his view of the Tiananmen demonstrations, now declaring them a tragic mistake. He believed the students' decision to stay in the square following the declaration of martial law set back the pace of reform years, if not decades. Song also held the student leadership responsible, at least in part, for the deaths that occurred that day in June. Blame no longer lay completely with Deng Xiaoping but shortsighted hotheads such as Chai Ling, who, on the eve of the crackdown, told an American interviewer that she hoped for a violent end to the protests.

Becoming a father cooled Song's ardor for radical political change in China, although he remained committed to the ideals of democracy.

Instead of politics, Song now focused on his daughter, his wife, and a passion he had only recently rediscovered: soccer.

Italian soccer is among the world's best and in the 1990s stars such as Roberto Baggio became icons in China. The perennially poor showing of the Chinese soccer team only amplified the popularity of foreign players. While the government had forbidden Chinese from speaking favorably about foreign democracy, it had a harder time preventing them from worshipping foreign sports stars. Chinese fans looked abroad for heroes and found them in the NBA and the Italian and British soccer leagues.

To help satisfy the national hunger for soccer news, Chinese sports magazines and newspapers began searching for Chinese living overseas who could file an occasional dispatch. Competition in the media was intensifying as state subsidies dried up. Words such as *advertising, circulation,* and *content* suddenly meant something.

A soccer buff since his early days at Nanda, Song was pleased when a friend from Nanjing contacted him to see if he would consider covering the Italian league for a small newspaper in Jiangsu. In the beginning, Song's pay could barely cover the cost of sending a fax from Rome. Appropriately, Song looked at the work as a hobby. He wasn't really a sports journalist, he would tell himself, he was a traditional Chinese intellectual. His Chinese characters were beautiful. He was a good writer with a deep knowledge of Chinese history and literature. He was still, formally, a PhD candidate at Nanjing University, and was the recipient of an academic scholarship from the Italian government. But over time his salary at the paper increased, and while he still would never feel comfortable calling himself a sports writer, he was happy to share his newfound salary with his family back home. His first savings went for his parents' first color TV.

Despite his success, Song remained worried that the Ministry of State Security, which kept close tabs on dissidents, would punish his colleagues at the newspaper for employing a member of the "anti-China forces." Song called his editor and stressed that he had political problems. "The ministry knows you are working for us," the editor replied with a laugh. "They said it was okay."

In August 1997, Song received a phone call telling him that his father had stomach cancer. The question was not whether, but when, the cancer would kill him, as it was not diagnosed until its late stages. Song had always been a stranger to his parents. Yet now, in spite of all the beatings his father had inflicted, the old man was calling for his eldest son. Song made plans to return home.

His first step was to write officials at Nanjing University's history department, requesting permission to visit China. As Nanjing University remained Song's work unit, so it was there that Song needed to direct his request. In the letter, he waxed patriotic, invoking the glorious return of the former British colony of Hong Kong, in July 1997, to the embrace of the motherland. Song offered to give up his standing as an Italian political refugee in return for being allowed back home. Within a few weeks, Song received a reply from the embassy in Rome. While he would be allowed to return home on a Chinese travel document, the government would not issue him a passport, nor was there any guarantee that he would be allowed to leave once he got to China. Would he be thrown in jail? Again, no guarantee. As the weeks passed and Song deliberated in Rome, his father's voice over the phone weakened progressively due to pain. His sisters described the old man as so thin that one of them could easily lift him out of bed.

Yang Su, Song's eldest sister and a government official in Yancheng, contacted the local state security bureau to inquire if Song would be arrested if he returned. For months, there was no reply. Song started making plans to send Maria Luisa and their daughter to take his place at his father's bedside. He would discuss these plans repeatedly with his family in Yancheng, figuring that security officials, who were bugging his parents' phone, did not want to internationalize this problem by having an Italian stand in for the family's eldest son. In March 1998, his sister called Song and said the state security officials had assured her that he would not be arrested and would, in fact, be issued a new passport and permitted to return to Italy after seeing his father. Based on nothing but the word of a bureaucrat, Song went to the Chinese embassy in Rome and said he would accept their terms. But there was one more condition. The embassy ordered Song to place an ad renouncing his dissident past in a monthly Chinese-language newspaper published throughout Europe called the *European Chinese Times*. The ad would read as follows: "I vow to reject my political asylum status, formally break my ties with the so-called Chinese democracy movement, and pledge not to partake in any anti-Chinese activities."

Embassy officials demanded to see the ad before they would issue a travel document. Song paid the fifty-thousand lira (twenty-five dollars) to buy space for the ad. Another month passed. The newspaper hit the stands, and he carried it to the embassy. An official handed Song a travel document to return home. Song felt "like a dog crawling on his belly." To commemorate this indignity, he changed his e-mail address to "yesman."

Song arrived in Yancheng in April 1998, nine months after beginning the process to visit his father. By this time, the old man was barely able to speak. Song spent his first day at home sitting by his father's bed. The next day, agents from the Bureau of State Security took Song away. The experience of having his son led away by agents agitated his father, who was now close to death. "Make sure you tell them you love China," his father whispered.

Song's interrogation lasted that whole day and well into the evening. His chief interrogator had traveled two hundred miles from Nanjing just to question Song. She began by asking Song to list all of his anti-China activities; when he forgot a few, she filled in the details. Song was awed by the fact that, though he had played only a bit part in the overseas democracy movement, the agent had amassed a raft of information about his life as a dissident. Brandishing a photo of a closed-door session of Chinese democracy activists that Song had attended in Moscow in 1997, one agent remarked, "It seems you were plumper then."

Song's grilling was designed to ensure that he understood just how powerless he was, like all exiled dissidents. The interrogators also stressed that the only reason Song was allowed to return home was due to China's benevolence. "They wanted me to thank them," Song said. "They wanted me to feel like I owed them a favor."

Song's father remained ignorant of the fact that he had inoperable stomach cancer, kept in the dark by his daughters and wife. For Song, this was even more upsetting than the interrogation. Though he selectively took part in Western society, he nonetheless appreciated that when it came to matters like death, truth was generally better than obfuscation. The experience of his father's terminal illness drove home for Song the broader problem of how Chinese confront reality.

"It was a horrible game," Song later recalled. "You wanted to make him feel better, but you never could because it was like this great big lie. Everyone knew it was cancer, but no one ever talked about it. We Chinese live with contradictions better than people from the West, but sometimes people need to speak the truth."

A week after Song arrived in Yancheng, his father died. The State Security Bureau approached the family with an offer. Even though Song's father had failed to join the party during his lifetime, the bureau was willing to secure him a posthumous entry, affording his mother an extra twelve dollars a month in death benefits. Song turned down the offer.

The funeral was simple: a meal at a big restaurant. As was the custom in urban China, the family had the body cremated. Song hadn't expected his father to die so soon. He had a few days left in Yancheng. He set out to reacquaint himself with his hometown.

Yancheng, like the rest of China, had been significantly transformed by economic development and other changes since Song had left China a decade earlier. He tried to find traces of his family's old home in a dormitory in the grain bureau, but the office had been moved and the dormitory had been torn down. He could not even find the street.

During Song's stay in Yancheng, workers were protesting layoffs and trying to form an independent labor union. He was in a cab one day when demonstrators blocked the road. The authorities would eventually crack down on them, arresting the leader of a group of laborers at a failing silk factory and placing him in Yancheng's No. 4 Psychiatric Hospital. "In 1989, students protested for democracy. By 1998, protests were about pay and conditions for workers," Song observed.

By 1998, most intellectuals had abandoned the idea of trying to mount an organized challenge to the Communist regime. The few who did were rounded up starting in November 1998, when the security apparatus launched another crackdown—this time on the newly formed underground China Democracy Party. Two decades had passed since Song had entered college. The idealism and zeal displayed by his generation and the generation that followed his had faded, replaced by a practical complacency. Among the elite, patriotism was also on the rise, stoked by the party's propaganda machine but also founded on widespread pride in China's remarkable economic transformation.

Most university students and recent graduates were generally happy with the direction in which China was heading. They had benefited greatly with high-paying jobs upon graduation. They could choose where they

1. Zhou Lianchun (Book Idiot Zhou) (*top row, left*) with parents and sister at Shen Kitchen Commune, standing outside the house Zhou built, circa 1976

2. Zhou at his first job after graduating from Nanda, at the Bengbu Tank Institute, fall 1984

3. Zhou along the banks of the Huai River, near Bengbu, 2004

4. Guan Yongxing (Little Guan), in pigtails, with her parents and sisters, at the White Pasture Commune, a few months before the Cultural Revolution began, March 1966

5. Little Guan's surprise birthday party at Nanda, 1979

6. Little Guan with her husband, Ding Bangjun, and their son, Ding Xing, in Hefei, circa 1992

7. *Left to right:* Little Guan's Nanda roommate, Mary Boyd; Xiaodan's mother; Little Guan; Guan Xiaodan, 2004

8. Wu Tianshi, father of Wu Xiaoqing (Old Wu), who was murdered in 1966. Photo circa 1955

9. Old Wu's mother, Li Jingyi, who was murdered with her husband in 1966. Photo circa 1960

10. Old Wu stands in front of the field where his parents were killed, on the campus of Nanjing Normal University, 2004

11. Song Liming (Daybreak Song) (*bottom right*) at a park in Nanjing, with Antonella Ceccagno (*bottom left*), circa 1982

12. *Left to right:* Daybreak Song; Hu Jia, daughter of classmate Hu Youxiang; and Leila, 2004

13. Ye Hao (Big Bluffer Ye) is in the top row, *far left,* 1982

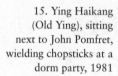

14. Big Bluffer Ye, without a jacket, walks down Hunan Road with Vice Premier Li Lanqing, who is waving his hand, fall 2003

15. Ying Haikang (Old Ying), sitting next to John Pomfret, wielding chopsticks at a dorm party, 1981

16. Old Ying on the hunt for antiques in Southern Anhui Province. The slogan on the wall says "Long Live Marxism Leninism," 2004

17. Xu Ruiqing (Old Xu) is in the top row center with his arm around classmate in black jacket, 1980

18. Old Xu in Changzhou after he was fired from his government job, 2004

19. Du Mengxi (Lucy Du) with her husband, Tom Zhou, and their children, Amy (*left*) and Mary (*right*), in front of their home in Livingston, New Jersey, 2004

20. Pomfret in his dorm room with Bing, who is eating sunflower seeds, and Hu Youxiang, 1982

21. Pomfret, working for the Associated Press, at an open-air press conference held by student leaders Wu'er Kaixi, *right,* and Wang Dan, during the Tiananmen Square demonstrations, 1989

22. Alan Pessin of the Voice of America and Pomfret on June 14, 1989, the day they became the first two foreign correspondents expelled from China following the Tiananmen Square crackdown.

23. Pomfret and Zhang Mei on their trek to the isolated Tibetan village of Yubeng, October 2000

worked, buy their own apartment, take out a car loan, travel overseas. Things Song and my classmates fought for had become commonplace. Discontent was now concentrated among the lower classes—the tens of millions of workers fired from moribund state-owned enterprises and the hundreds of millions of peasants whose meager income was now threatened by onerous taxes and random fees.

The biggest shock for Song was the explosion of prostitution, dance halls, and the easy accessibility of casual sex. Sex was everywhere. Barbershops, fronts for small-time massage parlors, lined Yancheng's grubby streets. Song's richer friends boasted openly of having mistresses—young, pretty women from the countryside—set up in apartments around the city. One man, a real estate developer, bragged of having four.

To ensure that Song would stay under their watchful eyes, state security agents arranged his trip to Nanjing. Song stayed at a guesthouse inside Nanjing University—also booked by state security. Song had returned to Nanjing to wait for his Chinese passport—part of the original verbal deal with the ministry. But months passed and no passport arrived. Leila, who had stayed in Rome with her mother, was missing her dad. Song again broadcast his exasperation across international telephone lines in the hope that state security was bugging his phone.

On June 22, he and Maria Luisa decided in a phone conversation that she would bring Leila to Nanjing. The next day, Nanjing police brought Song's passport over to the guesthouse. Maria Luisa and Leila traveled to Nanjing nonetheless, and accompanied Song to a a dinner hosted by the department chief in the provincial state security bureau, the same woman who had interrogated Song a few months earlier in Yancheng. With an ear-to-ear grin, the security agent presented Leila with an enormous furry stuffed animal, which dwarfed the four-year-old. She fawned on Maria Luisa, praising her Chinese and treating her as if she were a long-lost friend, which made sense in a perverted kind of way as she, no doubt, had perused copies of Maria Luisa's letters to Song, eavesdropped on their phone conversations, and opened a special file on the Italian as well. Song's friendliness toward his case officer perplexed Maria Luisa. Song even volunteered to donate money to a ministry project to help poor villages in the province.

To Maria Luisa, it seemed as if Song was cozying up to his captors.

Despite his beliefs in a freer China, something happened to her husband when he was in the presence of state power. He suddenly craved acceptance more than anything else. For all his attempts to break with his father, Song shared something very fundamental with the old man. He wanted to prove, even to these state security goons, that he—just like his dad—loved China.

25

HOMECOMING

Soon, I, too, would be asked to prove that I loved China. After three years based in Hong Kong, I left the Associated Press at the end of 1992 to join the *Washington Post*. The AP had sent me to cover wars and their aftermaths around the world: Afghanistan, the Gulf War, the Kurdish exodus from northern Iraq, Yugoslavia's civil war. The *Washington Post* wanted someone who knew the ropes to go back to Yugoslavia and chronicle its disintegration. They also asked whether I thought I'd be allowed back to China to work full-time again. Sure, I said confidently, though in reality, I had no idea. By April 1993, I had landed in Sarajevo as a reporter for the *Post*, and would spend the next four years in and around Bosnia. Winters I spent skidding down icy roads in the bureau's partially armored Land Rover; in the summer, when the fighting escalated, I zigzagged the same roads, flinching at the sound of exploding artillery. As the war droned on, I could hear the ennui in my editor's voice on the other end of a satellite phone, while outside my window, the country grew more dangerous. I began to wonder what I was doing with my life.

After Bosnia, it was Zaire in 1997 and the fall of Mobutu. Shortly after that, a job opened up at the *Post*'s bureau in Beijing, and my name was submitted to the Chinese embassy in Washington. "Please try another name," the embassy responded. My crimes during Tiananmen Square had not been forgotten.

It was my good fortune that Katharine Graham was running the company. Mrs. Graham did not take kindly to anyone, much less the Chinese

Communist Party, telling her what to do. She took on my case personally, inviting the Chinese ambassador over for tea to lobby him. To follow up, she asked Henry Kissinger to put in a good word on my behalf with Vice Premier Qian Qichen, China's top diplomat, during one of Kissinger's frequent business trips to Beijing. Meanwhile, in the trenches, I and my reporter-colleagues at the *Post* launched a campaign designed to whittle down Chinese resistance. I met with every Chinese reporter in Washington, figuring at least one of them was connected with the Ministry of State Security, whose agents, I subsequently learned, had been the ones grilling me in Beijing. I brownnosed officials from the embassy, slowly working my way up the diplomatic food chain. I got the feeling that the Chinese embassy was giving me a loyalty test, not unlike the one it gave Daybreak Song. An embassy official requested that I write a letter applying for the position in Beijing. He called it a "self-examination"—an expression snatched directly from the Maoist lexicon of brainwashing and thought control. I wrote my self-examination, saying only that four years in Bosnia had shown me enough chaos for a lifetime—a backhanded way of acknowledging the party's obsession with societal control.

Though I did not know it then, by 1996 the Chinese government had begun to modify the way it handled cases related to the June 4 crackdown. While scores of Chinese remained in jail on charges of participating and organizing marches, low-level participants in the demonstrations who had fled China after June 4 were now being allowed to return home. The government had ceased referring to Tiananmen as "turmoil" and began calling it a "disturbance" and even the more anodyne "incident." Against this backdrop, and with the support of the paper and several officials, the Chinese government relented. On Christmas Eve 1997, I was informed that my visa had been approved. By April 1998, I had moved back to Beijing.

The first thing I did upon my return was to change my Chinese name. Pan Aiwen (Pan Loving Culture) became Pan Wen (Pan Culture). Pan Wen was simpler and less feminine. The Ministry of Foreign Affairs signed off on the name change, although the security services would know who I was.

In the decade that I had been away, foreign influences and investment had reshaped China's landscape, tastes, and culture. In the 1980s, China had hundreds of beverage companies churning out something called *qishui*, a fizzy, sickly sweet soft drink that ranged in color from piss yellow to orange depending on the day. By the mid-1990s, Coca-Cola was the drink of choice, leaving all those lumbering state-owned manufacturers in its wake. Kentucky Fried Chicken had opened its first store in 1987. It would soon have 1,200 branches in China, while McDonald's and Pizza Hut would operate 600 and 150, respectively. When Chinese were asked where they would like to take someone on a date, a majority of university-aged men and women picked a Western fast-food joint.

In 1994, BMW opened its first sales office. Sales of Mercedes-Benzes and other luxury automobiles were skyrocketing as government officials used state money to buy themselves fancier cars. The gap between rich and poor, which had been comparatively narrow during my last stay, had widened with great speed. Bands of beggars plied the streets of major cities, a vivid throwback to prerevolutionary China. There were still waiting lists in the 1990s, but they were for Ferraris, not meat.

Also in 1994, the first of the Western big-box retail stores started business in China, heralding a consumer revolution. The shopping experience marked a huge change for the Chinese, who were accustomed to garrulous shop assistants tossing items at them from behind counters; now, for the first time, Chinese were allowed to inspect the merchandise before buying it, and even return it if they changed their minds.

Language had evolved, too. When I first came to China in the early 1980s, *pusu* (frugal) was a compliment. Now it had become a put-down, implying poverty and stupidity. *Kaifang* no longer meant "open-minded"; it meant "promiscuous." *Xiaojie* no longer meant "Miss." It meant "hooker." Most notably, the all-purpose Communist greeting *tongzhi* (comrade) had all but disappeared from everyday speech, replaced by formal titles like Mister and Doctor—underscoring China's new obsession with class and rank. The only place *Comrade* still flourished was among the Bohemian demimonde in Beijing, Shanghai, and Guangzhou; it was what homosexuals called each other. New words appeared. *Little honey* meant "mistress." *Ku*, an import from Taiwan, meant "cool," and *hei ke* (black guests) meant "hackers." On the streets of Shanghai, people bumping into each other said "Sorry," in English, not *duibuqi*. A popular book posed the question "Are You Middle Class?" employing another new term in a society that just a few years ago had fancied itself classless.

The late 1990s and early years of the twenty-first century were a golden era for foreign reporters. On paper, our restrictions were the same as a decade earlier. Every time we left Beijing on a reporting trip, we were supposed to have the approval of the government. The reality was that China was morphing into a society with voluminous rules and regulations that few bothered to obey or enforce. Foreign correspondents were no exception. I traveled everywhere, and only rarely over the course of six years did I ask for permission from the authorities. Both the Ministry of Foreign Affairs and the Ministry of State Security were aware of my travels, since my stories would appear in the *Washington Post* with datelines from places I had no official permission to visit. But they rarely complained. When they did, their criticism often came with a nod and a wink. Many of the officials admitted to having wearied of enforcing group-think in the Internet age.

My personal relationship with China was very different as well. In the 1980s, China to me was an adventure. By 1989, it had become an obsession. By my third stint living there, after years spent in war zones, I was able to put China's challenges in perspective. My experience in China was no longer caught up in my becoming a man. For better or worse, I already was one.

On February 19, 1997, China's supreme leader, Deng Xiaoping, died at age ninety-two. According to Communist practice, solemn tunes were broadcast on state-run television, on radio, and on the streets. The nightly news extended its broadcast from thirty minutes to three hours to pay tribute to the four-foot-eleven-inch-tall man, known as "the short giant," who had opened China to the outside world. Five days after Deng's death at 10 a.m., the nation paused in silence for three minutes.

Deng's passing was remarkable precisely because it was *not* remarkable. For the first time in Communist China, a leader's death did not trigger an upheaval. Zhou Enlai's death had sparked demonstrations that left hundreds dead; Mao's demise heralded the end of the Cultural Revolution. Hu Yaobang's death led to the Tiananmen Square massacre. But Deng's departure brought no major changes. Unlike Mao's, his body was not mummified and stuck in a grotesque "Mao-soleum" in the middle of Tiananmen Square. Deng was cremated, his ashes scattered, according to his wishes, over China's rivers.

The stability that followed Deng's death owed much to Jiang Zemin, whom Deng had elevated to the party's general secretary following the Tiananmen Square crackdown. For years following his ascension to power, pundits daily predicted Jiang's fall. Publicly, he acted like a Communist Liberace, staging sing-a-longs with foreign leaders and waltzing with their wives. He looked like a stand-in at a wedding when he presided over Hong Kong's return to Chinese rule on July 1, 1997. Deng had done all the heavy lifting with Hong Kong's old colonial masters, the British, but died five months before the handover. But Jiang was no dummy. He excelled as a political infighter. By 1995, he had purged the party and army of all rivals, consolidating control. He kept the party united, thereby avoiding the internal struggles that allowed the 1989 demonstrations to get out of hand. His economic team tamed inflation, and he cultivated China's growing elite.

On July 1, 2001, the eightieth anniversary of the founding of the Communist Party, Jiang announced that the party would accept private businessmen as members. Capitalists in the Communist Party? But Jiang's speech just acknowledged reality. More than 150,000 party members, such as Book Idiot Zhou, already ran businesses, and in the years since the Tiananmen crackdown, the party had abandoned its proletarian roots and catered increasingly to the economic and intellectual upper crust. I only met Jiang once, in March 2001, when my editors came from Washington to interview him. At the end of what was a generally unsurprising interview, Jiang stood up and began what the Chinese like to call in English a "free chat."

"I know some people no longer believe in communism anymore," Jiang declared, "but I still believe." But his was a very different type of communism than that of Mao or even Deng.

Indeed, the Ministry of Foreign Affairs had finally discovered spin and understood that influential newspapers like the *Washington Post* could be used to communicate China's point of view to the United States more efficiently than its own staid state-run press. As the *Post*'s bureau chief, I was granted background briefings and interviews with Chinese officials who for years had hidden themselves behind a veil of unreturned phone calls. Still, I was vigilant about protecting sources. The memory of Liu Gang, my jailed composer friend, weighed heavily. This may have been a different kind of communism, but it was communism nonetheless.

In the years since the Tiananmen crackdown, the party had worked relentlessly to airbrush the killings from living memory. At the yearly press conference with China's premier, a Western reporter would invariably raise a question about Tiananmen. The premier would obfuscate, and the issue would be forgotten for another year. Work teams had long ago repaved Chang'an Boulevard and Tiananmen Square, erasing tank treads and plastering over bullet holes. Earlier traces of the Democracy Wall, the 1979 precursor to the Tiananmen student movement, had also been removed. A Starbucks and a shopping mall hawking Ray-Ban sunglasses and Victoria's Secret knock-offs sat in the place where Wei Jingsheng hung his posters calling for democracy and human rights.

Still, signs of China's troubled past surfaced in the strangest of places. One of the few undeveloped plots of land near the city's center had been a small wooded area owned by the Forestry Department; a businessman had turned it into a drive-in theater, the "Happy Auto Movie Palace"—a taste of Americana in Beijing, except that here cars were provided for those who did not drive. When I visited the drive-in one summer afternoon, the owner pointed to the concrete slabs beneath our feet. If you looked closely, you could see tank treads. He had bought the unwanted pieces of Tiananmen Square from a corrupt army captain to pave his theater. "How bizarre," I remarked.

"Not really," he replied. "It was a good deal."

26

THE ADMAN

Xu Ruiqing, the party's spook in my dorm room, had dozed along in the snooziest corner of the Communist Party for years. Since graduating from Nanda in 1982, Old Xu had labored in the Communist Party History Office in Changzhou, his hometown sixty miles east of Nanjing, pushing pencils and writing essays that no one read. But as China softened its austere Maoist line in the years after the Tiananmen Square crackdown, Old Xu woke up and seized on the chance to get rich.

It was 1992, and the Chinese New Year Spring Festival was nigh. Old Xu had been promoted to the head of the office—a promotion he had been awaiting for years. He wanted to celebrate. For two years following the crackdown, Chinese officials had been instructed to keep the Chinese New Year Spring Festival celebrations to a minimum. But in the run-up to the 1992 holiday, no such instructions came.

Old Xu threw a party for his office staff at Changzhou's one disco, which had only recently reopened. Several aging Communists had opposed the celebration, but Old Xu pushed ahead, ordering Christmas tinsel and party hats. The bash would prove an enormous success. Everyone spent the night crooning old revolutionary songs and Canto-pop hits from Hong Kong. Old Xu was particularly pleased that even the aging officials showed up and danced, albeit bearlike, under a rotating disco ball.

Old Xu could breathe again, and so could Changzhou. The 3.5 million people of the city were furiously pursuing some plan or other to get rich.

Changzhou had been designated a center for what were called "township-village enterprises," a huge engine of growth in the early 1990s. Under this new policy, villages and townships would establish businesses, primarily in manufacturing, that appeared on paper to be state owned. In reality, they belonged to families or entrepreneurs who, to protect themselves against Communist ideologues in faraway Beijing, camouflaged their holdings as state-run concerns. The Chinese called them "red hat" companies. The hat might have been Communist red, but the body beneath was cold hard capitalist.

Traditionally humdrum places, Party History offices were a central cog in the vast propaganda apparatus, responsible for perpetuating Communist Party mythology. Bureaucrats spent their days airbrushing disgraced ex-leaders from municipal group photographs and censoring articles about China's recent history.

But with all the excitement erupting outside his window, Old Xu couldn't help but get swept up in the money-making fervor reaching ever deeper into Chinese society. Even during our university days, Old Xu was a bit of a con artist, hitting me up with requests to change money and buy him sugar and cigarettes at the Friendship Store. Now that Old Xu was the office boss, he decided to make a change: the somnolent party History Office of Changzhou became the Good Times Advertisement Agency. Old Xu named himself chief executive officer.

Old Xu's bold move was being repeated all over China as government bureaucrats transformed the agencies they managed—health centers, hospitals, schools, police departments, military installations—into for-profit ventures. The party backed these quasi-private businesses because as government subsidies dried up, revenue had to be generated somehow. "I ran the office according to the spirit of the central government," Old Xu said later. "I reformed it."

Good Times created ads for dozens of Changzhou's little firms, placing them on billboards and in magazines and newspapers. Revenues poured into the listless government office. Old Xu purchased two Volkswagen Santana sedans for the office and took his staff on junkets to Buddhist temples and sacred mountains. He installed air conditioners and bought himself a high-class swivel office chair and a vast desk. At forty-three, Old Xu had become the boss of a mini-empire. Among the delights of his new-found success was an affair with his thirty-five-year-old accountant.

In 1995, its third year of business, Good Times Ad Agency made $250,000 in profit. But who was to decide where the money went: the government, since it technically owned the agency, or Old Xu? Old Xu chose himself. He increased the wages and perks of his staff, providing them with a free lunch. He began distributing the agency's money to relatives and friends; he gave his sister funds to renovate her apartment in Nanjing; he paid for his daughter's education and bought a new apartment for himself and his wife. He also started a small magazine, giving the printing contract to a buddy for a 10 percent kickback.

Old Xu's efforts to work the system bred jealousy. As a Spring Festival gift in 1998, Old Xu's second-in-command gave him the finest set of clothes Old Xu had ever seen, an Armani suit. In government offices all over China, subordinates were expected to ply their superiors with gifts and money. In fact, promotions were generally secured by bribing the boss. But the suit was too ostentatious; Old Xu sensed he was being led into a trap and handed back the present. "I am not going to accept that," he said. The man was stunned.

"Please, Director Xu," he said. "I know how much you like good clothes."

Old Xu took the box and dropped it onto the floor. "I am not going to accept this!" he yelled.

Old Xu's number two gathered up the clothes and stomped off. Later that week, he wrote a report to party authorities. At the end of the Spring Festival holidays, a team from the party's Discipline Inspection Committee—the anticorruption squad—arrived at the office. Old Xu invited them in. "Actually, we'd like to invite you outside," the lead investigator said.

The men took Old Xu to a safe house run by the party, where he was forbidden to call his wife or his daughter. He was held there for three days and nights as four teams of men interrogated him. He was given no food, only water, and was forbidden to sleep. Old Xu was placed under *shuang gui*, a form of detention used by the party to investigate corruption among its ranks. He had no right to get a lawyer; in fact, he had no rights at all. Throughout his ordeal, the men told Old Xu that he had done nothing wrong. All he had to do was to admit to a little malfeasance—renovating his sister's apartment, pocketing twenty-thousand dollars for himself, taking kickbacks from his printer—and everything would be fine.

"Your problem is tiny," one interrogator assured him. Indeed, compared to some of the corruption cases erupting around the country, it was. One smuggling case in Xiamen, along the coast in southern China, netted dirty government officials and their business partners billions of dollars. In Old Xu's province of Jiangsu alone, investigators were seeking sixty officials—four of them from Changzhou—who had fled abroad, mostly to the United States, after bilking various state-run businesses out of $40 million.

"I was under a lot of pressure," Old Xu complained to me, "so I admitted to a little because I wanted the pressure to end. Who would have guessed what happened next?"

At forty-nine, just a few years from retirement, Old Xu was forced to resign his government post and given a reduced pension. A government prosecutor wanted to throw Old Xu in jail, but the party secretary of Changzhou quashed the case; he did not want his own term marred by the indictment of one of his department chiefs. As for Old Xu's deputy, he did not end up as the Good Times boss. Old Xu was able to pull strings to ensure that the man was reassigned elsewhere, to the Handicapped Association—a dead-end post.

I traveled to Changzhou to see Old Xu in the spring of 2004. He met me at the bus station. Though I had not seen him since 1982, I recognized him immediately. He had shed his Mao jacket for a plaid sports coat and a black-and-white checked tie, and was driving a blue VW Jetta that his new boss, a private businessman, had given him. He looked well, and, when his lizardly lips broke into a sensuous smile, I felt like we were suddenly back in our musty dorm room. Old Xu was still a hapless operator, but his desire to survive, to bend his personality around the permutations of the Communist Party's edicts, struck me as both pathetic and endearing.

We swung by his old house for a look. Migrants from the countryside inhabited it. Old Xu had a new apartment across the street—in a gated development of new buildings and townhouses with a manicured lawn and Muzak piped into the elevators. After a quick tour through the compound, we headed into town. Old Xu had found a new job working for a fellow villager named Boss Liu, who wanted to take us to dinner.

I asked Old Xu about his corruption case; it had become a hot topic on the classmate grapevine. "How many years did I work without pay?

On Sundays! Weekends!" Old Xu screeched as he veered down the street in his Jetta, driving perilously like Mr. Magoo. "My father died, and I passed the time working on ads as I kept vigil by his body. This was really unfair!"

We ate in an old section of Changzhou. In the early 1990s, the city had demolished a neighborhood of Qing Dynasty houses to make way for gimcrack office buildings. By the end of the decade, realizing their mistake, city leaders tore down the buildings and replaced them with reproductions of the ancient houses that had been demolished. Simulated bricks were etched into plasterboard walls. Wooden beams were painted on plywood ceilings.

Boss Liu was big for a Chinese. On his right wrist, he wore a huge Rolex. ("It's real!" he yelled when he caught me ogling it.) On his left dangled Buddhist prayer beads. Liu was one of the so-called red hat capitalists who had managed a township enterprise and then came out of the closet as the real owner in 2000 when party policy caught up with economic reality. The business manufactured railroad equipment and had sales of $1.25 million a year. His son was studying in Germany and had plans to go to business school in the United States. "Not bad for an uneducated farmer," Boss Liu brayed from across the table, stretching out his glass of grain alcohol for a toast.

Like many successful entrepreneurs, Liu had had a checkered past.

"With me it began even before I had pubic hair," he said as we clinked glasses again. In 1967, when he was eleven, Liu was accused of being a counterrevolutionary; his alleged offense was scrawling "Down with Chairman Mao" on a wall. Liu had merely reported seeing the grafitti—he had not drawn it—but the Revolutionary Committee accused him anyway. He was beaten until he confessed, jailed for six months, and, subjected to weekly public-humiliation sessions, during which he was forced to wear a placard around his neck that read "Counterrevolutionary."

Old Xu was living in the same village and was seventeen at that time. Their families were close, and Old Xu treated Liu like a younger brother. A few years after Liu was released from jail, Old Xu used his family's connections to get Liu an appointment as a leader of one of the commune's production teams. Liu learned some management skills and later attended a polytechnic institute run by the Ministry of Railroads, where he was assigned a job as a worker in a railroad parts factory.

In 1988, Liu went into business for himself, first trying to grow mushrooms in the basement of his apartment building, a popular business venture among first-time entrepreneurs. That failed. He then borrowed four hundred dollars, rented a workshop, and began producing spare parts for the railroad. His first deal, in which he leveraged the difference between the low state price and the high market price, garnered him a profit of $1,250. He delivered his first products on a bike, graduated to a gigantic tricycle with a flatbed, then to a truck.

Liu was not satisfied with his success. First among his complaints was that he was tired of bribing people all the time. To sell to the Ministry of Railroads in Beijing, he made several trips a year to the capital to pay off the ministry's purchasing agents. "China's economy is an economy based on connections," he said. "It's not what you make; it's who you know. I have to make payoffs to do any business.

"I feel that I am a distorted man. I have a twisted personality. The system has twisted me."

When Liu learned that Old Xu had been caught up in a corruption probe and forced to retire, he contacted his old friend and returned the favor of years ago. Liu appointed Old Xu the director of his company's front office. Old Xu became Liu's local bagman. He did deals for Liu with the local taxman, the local environmental protection people, the land bureau—all the offices that hand out administrative approvals necessary to do business. As for the corruption charge that led to his dismissal from his government job, Old Xu felt no remorse. He was just angry about getting caught.

"There is a cost of doing business and a cost for getting things done in China," Old Xu told me, cracking a mischievous grin. It was the same grin that used to crinkle his face twenty years earlier when he would ask me to head down to the Friendship Store to buy him a bike. "China's market economy has Chinese characteristics. I am a purveyor of lubricants for China's economy. I help keep it oiled and running smooth."

27

THE CHINA PRICE

By the early 1990s, China's urine-extraction business had become completely private, mirroring a similar shift in other sectors of China's economy. As the state stopped blocking private enterprise, more and more businessmen were seeking a piece of the action—any action—that could make them a *yuan*. Book Idiot Zhou suddenly faced new competition for access to municipal urine supplies.

His luck in Beijing continued to be lousy. The vats at the processing plant routinely overflowed and flooded nearby houses in a tide of stale urine. One time in the summer, the stench was so bad it forced farmers to flee their homes, and Zhou had to spend hours mopping the effluent off their dirt floors. Meanwhile, competitors elbowed into his territory, hiring gangs of toughs to beat up his drivers and steal his vats. This was hardly the sort of life he envisioned as the university-educated boss of a private company.

Zhou's business, like Boss Liu's bribery-riddled railroad operation, was a window on Chinese culture and its booming no-holds-barred economy. The more Zhou looked through it, the more distraught he became. Taiwanese and Japanese investors had been involved in the urine-extraction business in its early days. They'd since bailed out because of the escalating corruption and violence.

Unbridled competition brought a crash in the price of enzymes. This was similar to what was happening in other businesses across China. Across the oceans, Americans and others worried about the rise of China, the unstoppable economic juggernaut, with its "China price" of ever-lower costs and constantly increasing production. But at home, Zhou and thousands of other businessmen watched their margins all but disappear as they continued to brawl—often literally—to win a slice of the market-place. The "China price" was hurting Chinese, too.

After his semester-long study break at Beijing University in 1992, Zhou continued running the Beijing operation while commuting from Bengbu, where he also had a factory. During the Spring Festival holidays in 1995, Zhou lugged about a hundred pounds of enzymes from Bengbu to a phar-maceutical plant in Guangzhou. Zhou handed the product to his buyer and waited at a shabby inn to collect his money. The next day the factory manager asked Zhou to come over.

"Look at it," he said to Zhou, opening the box containing the urine enzymes. "It's red. It's useless." The manager asked Zhou if his workers in Bengbu were using new equipment. No, he replied, they used the same stainless steel vats and plastic tubing as before. "Well, whatever is going on, this is not the right stuff," the manager said. "It's tainted." Zhou brought a sample back to a Nanda chemical lab for testing. A chemical analysis revealed the product was laced with heavy metals. How had they gotten into the urine of the good people of Bengbu?

Bengbu is a grubby industrial center that spans the Huai River, China's third longest—and most polluted—waterway that flows for more than six hundred miles through five provinces. During the 1990s, as local gov-ernments encouraged village and township enterprises, the towns that lined the Huai were transformed from dozy farming hamlets to swarming industrial centers. Paper mills, cement plants, and chemical complexes sprang up like weeds.

With manufacturing came pollution. Nothing unusual about that; China was suffering from serious environmental degradation. Nation-wide, 190 million people were drinking water that was so contaminated it made them sick. Even by those standards, the condition of the Huai River was atrocious. Pollutants expelled into the river from various factories bonded into enormous bargelike collections of scum that putrified the river. At times the brown lather—a noxious mix of trash, effluent, and untreated waste—stretched more than sixty miles and stood six feet high in places. Local residents wore masks and wet towels across their faces to keep from retching. Drinking water had so damaged the health of those who lived along the river that the People's Liberation Army stopped conscripting Bengbu residents because they were unfit for service.

In 1996, Bengbu's primitive water treatment system collapsed. For weeks, the water flowed black and malodorous from the taps of the five hundred thousand people who lived there. Choosing not to inform the population of the potential health risks, the government banned state-run newspapers from publishing information about the harmful contaminants. But the city's urine didn't lie.

As word about the water coursed through China's efficient rumor mill, black marketeers descended on Bengbu and made a quick killing selling bottled water. A team of officials dispatched from Beijing vowed to clean up the river within four years. On January 1, 1997, government workers shut down hundreds of paper mills, chemical and cement plants in a textbook Communist-style command-and-control operation. Within two years, however, 40 percent of the plants had reopened. By 2004, when I traveled the river with Zhou, all the firms were back in operation, without pollution controls. Because of an electricity shortage, local governments had shut down smokestack scrubbers and waste-water treatment facilities. That July, another sixty-mile carpet of sludge swept down the river, killing millions of fish and devastating wildlife. To protect his business, Zhou installed special filters at the Bengbu plant to cleanse the locals' urine before processing.

In 1998, Zhou had to give up the Beijing factory. The man who had signed the lease with him, the party secretary, had lost his job because he and his wife had violated the one-child policy. The new secretary wanted Zhou to give him an additional kickback in exchange for allowing Zhou to keep the factory. When Zhou refused, his electricity and water were cut off and the party secretary tore up his lease. The official gave Zhou ten days to pack up or, he warned, local toughs would roust him out. Zhou swallowed a loss of one thousand dollars, and left the capital for good.

Zhou's next move was to spread his operation to Hunan, Shandong, and Hebei provinces. As business expanded, competitors continued to fight him, using the same combination of strong-arm tactics, guile, and bribery.

The chief of the sanitation department in one town in Anhui Province had been in Zhou's pocket for years, until a competitor came in to offer him a fatter payoff. Zhou won the bidding war when he promised the official an extra $1,500 a year for exclusive access to the town's urine supply. In Bengbu, the party secretary and his second-in-command exorted twenty-five thousand dollars from Zhou's firm as part of their citywide campaign to extract cash handouts from private firms. Instead of being denigrated by the party as "capitalist exploiters," private industry was now a bottomless ATM for the party machine.

One autumn, I went to Bengbu to visit Zhou, and had a boisterous dinner with him and his associates, including his partner, Sheng Hongyuan. (We drank only bottled water.) The Moon Festival, which celebrates the fall harvest, was upon us, but Sheng, who had just come from the office, was not in a festive mood. That afternoon, several government officials had arrived, demanding a payoff to ring in the holiday. They commanded Sheng to open a safe. It contained the equivalent of eight hundred dollars. "I'll take it all," said the top official in the group, extending his hand. Sheng tossed him the cash.

I first thought Sheng—a garrulous little man with a crooked grin, who wore threadbare clothes and holey shoes—was one of Zhou's laborers and not his partner. "Ha, I fooled you, too," he said, laughing. "I wear lousy clothes on purpose. If not, they'd steal even more." Sheng parks his car inside the gates of the institute where Zhou teaches. If party officials knew he had enough money to afford one, the extortion would only intensify. But for all their complaints about corruption, Zhou and Sheng were getting a good deal. They had dodged taxes, disobeyed local pollution regulations, and offered skimpy benefits to their workers. I asked Zhou if he would be willing to pay taxes in exchange for an end to the shakedowns. "No," he replied, after a pause. "If we had to pay taxes, we'd have to give the government much more."

After 1998, Zhou's financial outlook brightened. His firm was producing about two hundred pounds a month of raw material. While foreign demand for drugs composed of enzymes extracted from urine remained stable, in China the demand for the heart medicine was skyrocketing. The Chinese diet had become much richer in fatty foods (another consequence of increased prosperity), so heart disease had replaced cancer as the leading cause of death. On the downside, the introduction of indoor plumbing meant that fewer people were using public toilets, reducing the amount of raw material. In the 1980s and into the 1990s, the residents of Bengbu used to reliably deposit twenty-two tons of urine a day in public toilets. By 2004, the flow had dropped by half and continued to fall.

Still, Zhou had learned how to profit in the hurly-burly of China's capitalist system. He knew when to strike fast, as when a competitor was moving in on his turf and Zhou had to drive all night to deliver an extra payoff for the local district chief. He also knew when to bide his time.

In 2003, a business partner who had owed Zhou sixty thousand dollars for eight years paid him half of the debt. Zhou bought a new white Volkswagen Bora for twenty-seven thousand dollars. That same year he also purchased a sprawling, eighteen-hundred-square-foot apartment in Nanjing, directly opposite Nanda's northern gate. The apartment had belonged to a senior government official who had been convicted of corruption—extorting money from a teapot manufacturer—and sentenced to ten years in jail.

Zhou bought the apartment at auction for $110,000 in cash (mortgages were only available for newly constructed apartments) as a gift for the woman he wanted to marry. Zhou's previous affair had ended several years earlier because he could not come up with the money the woman sought to get out of her marriage. His girlfriend, Beibei, a former student of his at the Anhui Institute of Finance and Trade, agreed to marry him after Zhou showed her the place.

In the mid-1990s, while he was still married to his first wife, Zhou had noticed Beibei in one of the classes he taught at the Anhui institute. He found her pale complexion and bright eyes alluring. He encouraged her to come visit him during office hours and gave her books to read outside of class. He was twenty-two years older than she was. She used to say she looked more like his daughter than his girlfriend. But no one seemed to blink at such age gaps. Many women, seeking financial security and pining for fatherly love in a society with broken-down families, sought out older men. Relationships between students and professors, secretaries and CEOs were increasingly common. Huge swaths of real estate in southern cities had been transformed into "second wives' villages," inhabited by the mistresses of wealthy businessmen and corrupt officials. But Beibei didn't want to become anyone's mistress.

Zhou and Beibei began dating when she was a junior. Five years later, in 2003, the pair married, despite opposition from her family. At their wedding, she was twenty-eight and he was fifty. Soon after the wedding, she fulfilled her dream of visiting an orthodontist and getting braces.

Zhou loved the idea of himself, a child of China's dirt-poor countryside, sleeping in a king-sized bed once frequented by a corrupt party boss. He also liked the fact that the official had decorated the place in the favored style of China's nouveau riche: overstuffed leather couches puffy as the Pillsbury Doughboy, still wrapped in cellophane, chandeliers cut from ornate multicolored plastic.

Visiting Zhou one day, I was ushered into the guest bathroom where, with a flourish, he pointed to a shower that would have easily slept four and the toilet. I had always heard that Chinese officials favored ornate bathrooms, and this one did not disappoint. The official had installed a Toto Washlet, a Japanese toilet that advertises itself as "paperless." On the side of the bowl there was a panel with a multiplicity of knobs and buttons, similar to a TV remote. I began fiddling with the controls. A blast of chilly water shot up from the bowl, followed by a warm gust like that from a restroom hand dryer. Zhou said that he had to work the toilet by trial and error since the dials were all in English.

Zhou divided his time between Nanjing and his job teaching Marxism at the Anhui Institute of Finance and Trade, but he was growing weary of his old life and increasingly unwilling to toe the party's ideological line. Each year a handful of students, usually those applying for party membership, would express doubts about Zhou's loyalty to the party and to China. What was happening in Zhou's classroom was also happening across the country; students had begun to turn politically conservative. While their views on social issues were becoming more liberal, including their acceptance of premarital sex and even homosexuality, they were embracing a knee-jerk nationalism that made them even more sympathetic to the party line.

In 2002, the party secretary at the institute received a report from one of Zhou's students. Eight pages in all, it detailed Zhou's "crimes against the party" and included a systematic criticism of his instruction, describing Zhou as "antiparty" and "anti-Mao." The report went so far as to list the percentage of time Zhou devoted to criticizing the party (85 percent), praising the party (10 percent) and remaining neutral (5 percent). The student paid particular attention to one class Zhou held after U.S. cruise missiles in the spring of 1999 destroyed China's embassy in Yugoslavia, killing three people. The American attack was a godsend to the Chinese government, occurring right before the tenth anniversary of the Tiananmen Square massacre. Hundreds of thousands of Chinese students were allowed to demonsrate across the country, this time shouting "Down with American imperialism," not "Down with the Communist Party." In Beijing, students pelted the U.S. embassy with rocks and paint. In Chengdu, they set the U.S. consulate on fire. In his lecture, Zhou scoffed at the students' indignation. "Your anger is not sincere," he said, "because I know that all of you would trade it in a second for a visa to the USA."

The party secretary summoned Zhou to his office. The school's three other deputy party secretaries were there as well. Zhou was handed the document, which they had transcribed to protect the identity of the snitch.

"What's going on here?" the party secretary asked. "You are teaching Marxism and Maoist thought. This class is essential to the education of our graduates. If they do not have a correct understanding of Marxism and Maoist thought, they cannot be good citizens of the People's Republic of China." The secretary sat back in his chair, waiting for Zhou to say something. Zhou was speechless. "Will you change the way you teach?" the secretary asked. "Either you change the nature of your instruction or you will stop teaching Mao."

Zhou told the party secretary that he did not think that he was particularly antiparty or anti-Mao. The party secretary remained unconvinced. He informed Zhou that he was being switched from teaching Maoist thought to business administration. Zhou left the meeting shaking his head. Once they get into college, he would explain to me, students do not study hard, and cheat and plagiarize regularly. Yet, here was a student who had painstakingly written an eight-page critique of Zhou's teaching methods.

"I have thought a lot about why he might have done this," Zhou said. "Maybe he really thought I was anti-Mao. But I think the real reason is that he wanted to show he'd be a good party member. I think these kids have even fewer principles than even we did."

28

SPIRITUAL CIVILIZATION

On May 31, 1997, government officials gathered on Nanjing's redeveloped Hunan Road to celebrate Big Bluffer Ye's crowning bureaucratic achievement, designating the street one of China's 102 "national demonstration places"—a model for other municipalities nationwide. Just as Ye prepared to cut the ceremonial ribbon in front of municipal luminaries, a hunk of wet laundry fell from an apartment building at the entrance to Hunan Road, landing with a wet plop near the stage.

Livid, Ye vowed silently to get even with the residents upstairs. It was time to bring his modernizing influence not just to the stores on Hunan Road but to the apartments above them. Ye did not like the balconies, where residents, like those in buildings all over China, dangled their dripping laundry from long bamboo poles. Ye thought it looked Third World, and he wanted Hunan Road to be First World. He launched a campaign to force all residents of the 345 apartments on the road to enclose their balconies. The residents would have been happy to do so, since following Ye's order essentially meant adding another, albeit cramped, room to their units, but few had enough money to carry out that kind of renovation. Ye ordered his minions to subsidize the project, but not before ensuring that the contracts went to a construction company owned by a former colleague in the Drum Tower District.

Over the next few years, Ye battled against bicycles, banning from Hunan Road what was still the fastest, cheapest way for people to get around. He forced shopkeepers to dismantle the corrugated "ghetto gates" they used for security because he thought they didn't look modern; when merchants balked, he had police raid the stores on trumped-up charges of selling pirated software. Finally, he demolished a popular flea market and a textile factory, which he replaced with a ritzy restaurant.

Ye was promoted to chief of the Drum Tower government in 1998, and two years later he became the party secretary, making him the most powerful man in the district. With Ye's heightened status came highfalutin hobbies. While Big Bluffer still enjoyed playing gin rummy, he also excelled in tennis and horseback riding. "I like controlling big beasts," he said. A real estate developer had bought him a Mongolian pony which he boarded at an equestrian club on the outskirts of Nanjing.

Ye and I were eating dinner in another expensive restaurant. It had been turned over to a friend to manage, but Ye remained involved in its operation. He boasted that he had actually designed the whole place. "You see that?" he said, pointing up to a sky-blue ceiling with airbrushed clouds and a garish chandelier in the private room where we were eating. "I did that. Just think, this used to be a workshop in a textile mill." Ye had even given the restaurant its name in English: the Lion King Dainty Community. I told him it didn't make much sense. "It doesn't matter." Ye laughed. "Diners see English and think it's high class."

Yet for all Ye's efforts to blot out reality, Hunan Road was still a part of China. As the crowds on Hunan Road grew, so did the number of beggars. Ye declared war on them, too. Some were beaten; others were kidnapped by police agencies and put to work—for no pay—in factories run by the local bureau of public security, a practice that would only be outlawed in 2003 after police detained a college graduate because he forgot to carry his identity card, and slapped him in a work camp where he was beaten to death by the staff. "People come up to me and say this road is like heaven. 'No beggars and no itinerants,'" Big Bluffer Ye boasted with a big grin.

Within the space of two decades, China had changed from perhaps the most egalitarian society in the world, where a billion people were mired together in poverty, to one of the least. China's wealth gap in the late 1990s and early 2000s was greater than that of the United States. Gated communities boasted million-dollar mansions, golf courses, and Olympic-sized swimming pools, while the groundskeepers and maids servicing them made less than three dollars a day. Brigades of beggars, controlled by characters straight out of *The Three-Penny Opera,* ran entire sections of certain cities, staking out lucrative corners and paying the police and other security services to look the other way while they begged.

Ye continued to raise money for Hunan Road, strong-arming state banks to invest in his redevelopment plans. State-mandated lending is a secret of China's economic growth. The country's state-owned banks take depositors' savings and loan them out not to credit-worthy borrowers but to well-connected ones. Ye's position as a top official of the Drum Tower District allowed him to order, not request, banks to earmark millions of dollars to redevelop the road. First he had to widen the street. Then he built the pyramid of light. Then he knocked it down. Then he installed a twenty-four-hour electronic surveillance network. Then he outlawed all wheeled traffic and turned Hunan Road into a pedestrian walkway.

As the rich in Nanjing got richer, the number of automobiles rose sharply. In 1993, there were 65,027 privately owned vehicles in the city; a decade later, the number had tripled. Parking was scarce, especially around Hunan Road. Ye again forced banks and businessmen to invest, this time in a parking structure. Of all his schemes, Ye was most pleased about masterminding this one. The inspiration came to him during a trip to Venice, Italy, a city that is, as he put it, "one big pedestrian walkway." Ye had asked about the parking-garage business there. "I discovered the Mafia ran it, so I figured it must be good business," Ye said, cracking a self-satisfied smile.

Hunan Road brought in significant money for the local Drum Tower District government. In 2001, it generated $48 million in tax and fee revenues; in 2003, that sum jumped to $82 million, one third of the district's revenues and more than the total revenue of some of Nanjing's poorer districts. An average of one hundred thousand people walked down Hunan Road a day. Rents kept moving up, hitting two hundred dollars a square foot in 2004.

That year, Ye had another dose of inspiration. After spending a summer at the Wharton School of Business at the University of Pennsylvania, he, like most Chinese officials visiting the United States, made a pilgrimage to Las Vegas. The neon cacophony of the Vegas Strip "deeply impressed me," he enthused. "It was a revelation."

Ye decided that Nanjing needed its very own neon strip. He designed a one-hundred-yard-long arcade of multicolored lights along Hunan Road, which he named the "Light Art Tunnel." Unfortunately, he could only wheedle funding for fifty yards of lights, so Ye modified his design. Alongside Light Art Tunnel now stood a three-story-tall, red-eyed neon dragon that belched steam.

"When I take my future grandson on a walk on Hunan Road, I will say to him, 'See, I created this.' I saw Hunan Road more than I saw my own son. I did all the changes here," Ye bragged.

Ye framed his discussion of Hunan Road not just in terms of increased tax revenues but also in terms of culture. "What we've done with this street is to bring to life the concept of spiritual civilization," he said, while daintily placing a glistening chunk of abalone onto my plate. He sat back, then bent forward and took a giant slurp of his shark's fin soup, leaving me to ponder his words.

The party had been talking about "spiritual civilization" for years, yet I never really understood what it meant. At first, I thought it was an attempt to fill China's spiritual vacuum with some type of secular belief system. Now it hit me. What could fill China's spiritual void? Shopping. And indeed the way Ye had constructed it, Hunan Road, with its memorial arch and electric gas-spouting dragon, was a temple. Not to Marx. Not to Buddha. But to money.

Ye's dominance of Hunan Road—from the design of its restaurants, to its lights, security gates, and inventory—was a model for how the Communist Party wanted to run China: a father-knows-best paternalism layered over a partnership with the private sector. Ye had no interest in democracy. Democracy, he declared, breeds chaos and inefficiency. He subscribed, despite its anti-Marxist slant, to the Great Man theory of history. Great men fashioned modern nations out of nothing. Great men made Hunan Roads. And why did they make Hunan Roads? So people could shop.

The economy of Hunan Road, like that of the district and country, had turned private over the years Ye was in power. By 2004, 84 percent of the Drum Tower District's economy was no longer owned by the state. But it was a private economy different from others around the world. There was no invisible hand here. The imprint of Ye's dainty little paws was all over the road—ordering bank loans, randomly confiscating goods, dictating sales policies, designing restaurants, and picking winners. I asked Ye if he subscribed to the widespread belief in the West that economic development, and with it privatization of the economy, would lead to political liberalization and the end of the one-party state. "Ha!" he scoffed. "So far, it's only made us stronger."

Like many party and government officials, Ye, too, had to keep up the appearance of continually improving himself, one area of life in which a smattering of Confucian tradition remained, if only on the surface. He spent 2003 at the Central Party School in Beijing—a mecca for officials awaiting promotion. The next year, he was awarded a doctorate in political science from Nanda. In the middle of our first dinner at the swank restaurant atop Hunan Road, Ye boasted about his doctoral thesis. "I think I have made a breakthrough in the world's understanding of Western political thought," he said. "My thesis is deeply profound. I think it should be translated."

I dug up Ye's thesis and several other articles by him. The dissertation focused on how Western societies managed to check the authority of their leaders, something he praised. Another essay, which he wrote for a party journal, called for limits on the power of party secretaries. "Absolute power corrupts absolutely," Ye opined, not bothering to cite Lord Acton, the author of the quote. An image floated through my mind of Big Bluffer Ye playing Chinese gin rummy one winter evening in 1981 in our dorm room. He had won a huge hand and was guffawing at his friends: "You're so easy to cheat. You're such suckers." Ye Hao was, indeed, a Big Bluffer, I thought.

After we finished our meal, Ye and I walked with a police escort toward his three-story smoking dragon at the end of Hunan Road. Along the way, we passed thirty-eight restaurants—Thai, Indian, Korean, and Japanese—plus a karaoke bar and a massage parlor called the Big Rub Gate. We paused beneath the memorial arch, thirty feet high with a menagerie of gremlins and lions carved into its cement columns.

Crowds of people were out in the late-summer air—teenagers, families with their single children, businessmen staggering out from boozy dinners. Before us was Ye's Light Art Tunnel and above it the dragon, spouting steam and emitting an electronic roar. Ye had switched everything on just for me. The lights had been dark all summer because of electricity shortages in the province, another sign that China's economic juggernaut was straining its outdated infrastructure.

"People said this is all too foreign," Ye said, pointing at the Light Art Tunnel twinkling behind the puffing dragon. "We have McDonald's over there, so how can we have a memorial arch? We have Kentucky Fried Chicken over here, so how can we have a Chinese dragon? They said this street is like Europe and we're in China. They said it's like the USA but we're in China. But I say China can be all this and more."

Ye looked up at the dragon and sighed.

"You know, I wanted him to breathe fire, but he only blows smoke."

29

GODS AND ANIMALS

I found myself blowing my share of smoke as well.

By the late 1990s, the government had stopped caring about foreigners' relationships with most Chinese. I began to actively date Chinese women. I made friends with women via the Internet, in airplanes, and the lobbies of office buildings. While I never was particularly good at pick-up lines in English, speaking Chinese freed me from my concerns with sounding utterly ridiculous. I was bolder in Chinese.

It used to be that the main motivation for women to spend time with foreign men was either a ticket out of China or money. Now the rules had changed. In Beijing and Shanghai, it had become trendy to have a *laowai*, a "venerable outsider," as a boyfriend. Casual sex became the norm for single foreign men in China's big cities. For a man who had been living in dangerous places for the past eight years, this new China was a welcome change. The courtships were swift, very swift, and expectations were minimal. Gone were the days of Daybreak Song's slow-boil courtship. Westerners idealized China as a culture that cultivated patience and the long view, but China at the turn of the century was a nation consumed by the fast buck and the quick fix—from the boardroom to the bedroom.

One winter day in early 1999, I received a picture of a beautiful woman from an Internet dating site I frequented. The note read "Little Flower want know you." I responded, and in reply the writer sent me more pictures of the same stunning woman. We set a date for an early afternoon meeting in a Starbucks in downtown Beijing.

I arrived at the appointed time and settled into an overstuffed chair with a decaf latte. A few minutes later, my cellphone rang. I looked up, and a man was facing me, holding his phone. "Are you Pan Wen?"

"Yes," I replied.

"I have a message from Little Flower," he said. "She can't come today. But can I sit down?"

It turned out I had been scammed by the guy. Zhou Aihua was gay and seeking a foreign lover. He had liked the picture I had posted on the Web site and had lured me out with photographs of a Chinese starlet.

"But surely you can find lots of foreign gay men in China," I remarked.

"I wanted to meet a straight man," he replied. "I want to seduce one. That would give me a sense of accomplishment. That would be very stimulating!"

My friendships with Chinese men never approached the depth or variety of my friendships with women. I was not alone. I would often hear Western men and women add the adjective "Chinese" to the word "friend" when they described their same-sex acquaintances from China. It was a special category; the relationships rarely approached the level of intimacy or honesty of their Western friendships. "This is my Chinese friend," they would say, with the emphasis on "Chinese." Politics played a role in inhibiting closeness, at least with the men. Unlike their cousins in Hong Kong or Taiwan, mainland Chinese men had been brought up with decades of anti-American propaganda and they seemed to believe it more readily than the women. Part of it was also cultural.

"The Chinese have two ways of looking at foreigners," wrote Lu Xun, China's greatest twentieth-century writer. "We either look up to them as gods or down on them as animals." It was still true. Rarely in China was I treated as an equal. For a while, I enjoyed being treated like a god, even an animal, by Chinese women. But I couldn't stomach it from the men.

I had made one good male friend at Nanda, Ying Haikang, the guy whom I relied on for advice about my girlfriend, Fay. In late April 2004, Old Ying told me he was heading to the Huang Mountain resort area to look for antiques for the remodeling job he was doing on his new apartment. Keeping up with the Wangs had become a national obsession, especially among the new urban middle class. He asked me if I wanted to come along.

Tall for a Chinese and already balding during our time at Nanda, Old Ying was often too blunt for his own good, but he had a strong sense of justice and could appreciate the absurdity of life in his own country. I loved his laugh—a bawdy guffaw that would explode out of his fat face and shake his substantial paunch. He was one of the few Chinese men with whom I could be myself. He accepted me, rarely hit me up for favors, and seemed to enjoy my company as much as I enjoyed his. He called me Little Pan or, in a deliberate mispronunciation of my old Chinese name, Pian Aiwan, the Partying Fool. Born in 1957, he was two years older than me, so that gave him the right to call me Little. Old Ying had been in the antique business, but his shop went bust in the late 1990s after he bought too many fakes and could not unload them. He was now in the paper business—selling high-quality stock to Chinese firms for their annual reports and ad brochures.

Old Ying picked me up on a Friday afternoon in Nanjing in front of my hotel. My first inkling that this was not going to be an ordinary shopping expedition came when I opened the trunk of our borrowed car to stow my suitcase. A noxious blast of Chinese grain alcohol nearly bowled me over. Old Ying had crammed five cases of the stuff in the trunk along with three cases of Nanjing's most expensive cigarettes. He had corralled two fellow travelers—a friend who introduced himself as Tom Lee and an overly serious bespectacled twenty-something who went by the English name Henry. Henry was the son of one of Ying's business partners who had lent us a car for the trip. After stopping for bottled water and a huge sack of sunflower seeds to nibble on the way, we took off, Henry behind the wheel.

About two hours outside of Nanjing, the industrial suburbs gave way to the countryside. We headed south on a two-lane road snaking through the mountains of southern Anhui Province. Stands of bamboo cascaded down the hillsides and swayed in the wind. The azaleas were in bloom, punctuating the sea of bamboo green. In the Ming and Qing dynasties, merchants in the Huang Mountain region did a thriving business in salt, sending their goods along the myriad waterways that connected their towns with China's major cities. The merchants plowed their profits into the construction of enormous courtyard palaces as high as four stories, made from stone and wood. The timber in the region was soft—pine and camphor—good for carving. The best doors and windows were intricately decorated with small scenes of rural life: peasants on bended knee pleading to hard-hearted officials, bandits in the grips of sword-wielding imperial guards, scholars debating trivia on top of an arched bridge in a garden. Over time, trains and roads replaced canals and rivers for transportation, the waterways silted over, and the region fell on hard times. The area's isolation protected its cultural heritage—especially from the Cultural Revolution's Red Guard—until the 1990s, when antique smuggling boomed throughout China.

As we headed south, I realized that antique hunting was not the only reason that we were heading to Huang Mountain. Business mixes easily with pleasure in China, and the men I was accompanying had business in mind. A call came on Old Ying's cell phone. "Okay! Okay! Big Brother," Old Ying shouted, "we'll meet you at the Fish Lips Restaurant by the river. They've booked a room, a big room. Rest easy, Big Brother, we've arranged everything. *Hee hee.*"

Someone named Big Brother was going to meet us at Huang Mountain, flying in from Beijing. The booze and the cigarettes in the trunk were for him. Old Ying had also promised him antiques and girls.

Big Brother turned out to be a Beijing-based businessman married to the daughter of a senior party official involved in China's security services. Big Brother made his living selling truncheons and sirens to China's police and trading his connections to other businessmen interested in the police market. Government contracts in China are doled out on the basis of relationships, and this fellow was better connected than the rest.

Meeting Big Brother was important to Tom Lee. He ran an Internet security company that sold technical equipment to China's police, allowing them to monitor Internet users and spy on people's e-mail. China's Internet use had ballooned to more than 100 million by the end of 2005, from just 620,000 in 1997, and hundreds of police departments had established bureaus to electronically snoop on everyone. Tom believed he had a good product but, like many Chinese businessmen, he needed a government connection to sell it.

Henry had a different story. A fresh-faced graduate in computer sciences from a prestigious university in Nanjing, he had been hired by the Jiangsu Provincial Internet police bureau, one of five hundred around the country. His job was to protect "internal security," which meant he was one of the snoops reading people's e-mails, monitoring their accounts, policing Internet chat rooms for antigovernment discussions, and generally ensuring that the thoughts of China's Netizens stayed pure.

Earlier that year, Henry had been traveling in northern Jiangsu with his supervisor. One night at dinner, his boss got drunk. Henry went back to his hotel while his boss continued carousing. Returning to the hotel, Henry's boss plowed his vehicle into three cyclists and sped off—a fatal hit-and-run committed by a cop. Following orders, Henry lied to investigators to protect his boss but ultimately was forced to come clean. As so often happens in China, the boss escaped punishment and was able to retire with a full pension. Henry was fired. Henry hoped Big Brother could use his connections to get him reinstated.

Big Brother was waiting for us at the hotel, a squat man, balding, teeth stained with tobacco and tea. In his hand was a black leather clutch bag, a kind of male purse favored by Chinese businessmen. Big Brother was shouting orders into his mobile phone and grunting loudly. He seemed like a cartoon character of a Chinese wheeler-dealer—powered by a ferocious appetite for cash, sex, food, and booze. He turned out to be a very nice guy.

I had come on this trip in part to witness the ritual of Chinese men being men together. It was a world from which foreigners were excluded—either by the Chinese or by their own choice. Because Old Ying welcomed me, the tone was set for everyone else. Old Ying was unusual in that he did not varnish or modify his behavior or opinions when he was with foreigners. Once during a meal in Nanjing, as he was recounting a dalliance he had had with a nurse, he looked at me through a haze of cigarette smoke and said, "No other Chinese man will ever tell you about his sex life."

The Fish Lips Restaurant was as big as a hotel—four stories tall and lit up like a Christmas tree. On the first floor, scores of tables filled a hall as big as two basketball courts. Private rooms, equipped with karaoke sound systems, dominated the upper floors. Girls in shiny red cheongsams escorted us to the third floor, tittering about my big nose.

Old Ying was a smooth master of ceremonies, sensitively introducing Tom Lee's company and telling Henry's story to Big Brother. After the meal, all four of them said they wanted to go for a sauna, a massage, and, I figured, something extra. I left them to it. I was reading in bed when Old Ying returned. He lit a cigarette and began to speak about his love life. He had married late but his marriage was not working out. The couple almost got divorced in 2003 after Old Ying hired his wife's sister as his accountant and the equivalent of $1,500 disappeared from the corporate bank account. Old Ying and his wife agreed to a tentative truce. During the week, Old Ying would live in a new place, the one he wanted to renovate with antiques from Huang Mountain; weekends he would spend with his wife and daughter. Although more or less separated, they maintained a facade of togetherness for the sake of their child.

The next morning we visited a village that had been restored by a group of Western antique collectors. A man who introduced himself as Mr. Wang, a wiry fellow with an easy smile and a mobile phone that rang ragtime jazz, was our tour guide. Mr. Wang took us down six-foot-wide lanes lined on both sides by wooden houses built around central courtyards. The doors were stunning—massive planks of wood, ornately carved with scenes from Chinese myths. Windows were ornately decorated with animals and gremlins; others were lattice patterns, beautiful in their simplicity. Old Ying would stop Mr. Wang every so often as we passed a particularly fine example. The two would whisper. Mr. Wang would make a mark in his book. I figured he would come back the next day with an offer to buy it off the wall.

Mr. Wang invited Old Ying to his house to discuss the antique sales. While they chatted business in one room, Tom Lee, Henry, and I waited in the next. In 1989, Tom was a young university lecturer, teaching computer sciences in Nanjing. That spring, he led students on marches for democracy and freedom. In the investigations that followed the crackdown, he was fired from his job. Despite his political mistakes, Tom was allowed to leave China for the United States, where he got a PhD in electrical engineering. He returned home in the mid-1990s.

Tom partnered with several other Chinese computer scientists and began working on technology to sell to China's security services. This was ironic, to say the least. It was telling, too. The party structure had been assiduous in co-opting a broad spectrum of China's elite. From a dissident, Tom had been transformed into a defender of the Chinese system. "I have struggled to win my piece of the pie in China," Tom said, referring to his good salary, his house, his car, and the substantial dividend he receives each year as an executive in his tech firm. "I want to protect it. I don't want a revolution anymore. Anyway, a revolution would be horrible here.

The West has religion and moral values to hold people back, but China these days doesn't have anything like that. So, if a revolution happens, China would be destroyed."

On the final evening, we left Huang Mountain and headed back toward Nanjing. We stopped at a small roadside inn to spend the night. At about 10 p.m., there was a pounding on my door. I opened it, and Old Ying was there with a huge grin on his big face.

"Little Pan, we've hit the big time. It's a gold rush. It's raining women!" he enthused, barging into my room. "They're girls for eight dollars, ten dollars, twelve dollars, fifteen dollars, and twenty dollars, but they knocked the top price down to eighteen dollars! Cut rate! It's a steal, and, man, are they beautiful!"

Every hotel in China offered prostitutes. One establishment in Beijing, run by the People's Liberation Army, featured something called a *yang rou quanr*, a "goat-meat shish-kebab," which involved getting into bed with six naked lovelies and rolling around like a hot dog with too many buns. My close Chinese male friends all seemed to have something romantic or at least sexual going on the side. It was not that I ran with a particularly fast crowd—these were college professors, businessmen with graduate degrees, lawyers, investors—it was just the way things were. By way of justification, they would point to China's tradition of concubines. I thought the real reasons involved recent history. This was a country that for decades had instructed its people that sex was bad, that masturbation took energy away from economic development, and that women must desex themselves to the point of dressing like men. Then, suddenly, all the values changed. Or, more correctly, they just disappeared.

The phone rang. "Mister, are you lonely?" a smoky voice croaked from the other end of the line. "Would you like someone to come upstairs and play?"

"How much?" I inquired.

"The best are twenty dollars," she said. Apparently, I was not going to get a discount.

There was a knock on my door. I opened it and a thin girl in a shiny chartreuse tank top, dyed red hair, and stonewashed jeans greeted me with a blast of cigarette smoke.

"You want to play?" she asked, her arms akimbo.

I mumbled an apology and closed the door.

PART V

SPRINTING TOWARD LITTLE COMFORTS

30

PINE ON A CLIFF

When Little Guan asked Ding Xing whether he missed his father, her son would reply "not so much." She sensed he was trying to comfort her by hiding his pain. At the end of the summer after Old Ding died, Little Guan pulled out the family's electric fan and began sobbing. Traditionally, Old Ding would dismantle the fan, scrub down each part, and store it for the winter. Little Guan had never cleaned it. Her twelve-year-old rushed to her side and pushed her away. "This work is not something for a woman to do," he lectured her. At night, when thunderstorms erupted, Little Guan would rise to close the windows. Ding Xing got up, too, commanding her in his boy's voice: "Go back to sleep. Women are afraid of thunder. I will shut them."

Despite Ding Xing's protestations, his father's death set the boy back. His grades faltered. Always at the top in science and math, he fell behind. Ding Xing explained it by saying, "It's natural to lose your place." Nonetheless, Little Guan worried that the rigors of China's educational system were squeezing the life out of the boy. Before he turned eleven, Ding Xing was already up past midnight doing homework. One morning, as her son dressed for school, Little Guan discovered he had dozed off while putting on his socks. She complained to the principal that the children did not have enough time to sleep, play, and learn social skills necessary for life. The principal smirked and remarked that it was the first time he had heard a complaint like that. All the other parents wanted their children to study more, not less.

At eighteen, Ding Xing tested too low on the college entrance examinations to qualify for the major he wanted, information technology. But Little Guan, using her connections, got Ding Xing into the department anyway.

With her boy at college, Little Guan felt free for the first time in her life to spend some of her savings. She purchased an eighteen-hundred-square-foot apartment on the fifth floor of a building in Century Garden, one of many gated estates recently built in Hefei. She installed an American-made central air conditioning and heating system and a hardwood floor, which she had stained walnut brown. She scoured Hefei's antique markets for a Qing Dynasty door that she had workers fit to the space separating her kitchen and dining room. On the walls, she hung traditional Chinese calligraphy and classical paintings. On her balcony, she hung a hammock. She installed an imported showerhead and bought shower gel made from snake oil. In the summer she slept on a finger-thin mattress fashioned from reeds that allowed the sweat to evaporate. In the winter she used puffy cotton quilts with silk duvet covers. She bought a fine stereo system and had two good computers with broadband access. The place was both spotless and lived in.

In the early morning of October 4, 2002, after the renovations were complete, Little Guan and her son took Old Ding's memorial photograph and the pot they used to burn incense for him to their new apartment. In the back of a taxi, they spoke to Old Ding as if he were alive, telling him at each intersection where they were heading for fear that his soul might get lost on the way to their new home. For a month after they moved into the new apartment, Old Ding didn't come to Little Guan in her dreams. Thinking that he'd gotten lost, each day she burned incense and repeated the directions. Finally, he appeared.

Little Guan's relationship with her deceased husband was a living thing, and she would consult him on major changes in her life. In early September 2004, she noticed a hairline break in the metal of the gold wedding ring Old Ding had given her six years into their marriage. Little Guan had worn it since his death. That night Little Guan dreamed of her husband. He seemed at peace. She had believed that being single all these years was good for her boy. It would have been easy to find another husband but not easy to find another father. But now, Ding Xing had entered graduate school. He had joined the Communist Party, more for access to a good job than out of ideology. He was a man. The next day, she prayed in front of

Old Ding's portrait and asked, "Should I get married again?" Five times she flipped a one *mao* coin. Five times it came up heads. "He was telling me it was okay," she said. Little Guan decided not to repair her wedding band and commenced a search for a suitable husband.

In early 2005, Little Guan gave herself a Chinese New Year's present: she registered on an Internet dating Web site frequented by foreigners and Chinese. She'd had boyfriends over the years, but she wanted to try her hand at online dating. One suitor from Texas requested that she improve her English so they could communicate more deeply. "Why don't you learn Chinese?" she fired back.

"I've planted rice, raised pigs, been beaten, been married, raised a son, had lovers, but I never had an Internet love affair," Little Guan said with a chuckle. "I wanted one. So here I am." Little Guan didn't really believe she would find a husband online, but it satisfied her curiosity and bolstered her self-confidence. In two months she got forty responses, thirty-eight of them from non-Chinese.

Little Guan's emotional exploration was courageous and increasingly common among women her age. Hefei was a social, cultural, and economic backwater. But even here people were exploring new ways of living together, new ways of understanding themselves, within the confines of communism's strange jumble of repression and freedom. Little Guan wrestled with the idea that she might be a wayward woman. Widows were supposed to remain chaste, while she had not. She also grappled with her desire for love, which stood in contrast to her determination that her personal life not impede her son's growth, education, and career.

"Do you think I'm bad?" she asked. We were sharing a cup of tea at her kitchen table, a small pot of heated chrysanthemum oil filling the room with its scent. "No," I said. "I think you are brave."

Most of the time she went easy on herself. For generations, Chinese had been taught that all romantic relationships had to end in marriage and that only men were allowed to enjoy sex. But Little Guan and women of her generation had begun to break with this tradition. They had no role models to guide them.

"You say our generation has no model, that's true," Little Guan said, "but do you really think you need a model to survive? Have you seen the pine trees living on the ledges of Huang Mountain? They have no role models either. They can only adapt to the barren soil in the crevice between rocks, adapt to the trials of life, its winds and frosts."

Little Guan worried, however, that her son wasn't as adaptable. Already in his twenties, he had never had a girlfriend. Little Guan had decided that it was time. But Little Guan was different from most meddling moms. While other parents wanted their son or daughter to be looking for a relationship that would, as they'd say, "bear fruit," Little Guan urged her son to simply fall in love. "Many beautiful flowers don't bear fruit," Little Guan quipped.

Little Guan encouraged Ding Xing to invite girls over to their apartment. One evening, he asked several over for dinner. Little Guan chaperoned. Her favorite was a girl who came from a good family. But another girl, who was the product of a broken home, was sweet on her son. Little Guan disapproved.

"I want Ding Xing to be associated with a good family," she explained to me. "I don't want two broken homes together. And I worry that this girl would hate men because her father walked away from the family."

Little Guan plied Ding Xing with advice about how to approach her favorite. She was nervous about her son. He seemed to lack the mettle of his father. Ding Xing should fall in love at least once, preferably five or six times, in his life, she declared. Love makes you grow, she remarked. If you don't fall in love, you won't grow up. As far as finding a wife, she said, well, that's up to fate.

"It's like the cleaver we used for cooking in the countryside. When it's put into a hot fire and then cold water, it tempers the steel," she said. "If it is a bad knife to begin with, it will break fast. But if it can take the changes, it becomes better and better. That's the type of knife I am. That's the type of knife I want him to be."

My classmates candidly shared their stories of using connections and paying people off to help their children get a leg up—in school, jobs, even their love lives—in what was fast becoming one of the most competitive societies in the world. Their actions were fueled, in part, by the understandable wish to shield their kids from the deprivations of their own youths. When my classmates tested into college, their parents were of little use in advising them about majors or jobs. Back then, China was changing in ways that the older generation neither anticipated nor fully understood.

But having remade China, my classmates now had connections that were powerful and deep.

University enrollment was more than ten times what it had been in Little Guan's day, but competition for good schools was even more intense. The government had done away with the job allocation system and with it a guarantee of employment upon graduation. Finding a good job, like winning a spot in a good university or even finding a girlfriend, had become a blood sport. Thousands of college graduates were unemployed, and, thanks to China's skewed gender birthrates, thousands of men had no girlfriends. Known in slang as *guanggun* ("bare sticks"), more than five hundred thousand singles between the ages of thirty and fifty lived in each of China's two main cities, Beijing and Shanghai, a fivefold increase from 1990. In many cities, the average marrying age had jumped from twenty-four for men and twenty-three for women to around thirty.

Employment and relationship troubles were indicative of a major shift in how the government interacted with its people. Jobs were no longer guaranteed by the state, and neither were housing, medical care, schooling, matchmaking, or pensions. The iron rice bowl, the cradle-to-grave welfare and employment system, had been smashed for good. While life had improved significantly for those able to keep up with the times, it also had been made tougher. The Chinese state used to treat its people like infants. Suddenly, people were expected to act like adults.

While she struggled to help her son succeed, Little Guan fretted about the world he would enter when he received his master's degree in information technology. She hoped Ding Xing would move abroad—a sentiment expressed by many of my classmates. Some wished this because of China's severe environmental problems (60 percent of my classmates' children were asthmatic), others because no matter how fast China's economy grew, they believed the system was inherently unstable and destined for a calamitous collapse. Little Guan didn't worry so much about a political disintegration; her concerns were about a moral one.

"I don't want him growing up in an environment where to succeed he has to visit prostitutes and to go to karaoke halls," Little Guan said one day while he practiced dance moves around the apartment as he listened to love ballads on a new iPod. "It will change him too much."

In her own small way, Little Guan tried to improve the Chinese society she worried about. Several years earlier, she had chanced on a newspaper article detailing an eleven-year-old girl's victory fending off a jackal that had been stalking her for six hours along a mountain road. The girl's ordeal reminded Little Guan of her own encounter with a snake several decades ago. It did not hurt that the peasant girl, Guan Xiaodan, shared Little Guan's surname. And, like her son Ding Xing, the girl had also lost her father. Through a journalist friend, Little Guan checked the veracity of the story and determined that the girl's family was, indeed, destitute. Little Guan began sending her money—about $130 a year—to ensure that she stayed in school. The Chinese government used to provide basic education to its people (when it wasn't closing schools because of political campaigns), but elementary schools now charged tuition. With the collapse of the Communist safety net, the government lacked the funds necessary to support its schools. Indeed, China devotes only 3.4 percent of its GDP to education, half of what Western countries spend, and most of China's money goes to its universities, which cater to the elite.

In the summer of 2004, Little Guan and I traveled together to Shitai, a township nestled on the banks of a river in the mountains of southern Anhui. In the central plains, China was torrid, the thermometer pushing a steamy 102. But up in the hills, breezes wafted through bamboo groves. The air was clear; the only sounds were the swish-swish of farmers separating rice kernels from the husks. Little Guan seemed to shed decades as we traipsed around a rural landscape not unlike the one of her youth.

Little Guan's charge, Guan Xiaodan, was a shy thirteen-year-old with a sunburned face, wearing a frumpy, hand-me-down orange-checked cotton jacket. Her mother was tiny, even shorter than she was. They had walked all day from their village to meet us. Guan Xiaodan's father had died of leukemia in 2000. That same year, her elder sister had left the village for a textile mill that exported sweatpants to the United States. The fifteen-year-old worked eighteen hours a day, seven days a week, for five dollars a month.

After the death of her husband, Xiaodan's mother was left alone with a half acre of land on a mountain to farm. Her first instinct was to take her daughters out of school because the more hands she had around the house the better. The family's crop of wheat, corn, and vegetables barely fed them, and the local tax collector, despite laws to the contrary, still squeezed them even after her husband's death.

In the early years of the twenty-first century, China's economic reforms were clearly benefiting the middle class and the elite. But among the country's vast rural population, income had stagnanted for years while taxes and fees, often imposed illegally, continued to rise. The gap between the haves, such as Little Guan, and the have-nots, such as Xiaodan, was widening. When she sat down to a meal with us at a local restaurant, Xiadoan's eyes popped out of her head. She had obviously never seen so many dishes. But she also surprised us. The peasant girl began speaking in English. "I think America is good," she declared, looking straight at me. "I want to become a teacher."

Little Guan did not go through a Chinese charity to help Xiaodan and her family because officials in aid organizations, which were largely run by the Communist Party, regularly pilfered funds. Little Guan sent sixty-five dollars each semester directly to Xiaodan's mother by mail. But even that proved troublesome. Postal workers in Xiaodan's township stole the money. What's more, once the village chief learned of Little Guan's charity, he demanded a cut of the donation.

Little Guan pestered and cajoled the local authorities as she fought for the right to help Xiaodan, and her sister, who had returned from the textile mills because her left hand had gone numb after seven days a week on a sewing machine. Little Guan's contacts in the province's legal department threatened local officials in Shitai. The stolen money was returned, although the thieving postmen were not punished, and the village chief backed off. After lunch, as we strolled into the countryside with Xiaodan and her mother, I asked Little Guan if she thought she'd be able to fight her way out of the countryside if she were a modern-day peasant girl like Guan Xiaodan. "China was a different country then," she said. "I don't know if I'd be able to make it today."

Little Guan's life with Ding Xing was comfortable. Her income was bolstered by the books and articles she wrote and edited about Chinese culture, pottery, and painting as well as the occasional "red envelope" stuffed with money that she earned from matchmaking. Though she had used a big chunk of her retirement fund to purchase their spacious home, she still had some savings. Her job at the insurance company was as stable as one could expect in a country where state-owned enterprises had fired tens of millions of people in five years. Still, Little Guan hankered after a new challenge.

For years, friends and colleagues had been telling Little Guan she should go into business. She was a natural saleswoman, she loved people, and had a wide circle of friends. So when her fiftieth birthday rolled around in July 2005, she gave herself three more presents: she paid off her mortgage; invested six thousand dollars with eight friends in a nine-thousand-square-foot bar in Hefei; and registered the names of five companies. Little Guan had decided to jump into the sea.

The bar was located on a government-backed "entertainment street" in Hefei, a mini version of Hunan Road. In the second scheme, Little Guan and Ding Xing decided to try e-commerce, setting up a Web site to sell the products of Anhui Province, from tea to spices to preserved meats. E-commerce in China is still in its infancy. In 2004, Chinese spent $1 billion shopping on the Internet, 1 percent of what Americans spent. Few Chinese have credit cards, making it difficult to pay for items purchased online. Without any regulatory system, China is awash in bogus Internet businesses selling fictitious products. The lack of morality and the paucity of trust that pervade Chinese society have found their way to cyberspace.

Nonetheless, Little Guan was rejuvenated by the idea of taking a risk. For the first time since Old Ding died, she had stopped fearing failure. Her spirit seemed to be returning to the time at Nanda when, for the sake of love, she turned away from the acceptable path and went to Hefei as a jobless newlywed. It was an intoxicating feeling, she remarked, tempting fate again.

31

ENDURE

Fate seemed intent on a lifetime of humiliation for my sad classmate Old Wu. In 2003, his boss, the chief of the history department of Nanjing Normal University, came up with a moneymaking idea to write high school history textbooks. Old Wu was assigned the task of writing about the Cultural Revolution, which in Nanjing began with the murder of his parents.

Old Wu told me he didn't find it particularly galling to be asked to churn out nonsense about the events that caused his parents' deaths, but I was amazed. There is no word in Chinese for irony, perhaps because the whole structure of society is so infused with incongruity that the Chinese can't see it anymore: a Communist Party that is capitalist; an ancient culture hell-bent on burying its past; a workers' paradise of unparalleled exploitation, a son of political martyrs being told to distort in multiple ways the circumstances leading to his parents' deaths.

Old Wu did want to write something close to the truth. And he had planned on including a photograph of Liu Shaoqi, the head of state at the outset of the Cultural Revolution who, on Mao's orders, was beaten, denied medical treatment, and left to die. But the censors refused. In the end Old Wu's chapter glossed over the Cultural Revolution, blaming it on the Gang of Four and not China's Communist system. When I asked Old Wu how he felt about the party censoring his work, he cracked a pained smile and wrote out the character *ren* on a piece of paper. The character depicts a dagger on top of a heart. It means "endure" and encapsulates one of the central tenets of his life. The peculiarly Chinese instinct of knowing when and how to get along with authority governed Wu's decision and guaranteed his own future. In Old Wu's case, expediency once again vanquished principle.

When Old Wu first told me his life story, I found myself chafing at his passivity, meekness, even weakness. How could he so unflinchingly march to the tune of the state? First, it was painting posters vilifying his father; then it was lying about his parents' deaths in an application to get into the party. After the Tiananman Square crackdown of 1989, Old Wu had even acquiesced to a party decision to appoint him head of a team investigating the "antiparty" activities of teachers and professors at Nanjing Normal University, carrying out the same kind of interrogations that ultimately left his parents dead. And now this—putting his name to a chapter in a book that lies about the Cultural Revolution. The least he could have done, it seemed to me, was to have declined to write the chapter or to have called in sick when told to investigate whether his colleagues protested in 1989.

But over time my views on Wu changed. I realized that he was taking a very Chinese approach to vengeance. During the political purges after June 4, 1989, he was, by all accounts, the most lackadaisical inquisitor in Nanjing. Rather than giving in to official amnesia, he made a tremendous effort to dig to the roots of the actions that led to his parents' murders. More than any other classmate, he understood the capricious bloody-mindedness of the system, and perhaps because he knew it so well, *mei banfa*, "there's no way out," was his only logical response.

If Wu was a coward, he was a coward with the guts to openly display his fears. Each time I posed a question, he inundated me with information, files, and documents. It was Old Wu who gave me the party application in which he was forced to dishonor his parents; it was Old Wu who told me about the 1989 commission and the textbooks.

I began to see him as no less tragic but also heroic. Of all my classmates, Old Wu was the most adept at using the Internet, e-mail, text messaging, and other accoutrements of a modern life. With his wry smile, the alacrity with which he absorbed new technology, the joy he took in the success of his daughter (she was heading to Australia to study), Wu was consciously, even aggressively, enjoying life. Wasn't that a victory of sorts against the system and the people who had killed his parents? "People say that I am aloof," he wrote to me once. "They don't know what goes on inside me."

On a sparkling day in May 2004, I arrived with Old Wu at the gates of the Modern Times driving school, on the outskirts of Nanjing near Waterfield village, the place where, twenty-eight years earlier, he had learned of his parents' murders. On the parking lot sat a row of red Chinese-made Volkswagen Santanas, several with boom-box-sized dents in their sides. Wu's driving instructor was a middle-aged woman named Wang, who had earned her stripes as a Nanjing bus driver for fifteen years. Her real passion, she confessed, was dancing the tango. Chinese call their driving teachers coaches, so she became Coach Wang.

In spite of the fact that Chinese are generally dutiful students, China's roads are the most dangerous in the world. In the twenty years since Old Wu's graduation, the number of traffic deaths had grown faster than China's thundering GDP to three hundred a day, more than double the rate of the United States, even though China has about one-tenth the number of cars. For people between fifteen and forty-five, motor fatalities are the leading cause of death. The World Health Organization predicts that by 2020, traffic deaths in China will hit a million per year.

Driving tests? Many police departments issue driver's licenses to anyone with connections and the extra cash. Book Idiot Zhou got his driver's license for the equivalent of three dollars, even though he had never been behind a wheel. "Are you a cautious person?" the policeman asked. Zhou nodded. "Then you'll be a good driver." In their manic rush to become modern, the Chinese had become obsessed with the accessories of a more advanced life but somehow seem too distracted to learn how to use them.

For decades after the Communist revolution, the party banned car ownership, claiming it was "bourgeois," proof of the decadence of Western life. China legalized private vehicle ownership in 1979, but it took a long time for people to afford cars. Imported automobiles were hit with duties that doubled their cost, spawning a vast automobile smuggling industry, run by the police and the military. The navy devoted an entire base to its smuggling operation. Then in the 1990s, the government launched a program to encourage people to buy cars. In much the same way as the United

States did in the 1950s, the government looked to its nascent automobile industry as a new engine of growth. New expressways crisscrossed the country, and foreign automobile companies pumped in billions in investments. In 2003, there were 24 million cars on the road in China and 3 million new-car sales. The streets of Beijing, Shanghai, Guangzhou, Nanjing, and other cities now faced traffic congestion that rivaled that of Los Angeles. The average traffic speed in China's major cities declined from twenty-eight miles per hour in 1994 to seven-and-a-half miles per hour in 2005—a pace easily matched by a bike.

Coach Wang maneuvered the car to an isolated area of the Nanjing Industrial Development Zone, past a Philips plant, a military installation making radars for the People's Liberation Army, and a ceramics company. She stopped the car. Old Wu got out, walked to the driver's side, bowed his head, and yelped, "Reporting for duty!" Failure to bow and bark "reporting for duty" is grounds for automatic failure on the driving test.

Old Wu got behind the wheel. "Start the engine," Coach Wang commanded.

"Order received," Wu responded. Skipping this protocol would also result in failure.

Coach Wang wasn't wearing a seat belt. Neither was Old Wu. He guardedly pressed the accelerator and away we went, fluttering all over the road. Coach Wang never asked him what he saw out of the rearview mirror. When Old Wu came to an intersection, Coach Wang opined that "it might be best to look both ways" but that did not seem compulsory. So Old Wu would glide through intersections while I prayed in the backseat. Twice, Coach Wang sent Old Wu the wrong way down one-way streets.

"Step on the gas! Step on the gas!" Coach Wang snapped. "Change gears! Change gears!"

"Order received," Wu replied. He seemed very intent at grasping this new skill, as if he would never be allowed another chance.

Wu was moving at about ten miles per hour in first gear, but Wang wanted him to switch into second. Now at fifteen miles per hour, she ordered him to shift into third. Again, he complied. We hit twenty-five miles per hour, but she wanted to get him into fourth. He shifted, and the car started rattling like a clothes dryer. "You must shift quickly," Wang advised him. "This is the way to drive. Shifting early is the key to your driver's test. If you don't, you will fail."

Coach Wang was getting frustrated. In addition to not shifting quickly enough, Old Wu was having trouble driving in a straight line. Luckily, the road ahead was empty. Coach Wang threatened to give Old Wu the silent treatment if he did not obey her commands.

"I'm just going to shut up here," Coach Wang said. "I'm not going to talk to you." "Order received!" Old Wu yelled, a big smile on his gentle face.

Big Bluffer Ye didn't know how to drive; he didn't need to. He was chauffered everywhere—to business meetings, party confabs, his equestrian club, the party's exclusive tennis courts—in his black Audi 6.

One summer afternoon, Ye called and asked me if I was free for dinner. Of course, I replied. I had been waiting in Nanjing for four days to see him. He told me he'd pick me up at 6 p.m. in front of Nanda. I was at the gate waiting when the Audi swerved up the street, blaring its horn in the rush-hour traffic. Ye was sitting in the passenger seat behind the driver. As the car sped up to me, cutting into the bicycle lane, Ye reached over to open the door. The door smacked an old man on a bicycle, sending him face-forward onto the asphalt. "Don't worry about him," Ye shouted from inside the car as it screeched to halt. "Get in." Other bicyclists whizzed by, swerving to avoid me and the fallen cyclist. "Hey . . ." the old man shouted as he struggled to his feet. The click of the door silenced him in midsentence. The motor purred; the air conditioner blasted. Bicyclists glared into the car.

One of the things that struck me about Big Bluffer Ye was the ease with which he could jump from gentle words to tough deeds as if he had cultivated at least two personas, the engaging dinner host and the guy who runs over old men in the street. My classmates laughed at me when I told them I was trying to understand him better. "What's to understand?" one said. "He's a Communist, and there are two types. Those who go to hookers, gamble, eat big meals, and admit it. And those who do all that but don't admit it. Ye's in the second group."

That night Ye took me to one of Nanjing's ritziest restaurants in the penthouse of a Nanjing skyscraper; several other party officials joined us. During the meal, Ye held forth on Western society. First stop was religion. "You won't hear the Communist Party saying it, but most of us really think that religion is good. It's a glue that keeps a society together. China doesn't have such a glue. We could use one. We don't have anything keeping us together.

"Our policies in the past were too harsh on religion," he continued, gesturing with an ivory chopstick, its tip plated in silver. "The party needs to manage religions better and to understand that religious people actually make better citizens."

The other dinner guests shook their heads in agreement. "China needs something to believe in. The Chinese people have no beliefs," said one, a senior official in the Nanjing Party hierarchy.

"My daughter just believes in her mobile telephone," joked another.

Ye continued: "At the beginning of the Falun Gong crackdown, we just told them to stay out of the parks and keep quiet. But then . . ."

Ye's voice trailed off. One of the guests changed the subject.

Falun Gong exploded onto the world stage on April 25, 1999, when ten thousand members of this strange newly founded Chinese faith surrounded the Communist Party headquarters in Beijing. I was walking to my office that day when a Chinese friend called me on my cell phone. "Go to Zhongnanhai," he enthused, using the Chinese name for the party headquarters. "There's something going on."

A few minutes later I arrived outside the compound to find thousands of middle-aged men and women meditating five deep on the sidewalk in the early spring chill. None of them would talk to me or any of the handful of foreign correspondents who had rushed to the scene. Unbeknown to us, the demonstrators had someone else watching them: President Jiang Zemin, who was riding around the outskirts of the party's compound in a black government sedan.

Melding Buddhism, Taoism, Eastern mystical hocus-pocus, and martial arts, Falun Gong was started in the early 1990s by a feckless trumpet-playing government functionary named Li Hongzhi, who worked at a grain bureau in northeastern China. According to the myth, Li possessed magical powers, including the ability to fly and communicate with aliens. Initially, he was just one of many selling salvation to a populace dizzied by change and in search of an anchor in a society quickly jettisoning all beliefs.

At first, Falun Gong was tolerated, even encouraged, by the party. In the aftermath of the Tiananmen Square crackdown, the government supported it and other nativist sects, figuring that they provided an alternative to the obsession with Western democracy and individualism that swept China in the 1980s. The Ministry of Education published Falun Gong's early books. The Qi Gong Society, a party-controlled organization for martial arts, allowed Falun Gong practitioners to meet and worship in its facilities. Neighborhood Committees, the party's foot soldiers in cities, helped Falun Gong members reserve exercise space in parks.

Falun Gong promised good health at a time when thousands of people were losing medical benefits. And its message of predetermination was comforting to people who honestly didn't know what the future held in store. To aging Communists, retired high-ranking military officers, and other educated people, it offered a comfortable replacement for the Communist credo of their youth. Through its association with the party, the sect flourished, claiming millions of followers by the late 1990s.

Several weeks after the April 1999 sit-in, the party cracked down on Falun Gong, launching its biggest campaign of repression since Tiananmen Square. The party justified its actions by explaining that practicing Falun Gong made people crazy and drove them to suicide. In reality, Falun Gong's organization, not its theology, was the threat. For fifty years, the party had reigned supreme because it had never tolerated tightly knit networks of any kind outside of its control. The party's campaign against Falun Gong, which began in 1999 and lasted five years, would send hundreds to their graves and thousands more to jail.

In Nanjing, Falun Gong had made substantial inroads among university professors and engineers living in the Drum Tower District. Big Bluffer Ye battled the sect so fiercely on his home turf that the state-run Xinhua News Agency offered his techniques of interrogation as a model to the nation for how to break its members.

In 2001 the news agency praised Ye for forcing a Falun Gong leader in Nanjing to abandon the sect. Xinhua lauded the "careful thought work" Ye conducted with the man and his family. "After many rounds of reformatory education," the report said, "the family was back on the normal living track."

The report left out the details of exactly how Ye had compelled the man to renounce his faith. According to Falun Gong followers and other sources in Nanjing, Ye gave him an ultimatum: leave the sect or else your wife will be incarcerated for three years and your daughter for eight years, both in facilities where the male guards have a reputation for raping female prisoners. Three years after his interrogation, security officials continued to visit—and sometimes live—in the man's house to ensure that he had not returned to the fold.

For all the puff pieces on state-run media about Big Bluffer Ye, and for all Ye's success at turning Hunan Road into a cash cow, he found himself blocked in his once-effortless rise up the party hierarchy. On the morning of our class's twentieth reunion at Nanda in May 2002, Ye failed to get elected as the party's chosen candidate to join the city's Standing Committee—the pinnacle of political power in Nanjing. Even more remarkably, the local party bosses chose to allow the results to stand. Ye would have to wait until the next election, a year later, to join that elite club.

Party officials gossiped that Ye was too brash and boastful for a successful organization man. There were rumors about Ye's son, whom Ye had dispatched to a pricey boarding school in Singapore and then to Australia for college. There was no way Ye's salary could pay for the boy's tuition and living expenses of more than forty thousand dollars a year.

Another promotion was derailed when party investigators found close to $2 million stuffed in a refrigerator belonging to the head of the party's Organization Department in Jiangsu Province. The official, who had amassed the cash by conducting the biggest government job-selling racket in Communist Party history, had been preparing to promote Ye to the post of deputy secretary general of the provincial committee, a step up from the city level. His arrest scuttled those plans.

Then came a crisis.

On August 22, 2003, an unemployed laborer named Weng Biao was preparing to go buy a lunch of steamed fish and pickled vegetables for his wife when officials from the government Office of Demolition showed up at his two-room shack in an open lot in downtown Nanjing that was slated to become a shopping mall. They ordered him to come with them.

A thirty-nine-year-old part-time laborer with a bum leg, Weng limped to the office two-hundred yards away. Minutes later, several other officials barged into Weng's house and forced his wife, eleven-year-old son, and seventy-four-year-old father outside. A bulldozer arrived and flattened the house, even though residents of the neighborhood had been given eight more days to leave the area.

Back in the demolition office, officials had sprinkled Weng with gasoline and pretended they were going to light him on fire as part of a ploy to terrorize him into giving up his demands for more compensation for his condemned house. As they continued to threaten him, the embers of one official's cigarette hit the gas. Weng was hospitalized with third-degree burns over 90 percent of his body. By week's end, he was dead.

The party ordered Ye to deal with the problem, appointing him deputy director of the Office of Demolition. Ye ordered Nanjing's media to call Weng's death a suicide and say that Weng, despite his handicap, overpowered six men in the office, poured the can of fuel on himself, and deliberately sparked the fire that killed him. Ye instructed editors of Nanjing's newspaper to depict Weng as an unhinged malcontent who was unwilling to drop his unreasonable demands for more money to vacate his shack.

Weng was a casualty in a war over property that pitted China's haves against its have-nots. Across China, governments were condemning farmland and urban housing units and handing both over to developers at huge profits. Farmers and urban dwellers were generally offered a pittance to compensate them for their losses. An estimated 100 million people over the last decade had lost their land and houses in such schemes.

Big Bluffer Ye's speedy spin on Weng's death impressed the party. He allowed Nanjing's press to report the news, a relative breakthrough in a country that used to regularly ignore tragedies such as these, but he ensured that the government's version of events was the only one available. To muzzle the family, Ye locked Weng's wife in a hotel for a month and made her pay the bill when she was released.

In the summer of 2004, Ye was appointed chief of the city's propaganda department. Though the position sounded good, it was a side move at best. The Big Bluffer had gone from being a ward heeler, a real doer, making money and deals, to the dead-end position of chief censor, responsible for Nanjing's newspapers, TV, Web sites, and radio stations.

When Ye told me about his new job, as usual, he put on a brave face. He enthused about Western freedoms of the press. "We need that in China, too," he gushed. "The press should be free to report whatever it wants about whomever it wants. That's my view. We need more freedom like that in China."

Ye instituted a plan to award bonuses to reporters in Nanjing who had won praise from government officials while deducting pay from reporters whose articles angered the party. In January 2005, he chaired a meeting on propaganda in the city. After lambasting the editors of a Nanjing newspaper for failing to properly "manage" the news, he noted that too much "negative" news was being reported and that it must stop. He then announced plans to "rectify" the *Nanjing Daily*—the party's paper in the provincial capital. For decades the *Nanjing Daily* had been a tired rag that spouted the party line. In recent years it had begun to improve its journalism, daring to criticize the government for its failures to uncover scandals and report corruption cases. By no means a muckraker, it nevertheless had shed its image as a flaccid mouthpiece for the party's Standing Committee in Nanjing. Ye ended the meeting by ordering the dismissal of fifty reporters.

"The party paper must represent the will of the party," he said. "The *Nanjing Daily* is going in a bad direction. It is time to change it back."

"Who says China is going to have a Western-style free press?" Ye barked at the editors, just a few months after he had told me how much he admired one. "Not while we are in charge."

32

CRAWLING HOME

Despite the persistent vigilance of Big Bluffer and other censors like him, more than a decade after the Tiananmen Square crackdown, newspapers, magazines, Internet Web sites, and TV stations—all state-controlled—began to explore topics that had remained taboo since the revolution. *Southern Weekend,* a weekly newspaper based in the southern city of Guangzhou, broke stories on the AIDS crisis in Henan Province, reporting that the government had encouraged farmers to sell their blood to hospitals (where it was not tested for HIV), and blaming government officials for causing an epidemic among peasants. Other stories—about sexuality, official corruption, and police brutality—were published for the first time. Due to its comparatively benign subject matter, sports reporting was the freest and most competitive. Of the hundreds of sports journals in China, a Hunan-based paper called *Titan Sports* was the best.

After Daybreak Song returned to Italy following his father's death, *Titan Sports* hired him away from the Jiangsu sports newspaper, starting him on a monthly retainer of four hundred dollars, which grew to six hundred dollars after a year. By 2003, he was guaranteed one thousand dollars a month as base pay with extra cash for each story. The paper gave Song a zippy nom de plume, Qiao Wanni (Giovanni).

Titan had gone from a weekly to a triweekly, its circulation skyrocketing from 100,000 to 1.5 million. It had expanded its foreign staff to include bureaus in Spain, Britain, France, Germany, Argentina, Brazil,

South Korea, and Japan. Working three days a week, Song made thirty thousand dollars in 2003 and hit forty thousand dollars in 2004, placing him near the top of our class in terms of salary.

In January 2004 I went to Rome to visit Daybreak Song. A few days into my stay, we traveled by train to Modena, a central Italian city famed for balsamic vinegar and Ferraris. I wanted to see Song at work and catch my first professional soccer game. At the stadium, we went to the press box to pick up our passes. There was only one ticket, in my name. (Song had used my affiliation with the *Washington Post* to secure it.) We were told that we would have to find a second empty seat for Song once inside the stadium. Song snickered at the confirmation of his hunch. The Modena club had assigned me a seat, not him, even though he was the sports reporter.

"Westerners still look down on China," he said. "Millions of people in China care about this match and no one knows it's happening in the United States. But the Italians don't realize that. They are looking to America when they should be looking to us." After getting rousted from seat after seat, we finally found two good perches. Song explained the rules of the game, and we both oohed and ahhed when a Roman striker streaked ahead of Modena's defenses to score a dramatic first goal. Song filed a short article about the match, which ended in a tie, focusing on the fact that he'd been denied an assigned seat while his American friend had not.

Titan had a rule. Barring unusual circumstances, the photograph on its front page was reserved for a foreign sports star. The one regular exception was Yao Ming, the seven-foot-five NBA phenom who was famous in China because he played in the United States. Why were the Chinese so bananas about foreign sports? Well, for one, their own sports had become completely corrupt, explained Song's editor, Luo Min. More than half of the matches in China's professional soccer league, for example, were fixed.

Luo Min is an earnest, skinny man with sad eyes who junked a career in herbal medicine to write about sports. In addition to Song, he had nineteen journalists working overseas, with one reporter following Yao full-time. "People need something to believe in," he postulated when I went to meet him and tour *Titan*'s operation in Changsha, the capital of Hunan

Province. "We don't believe in Jesus, but we can believe in soccer. And it's a way to study foreign things."

In the summer of 2004, six years after his father's death, Song returned to China with Leila, who had recently turned nine. I went to the airport in Shanghai to meet them along with Song's eldest sister, Yang Su, a portly, no-nonsense, anticorruption official based in Yancheng. Two hours after their plane had landed, Song had still not made it through customs.

"I wonder if something's wrong," Yang Su whispered.

"Perhaps he's being interrogated," I quipped.

She responded with a throaty laugh and a shake of her head: "Anything's possible here."

Finally, the pair emerged: Leila, already overwhelmed by the crush of humanity, pulling her own tiny carry-on festooned with plastic flowers, and Song, looking rakish even after a bumpy landing through the clouds of China's rainy season.

Song's sister had hired a driver, and we all squeezed into a Volkswagen Santana for the four-hour trip north to Yancheng. The highway was new. Its smooth asphalt and gigantic Jetson-style tollbooths ablaze in neon was just the first of many sights that would amaze Song. I had come to spend time with Song, but also to meet up with other classmates. Yancheng was the home of more of my class than any other city—seventeen out of sixty-three of them hailed from here, although only a few lived there now.

I awoke the next morning in a Yancheng hotel poised by a river, its water running black and foamy with sludge. Like all of China's cities, Yancheng was a helter-skelter hodgepodge of China, a cacophonous, treacherous, malodorous mayhem. Wide boulevards divided rows of buildings with blue-tinted windows and tiny white tiles stained brown by the crusty drool from air conditioner vents. The side streets buzzed with the roar of East Wind trucks, their aging engines spewing black exhaust, buses with screeching brakes, government Audis honking their way through traffic. On all streets and in all directions, browbeaten cyclists pedaled against the tide of China's unruly modernization.

Later that morning, I met Song at a teahouse near the place where he had grown up. The dormitory where his family had lived had long since been demolished, replaced by a small department store and several whorehouses masquerading as barber shops. "Adult health stores," hawking plastic love dolls, dildos, and fake Viagra, dotted every neighborhood in Yancheng, each shop filled to capacity by gawkers fondling the merchandise.

"I don't recognize any of this," Song said as he squinted at the buildings. A classmate named Hu Youxiang, a portly, disheveled official who, like Big Bluffer Ye, was in charge of local censorship, arrived with his sixteen-year-old daughter, Hu Jia. We settled down in rattan chairs. Across from us, a young couple in their late teens snuggled over two fruit juices garnished with pastel umbrellas. The girl cooed over photographs her beau had taken with his cell phone.

Hu Jia sat next to me. She was a sensitive girl, her father explained, who cried easily but who was also full of opinions and not shy about expressing them. She told me she wanted to study chemistry but that her father would not let her because he said it might be bad for her health. He was also worried that because he had no connections in the scientific community, she would not be able to find a job. So she was turning her attention to economics. But economics, she confided, was boring. "In China, it just means studying corruption," she remarked. "We have a lot of corruption in Yancheng." That was certainly true. Her father's former boss had been sentenced to ten years in jail for taking in $1 million in exchange for arranging promotions.

Hu Jia was a so-so student. The pressure to succeed exerted on her by her parents and peers contributed to a nervous tic, a twitching left eyelid, and premature wrinkles from a permanently furrowed brow. She studied until 1 or 2 a.m. each night, fortified by the new drink of choice in China, coffee. "My generation doesn't drink tea," she opined with a proud smile. "We're modern."

During the weekends, she attended special tutoring classes to help her keep up in math, physics, and Chinese. She had not played any sports in two years, nor did she venture out with her friends, who were also closeted in their homes, memorizing. Still, Hu Jia was an adventurer of sorts. She had a boyfriend, a secret that she had recently revealed to her parents after they tried to arrange for her to spend chaperoned time with a friend's son. And she had begun attending a small evangelical church.

Both the boyfriend and the church-going caused a ruckus at home. Her parents were befuddled by her search for a deeper meaning in life and dumbstruck that, at sixteen, she had a boyfriend who she was very likely kissing (or worse). They had not even held hands with a member of the opposite sex before they were twenty-five. Hu Youxiang was against his daughter having a boyfriend. "But I can't stop her because she will find a way to disobey me," he complained. "Parents don't have any real authority anymore in China."

Tiring of the grown-ups, Hu Jia took Leila under her wing. The two moved to another table and nursed their watermelon juices. The difference between them was apparent to everyone in the room. "When I see these two girls, I feel sad for China," said Hu Youxiang.

Leila was not quite ten, but she held herself with a jaunty self-confidence. She would playfully punch her father, joke with his friends, and talk back without fear of reproach. During her travels, she made her own bed, packed her own bag, and figured out how to use the washing machine at Song's mother's house in Yancheng. For a Western child, her independence of spirit and action was routine. But the Chinese were amazed. Leila barely spoke Chinese, but nonetheless her personality shone: bright, creative, and fearless. Chinese call children *xiao pengyou,* "little friend." Leila hated it because she felt it was demeaning. "I am Song An!" she would exclaim when referred to as anything but her Chinese name.

Hu and our classmates from Nanda would tell me over and over that Chinese children were not this way. Competition, even at an early age, made them feel the strain of growing up. At the same time, they were much more coddled than Western children. My classmates paid lip service to the idea that too much pampering makes for a weird, unstable kid. But they spoiled their children all the same. Although she was six years older than Leila, Hu Jia had never made her bed, did not know how to operate anything besides her mobile phone and a computer, and exuded a world-weariness typical of many Chinese children. I asked Hu Jia what courses she was interested in at school. She replied that nothing really interested her. "We have to study it so I study it, but my favorite hobby is sleeping," she said. I had heard that line from scores of young Chinese. Sleeping? A hobby?

"I look at her and I am jealous," Hu Jia confessed at one point about Leila. "She's so free and independent."

Over lunch that day, our conversation turned to a string of recent food safety scandals that had killed scores of children. Pesticides had accidentally been brewed with a batch of soybean milk in Jiangsu Province, and a ham company in Zhejiang had acknowledged smoking its product with DDT. The head of the national food safety department had recently stated that he himself did not trust the food. Hu commended him. "This shows China is advancing," he said. "At least we can admit problems."

Song had the opposite reaction. "He should be fired!" he declared. "How can he say something like that? That's a serious dereliction of duty. In Europe, if he said that, he would have to step down."

Hu glanced sideways at Song. "Little classmate," he said, "you have been away for too long. This type of honesty is rare."

Song and Leila left Yancheng for an extended tour. Song wanted to show his daughter China and reconnect with his homeland. First stop was Shaoshan, the hometown of Chairman Mao, in Hunan Province. The town had become a capital of Chinese kitsch. Mao had been transformed into a kind of secular god, and the devotional Red Guards who had flocked there in the 1960s on their revolutionary pilgrimages had been replaced by avaricious touts hawking talismans.

In the mid-1990s, starting in southern China, drivers started dangling pictures of Mao from their rearview mirrors, claiming that the chairman's vibes, like a talisman of St. Christopher, protected them from accidents. The fad was fueled by nostalgia on the part of urban workers for the good old days, when their status was high and when the hucksters, smugglers, corrupt cops, rip-off artists, and gangsters who were now on top had been locked up in labor camps. This fad had grown to such proportions that truckers glued large portraits of the Great Helmsman over half their windshield, maximizing Mao's juju even as they expanded the blind spot.

In Shaoshan souvenir shops, the image of the man responsible for more deaths than Stalin could be purchased inside a snow globe that rained silver dollars and one euro coin. At a nearby temple, rebuilt in the 1990s after it had been destroyed by Red Guards during the Cultural Revolution, monks claimed Mao's mother had an immaculate conception and sold amulets of Mao as a reincarnation of one of the 500 *Luohan* monks who followed in Buddha's footsteps.

"Which reincarnation was Mao?" Song queried a grizzled monk selling a gold-colored charm of the Chairman.

"I can't remember," he replied.

"Were Deng Xiaoping or Zhou Enlai reincarnations, too?" Song asked.

"No, only Mao," the monk intoned, banging a small gong.

Song and Leila returned to Yancheng in August, and Maria Luisa joined them. Song had made plans to watch the Asia Cup soccer finals with his old high school buddies. China's team, playing under a foreign coach, was facing Japan.

Song and several friends went to a bar to watch the game on TV. Spectators in the stadium booed during the Japanese national anthem, and the few Japanese fans who ventured to Beijing to attend the game were pelted with garbage. "Death to the Japanese," read the signs. "Bomb Tokyo," "Exterminate the Jap Midgets."

The roots of Chinese hatred of Japan are twisted and deep. The obvious explanation is Japan's occupation of China, which began in 1932 and ended with the defeat of the Imperial Army by the United States in 1945. Japanese troops massacred hundreds of thousands of Chinese soldiers and civilians, raped tens of thousands of women, and ravaged huge swaths of countryside. Japanese scientists conducted gruesome human experiments, injecting Chinese prisoners with deadly molds and boiling others alive. Japan never sincerely apologized for the atrocities it committed.

But there are other, more invidious reasons why China hates Japan. One is China's sense of superiority. Chinese consider Japan a cultural upstart, an inferior tributary of the mighty Han race, a vassal to the Middle Kingdom. Japan took its writing system, its Buddhism, and even its architecture from China—all this more than one thousand years ago. As such, it drives the Chinese all the crazier that upstart Japan should have overtaken them throughout the last century.

The Communist Party has also encouraged Japan-bashing as part of a policy to replace the discredited ideology of communism with a resentful nationalism designed to keep the Chinese united through hatred or fear of the outside world. Since the 1970s, the Japanese have poured tens of billions of dollars in low-interest loans and donations into China—building airports, highways, factories, and ports as well as planting forests. These contributions have never been publicly acknowledged by the Communist

Party. After years of complaints from the Japanese government, China finally allowed a plaque to be erected at the gleaming new Beijing International Airport acknowledging that it was built with a low-interest Japanese loan. The plaque was hung in a hall in the administrative wing of the airport where no travelers would see it.

The bar was crowded with other fans who'd gathered to watch the soccer final. One Japanese goal appeared to have ricocheted into the net off the hand of a Japanese player. Song and his buddies cried foul. The referees seemed to look the other way as Japanese players flagrantly fouled the Chinese team. Song's friends shouted in outrage.

Japan won 2–1. In Beijing, the fans' frenzy for Japanese blood reached such a pitch that hundreds of riot police massed at the Workers Stadium to protect the Japanese team. In Yancheng, the crowd at the bar booed and pelted the big-screen TV with chopsticks. Song was again in the role of the ingenue, amazed and disturbed at his countrymen's fervor. The last time he'd witnessed such an outpouring of passion was in 1981 when Nanda students marched to celebrate the women's volleyball world championship. The emotions then were somehow "cleaner," he said, less angry. "We're bad losers," he remarked.

Song observed that nationalism had intensified since he had last been in China, a curious direction for the country to be taking since it was stronger and more respected than it had been in years. You would think we would be more self-confident, not less, he mused.

On the bus back to Nanjing, Song told me that despite China's changes—its crass commercialization, the harsh way people treated each other—he still longed to return. If he did, though, the price would be high: Maria Luisa could not follow him, which meant Leila would also stay in Rome.

Nonetheless, with his ballooning Chinese bank account, Song figured he could afford to live in China half the year. His sister, Yang Su, was in the process of constructing an enormous house for the family on a field in Yancheng—a sprawling three-story villa with a winding staircase and faux marble columns. To honor her little brother, she'd modeled it after a picture she saw of an Italian villa. When I saw it, it was just a concrete shell, but it was vast.

Song's personal goal, he confided, had never changed. He still wanted to be "free." But his concept of freedom differed from that in the West. "I don't want anyone to bother me," he explained, meaning not just Chinese state security, but also his wife, perhaps even Leila. As long as Song stuck to sports and did not write about Tibet or other sensitive issues, he would have a nice life. But it was unclear if Song would be satisfied being China's Red Smith. His spirit was too restless.

Living in Italy all these years had preserved Song's idealism, the infectious, blind hope that made China so vibrant in the 1980s. Absent during the Tiananmen crackdown and China's transformation in the 1990s into a society out for cash and kicks, Song maintained his innocence about the corruption, the swindles, and the general disintegration of whatever remained of traditional values.

How could he believe he could be free in China, of all places, I wondered. If he returned, what would stop state security from ordering his arrest? With just a click of the mouse, Chinese police could read all of the posts Song had made on Internet Web sites calling for China to begin negotiations with the Dalai Lama. People were routinely hauled off for lesser crimes. In 2004 and 2005, state security agents rounded up scores of people for posting their opinions on the Internet, slapping them with lengthy prison terms. In 2005, for the sixth year in a row, China had more journalists in prison than any other country.

Maria Luisa was right. Something of his father—the spurned supplicant to the Communist Party—remained in Song, exemplified by his slavish brownnosing of the Nanjing security agent and his dream of being welcomed back into China's embrace. Near the end of their stay, Song, Maria Luisa, and I went for coffee at a Nanjing Starbucks. As we savored our espressos, Song told a Taoist fable about a young boy who goes to another country to learn their way of walking. Before mastering the steps, however, he forgets his own and has to crawl home.

"Perhaps," he said, "I am this boy."

33

THE ENTHUSIASMS OF HIGH ALTITUDE

I had prided myself on knowing how to walk the Chinese way, shuffling and jostling in the crowds, but then something happened that reminded me that only my own way of walking, my own way of living, would lead me to where I wanted to go.

In October 1999, my boss at the *Post*, Phil Bennett, came to China on a visit. I gave him a choice: the bright lights of urban China or a poor Tibetan village. As his plans already included Beijing, he chose the Tibetan boondocks. Earlier that year, I had met an American couple who were working on a project sponsored by the Nature Conservancy, a U.S.-based environmental group, to create China's first national park. The couple, Ed Norton and Ann McBride, proposed that we fly down to Kunming, the capital of Yunnan Province, and trek to a Tibetan hamlet along Yunnan's border with Tibet—the same area I'd traveled to with Fay in 1982.

Phil and I flew to Kunming and met up with Ed and Ann. The next night at dinner, we were joined by a woman named Zhang Mei, who would be our guide. Two things struck me about Mei: her unnervingly steady brown eyes and her absolutely flawless English. When I pulled out a bottle of Australian Shiraz, she smiled. "I haven't had that in a long time," she said. My interest was piqued when, without an iota of self-consciousness, she poured a glass for herself—something I had never seen a Chinese woman do.

Mei was a native of Yunnan. She had received her MBA at Harvard in 1996, the only Chinese at the school who was neither a scion of a powerful family nor a longtime U.S. resident. After graduation, she returned to China to work for the consulting firm McKinsey & Company, but had since left to strike out on her own. Mei had recently started an adventure travel company called Wildchina. She had volunteered to lead our trek, figuring that she might cadge free press in the *Washington Post*.

Mei was impressed with my Chinese but also found me arrogant, another one of those know-it-all foreigners who think they understand China better than the Chinese. As for me, my interaction with Chinese women had been pretty much limited to floozies and opportunists. Mei definitely didn't fit either category. And just as I no longer needed a Chinese woman to get into Chinese society, Mei had no need of a foreigner to get out.

Nonetheless, Ann stoked my interest. "She's flirting with you," she whispered to me at one point during the party. "She put her hair up. That's a sign." I lost a few points, however, when, after dinner, Phil stopped to wait for Mei to get her bicycle and I blithely walked away.

Our trek began with an early morning flight to Zhongdian, eleven thousand feet above sea level in the mountainous far northeastern corner of Yunnan. In order to lure tourists to its lofty heights, the Zhongdian county government was in the process of changing its name to Shangri-La, a nonsensical moniker lifted from the 1937 James Hilton novel *Lost Horizon*. By breakfast time, Mei's opinion of me began to shift. We stopped at an eatery run by a family of Hui—Muslim Chinese who trade in animal pelts and run what are generally considered the cleanest restaurants in these parts. As we downed bowls of steaming beef noodles, I did what I normally do: slurp. Mei, perhaps because of her years in the United States, did not. I was the country bumpkin Chinese and she the polished Harvard girl. Our eyes met and we laughed.

After a full day's drive we reached Deqin, a small town clutching the side of a mountain. No longer the military zone it was when I last visited in 1982, the town was now a jumble of breakneck development and shambling old ways. We set off the next morning for a small village that would be our push-off point for the hike into the Yubeng Valley at the foot of Mount Kawagebo, the second most sacred mountain of Tibetan Buddhism. Mei turned green as the van careened up the spottily paved road that hugged the mountainside. I asked for her hand and dug into an acupuncture pressure point between her index finger and thumb that supposedly relieves nausea. She smiled. As the van swerved on, I watched her as she kneaded the point by herself.

We began our trek at eight thousand feet, climbing to twelve thousand feet through a deciduous forest laced with moss. Tibetan pilgrims, a monk carrying a motorcycle helmet, old women mumbling prayers, and young men in ragged shoes sprinting uphill without taking an extra breath were our only companions apart from our plodding pack horses. Tibetan prayer flags and mounds of rocks heralded the path's sacred spots.

It's hard to say exactly when and why two people fall in love. Certainly the prayer flags, the spinning prayer wheels, the ancient pilgrimage routes, and other man-made messengers of hope and mystery lent a helping hand. I had become so entranced by Mei that I had stopped trying to bond with my boss. I found myself walking behind her a lot, in part because she was in better shape than I was, in part because I liked staring at her legs. I cracked a lot of jokes. Mei got them all. I hadn't used English to chat up a woman in years. I was so rusty, I switched to Chinese for the punch lines.

Yubeng bordered a cascading river at the foot of a valley pointing toward Kawagebo's glacial peaks, 22,113 feet high. A waterfall splashing down the mountainside could be seen from the porch of the simple guest-house where we slept. I was used to Chinese relationships that were consummated quickly and withered soon after. But nothing happened during that week Mei and I spent in the hills: no hand holding and certainly no protestations of love.

As the trip neared its end, I began plotting to see her again. I suggested to Ann that she host Thanksgiving at her house in Kunming and even offered to bring a turkey from Beijing. "What are you doing for Thanksgiving?" Ann asked Mei. "I guess I'm eating the turkey," she replied.

Still, Thanksgiving was more than a month away, and both of us were growing impatient. I called Mei for the first time two nights after I'd returned to Beijing. Mei had a problem. The proxy server I installed on her computer was slowing her access to the Internet. Across the country, Chinese were downloading proxy servers that allowed them to access news sites, such as those of CNN and the *New York Times,* which the Chinese government blocked. Could I help? I had already sent her the first of what would prove to be 150 love letters. Soon we began writing, and calling, and writing and calling some more. I returned to Kunming to see her. My father, sensing my ebullience, warned "of the false enthusiasms of high altitude." Mei's father, noting that I was forty, was decidedly more matter-of-fact: "Hasn't he married already?"

During my visits to Kunming and to her family's homestead near the banks of Fuxian (Touching Gods) Lake, forty miles south of the city, I learned the history of Mei's family. In one of the strange and secret ways that life seems to double back on itself, I discovered that, twenty-five generations ago, the Zhangs had been natives of Nanjing.

In 1368, the first emperor of the Ming Dynasty decided on Nanjing as his capital. Because he feared spies and assassins, he exiled Nanjing's then three hundred thousand inhabitants to the outer regions of China's empire, mostly to Yunnan Province, up against the mountainous Tibetan border, and Qinghai, a desert region in the far west. The Zhangs were among the group of merchants and artisans sent to Yunnan. They fared well as landowners, businessmen, and educators. Before the Communist Revolution, the clan, more than one hundred strong, lived together in a compound of houses with connecting courtyards.

The Communist Revolution drenched the Zhang family in blood. The Communists executed one of Mei's great-grandfathers and her great-uncle because they owned land. Another great-grandfather committed suicide by overdosing on opium after enduring weeks of vicious beatings. Young revolutionaries ransacked his house and burned the last copy of the family tree, a record which dated to the fourteenth century.

Mei's father, Zhang Minqiang, was born in 1947, the third of five siblings and the only boy. Because the Communists labeled his elder sister a "rightist" in 1956, Mei's father lost the chance to finish elementary school. Instead he worked on dam sites from the age of eight, first as a guard and then as an electrician. During the Great Leap Forward, as famine swept through Yunnan Province, he witnessed his neighbors cooking and then eating the flesh of a dead peasant child.

In January 1968, Mei's father married Liu Rongzhen, also a child of parents with political problems and a laborer on the dam site. The couple received ten sets of the *Collected Works of Chairman Mao* as wedding presents. Mei's father coped with the madness of the times by cracking the occasional joke. At a political study meeting he came close to being named a counterrevolutionary when he posed this question: "If there's an electrical fire, should we stop studying Mao and put it out?" No one replied; after the meeting his superiors warned him to stop asking stupid questions.

The couple's first child was a son. Mei was born in 1971. Mei is a common name in China, but the character used for it is generally the one that means "plum blossom." Her father chose the character for rose because it is pretty but prickly, and not just anyone can pick it.

Four years later, Mei's younger brother was born. The family moved from dam site to dam site, living in shacks with walls fashioned from rammed earth, grass, and thatched bamboo. When the family spoke, even in whispers, their neighbors could hear. When they cooked, everyone knew what was for dinner. Mei's father made a ceiling out of newspaper, a process complicated by a regulation that all photographs of Mao, of which there were plenty, had to be pasted face out. They used a swath of burlap for a door and slept together on a skinny straw mattress atop two wooden boards. The only thing decorating their wall was a calendar. Drinking water came from a fetid stream and had to be hauled up a steep incline. They purified it by putting powdered aluminum into a rag, tying it shut, and sloshing it around in the bucket. The mud sank to the bottom; they drank the water on top. A clock and a flashlight comprised the only electrical items the family possessed. It wasn't until the 1980s that they owned a bicycle.

For years, Mei's mother had bouts of crippling depression. In the fall of 1979, while the rest of China was buoyed by the possibilities of economic reforms and new, unprecedented freedoms, Mei's mother sank deeper into despair. One day in October 1979, she drank a bottle of insecticide while eight-year-old Mei looked on. She died that day, with her daughter as a witness.

Mei's father faced a dark future raising three children alone. During the Cultural Revolution, the party secretary in charge of the dam had been placed under house arrest and was later beaten by Red Guards before being kicked out of his apartment and forced to live in a worker's shack, which by chance was next door to the Zhangs. Mei's father helped the former party secretary as much as he could—little kindnesses that were not forgotten. When the Cultural Revolution ended, the party secretary resumed his position. Mei's father asked him in turn for help in obtaining a transfer to the big city, Kunming, and he agreed.

A few years later, Mei's father remarried. Little Duan, as everyone called her, never accepted Mei or her two brothers as her own. As the years passed, Mei's younger brother lost his self-confidence, while her elder brother turned to drink. Mei took refuge in her studies. She excelled at an English-based high school in Kunming and then graduated with honors from Yunnan University. She took a job at a Thai bank in Yunnan. In 1994 she went to Harvard.

Mei arrived in the United States in August. Transfering in San Francisco to a domestic flight to Boston, she was perturbed that the airlines didn't offer a meal. "America's supposed to be advanced," she thought. "Why don't the airlines hand out food?" Arriving at Logan Airport, she searched for a luggage cart. Unlike in China, it cost one dollar. "That's eight *yuan*," she thought, the same amount she charged to tutor foreigners Chinese back in Yunnan. "No way."

Crossing the Charles River on the T-line, she saw the trees had already begun to change. She got off the train at Harvard Square, and cried. In her college journal, she had promised herself she would attend Harvard. Now that impossible dream had come true.

Mei was amazed at the choices Americans had—from toilet paper and milk to relationships, jobs, spiritual pursuits, and lifestyles. She was flabbergasted by how poor she was compared to the other students studying at the bastion of American capitalism. In the last job she'd had in China, she had made the equivalent of twenty dollars a month. Academically, she felt miles behind and worried that the business school's policy of forced attrition would catch her in its net. She'd never heard of Goldman Sachs, Morgan Stanley, and her employer-to-be, McKinsey & Company. She didn't know the difference between international trade and international finance and couldn't read a balance sheet. As she sat through lectures, she'd understand each individual word but collectively they made no sense. And who was Ross Perot anyway? she asked herself.

I had known Mei for barely two months, but I knew I wanted to marry her. I loved her hair, her wit, and her mind. If her life was a movie, I said to myself, I wouldn't want it to stop. I wanted to be a part of it. Unlike many of the women I had known in China who seemed to have misplaced their roots, Mei embodied the best elements of the eternal Chinese character: diligence, adaptability, and a reverence for family. And unlike many Chinese, she took me for what I was—a man, not an animal, a god, or a foreign devil.

After Thanksgiving, Mei visited me in Beijing. One morning, I made her breakfast in bed, got down on one knee, and proposed. She smiled and said, "Yes."

In the fall of 1999, Mei took me to the family compound near Kunming to meet her eighty-year-old grandmother, whom everyone called Nainai. Nainai, who came up to my waist, gave me the once over and pronounced herself satisfied. Upon hearing of our decision to get married in 2000, Mei's father nodded, but Nainai was living on a different time line.

"That's too late," she declared. "Why not before New Year's Day?"

It would be neither proper nor propitious, she said, for Mei to marry in the same year as her younger brother, who was planning a wedding in 2000. We had a few weeks left.

Mei and I went back to the United States for Christmas with my parents, who had retired to Seattle. On December 22, we awoke in a guest room at the Washington Athletic Club and pondered our future. Without much discussion, we went down to the King County government building, to an office that sold marriage, business, and pet licenses. The process was eerily simple. Raise your right hand, swear, sign, and, in three days, you can wed. During lunch at my parents' house, as we passed around a bowl of romaine salad, I remarked that we had done something "productive" that morning.

"We got a marriage license," I said.

My mother's jaw dropped. I'd spent my life springing surprises—good and bad—on my parents. This was a whopper. We needed to find a judge. After scrolling down a list of district court judges, I called Eileen Kato.

"Hello, Judge Kato's chambers."

"Ah, does Judge Kato do weddings?"

"It's the favorite part of my job!"

On Tuesday, December 27, at 4:31 p.m., we were wed. Judge Kato, a third-generation Japanese American, performed the ceremony in her courtroom, blew bubbles, and read from Kahlil Gibran's *The Prophet*.

34

SEVERE AND ACUTE

In early 2002, Mei became pregnant. I noticed that as her belly expanded, people looked at us differently. I was no longer stealing one of China's maidens. I had been transformed into "a son-in-law of China." On September 27, 2002, at 3:30 a.m., Mei woke me up. "It's time," she said.

Late that night, our son was born after an emergency cesarean. We named him Dali—a homonym for a town in Yunnan where Mei spent her early years. The characters mean to "arrive standing." But Dali came into the world pretty much flat on his back, with an infection and his lungs full of mucus. Our obstetrician had prematurely broken Mei's water, she'd spiked a fever, and the antibiotic the doctor gave her hadn't worked. (Like many drugs in China, it turned out to have long expired.)

Luckily, Dali's first few months were not as eventful as his first few days. The birth had weakened his lungs and, aggravated by Beijing's noxious air, he was sick often. But we all learned to cope.

Then, when Dali was about thirteen weeks old, we had a health scare that rocked not just my small family but all of China. And it came from a source none of us had expected to be so lethal.

There is a joke with a punch line that says Chinese eat everything on four legs except a table, and everything that flies except an airplane. That joke became ever truer with the emergence of high-class restaurants and the continued flow of state money for sumptuous banquets. In the late 1990s,

Chinese cuisine experienced a renaissance. Cities where the lights had gone out at 10 p.m. now bustled into the wee hours, brimming with neon-encased restaurants, steamy noodle stalls, and hot-pot outlets serving up hefty portions of calf's liver, pig's brain, and cow's throat.

The most adventurous eaters in a country of dining daredevils are the Cantonese in China's south. The San Diego Zoo pales in comparison to a stroll through a live food mart in Guangzhou. I have seen rats, dogs, cats, owls, a menagerie of waterfowl, monkeys (favored for their brains), and bears (favored for their paws) locked up in wire-mesh cages, their contents so valuable that night watchmen loll atop them in bedrolls. Water tanks teem with sea cucumbers, abalone, scallops, and an aquarium's worth of fish.

In late 2002, before my son was one hundred days old, a virus, somewhere in Guangdong Province, jumped to a human from one of these animals, most probably a civet cat, a fruit-eating creature that looks like a small fox crossed with a raccoon. (The Cantonese like to eat civet cat braised with ginger.) Within weeks, people were dropping dead from a strange respiratory disorder that the experts named Severe Acute Respiratory Syndrome, or SARS. Southern China is an incubator for flu viruses because people live cheek-to-jowl with farm animals. Influenza viruses routinely jump from ducks to pigs and then from pigs to people. In the farms of southern China, all three species cohabitate.

In February 2003, I flew down to Guangzhou to write about the disease, encasing my face in a surgical mask. Air travel had become a deadly efficient vehicle for spreading SARS. Speaking with doctors, government officials, and journalists, I learned that by December 2002, the Communist Party in Guangdong knew it had a serious health problem. Nonetheless, it kept quiet because it did not want to scare off the millions of tourists who descend on southern China every Chinese New Year, which in 2003 fell on February 1. Faced with a rampaging disease which the party refused to acknowledge, residents in Guangzhou turned to folk remedies. A special type of vinegar was rumored to kill the virus, so scores of people headed from Guangzhou to the farms where it was produced in Shanxi Province, one thousand miles away. The virus spread with them.

When one of the afflicted from Shanxi traveled to Beijing, the virus jumped to the capital. SARS exploded, infecting thousands. What was worse, it touched ground in Beijing in a facility run by the People's Liberation

Army, an independent fiefdom outside government control. The PLA declined to cooperate with any government authorities and also refused to hand over information, especially once the World Health Organization got involved.

After two weeks in Guangdong, I returned to Beijing, my face again wrapped in a face mask. I had a scratchy throat when we took off, and by the time we landed three hours later it had turned into a full-blown viral infection. I had a five-month-old boy with bad lungs at home. Did I have SARS? Would he contract it?

Mei quarantined me, forbidding me to touch Dali and exiling me to a room in the back of our apartment. It took the greatest self-control to keep my hands off my boy. At the time, the World Health Organization said that only patients exhibiting a fever had SARS. I never had a fever. Only later did they discover that many SARS cases never broke temperatures of 98.6.

China's Communists had been covering up disasters for decades. Dams split apart in the 1960s, killing tens of thousands, and no one knew about it outside the afflicted locale. AIDS ravaged the countryside in the late 1990s, and the authorities ignored it for more than five years. SARS showed that the party's priority was self-preservation; the well-being of the people came second.

For months, officials lied publicly about the death toll. The party was particularly gung-ho about suppressing news of SARS because China was going through its first leadership transition since Jiang Zemin took power in 1989. In November 2001, Hu Jintao, China's vice president, was given Jiang's job as the party general secretary, the first handover in Communist Chinese history not marked by bloodshed or the death of a leader. SARS exploded in Beijing just as Hu and the rest of the new government were preparing for the annual legislative session in March. No bad news could be reported at this time.

Hu was also proving to be much less tolerant of the press than his predecessor. Whereas Jiang had at least lived through a few years of China before the revolution, the younger Hu knew nothing of that freer world. Hu was devoting himself to creating a more efficient authoritarian system, tightening surveillance on dissidents and toughening restrictions on the press. He preached an asceticism that harked back to the medieval authoritarians—the neo-Confucianists. His goal for China was *ben xiang xiaokang*, literally "to sprint toward little comforts," in other words, a middle-class existence—minus free speech. Under Hu, scores of dissidents were arrested for posting opinions on the Internet, while chat-room Web sites established by students at leading universities, including Nanda's, were shut down.

The party's edifice of obfuscation began to crack on April 4, when a senior military surgeon wrote a letter to the Chinese press accusing the health minister of lying on state-run TV. The Chinese press could not report on the letter's contents, but a copy found its way into the hands of a *Time* magazine correspondent and from there to the Internet and back into China. Recovered from my flu, I met the surgeon, Jiang Yanyong, shortly after his letter had appeared on the Internet. "In today's China only the old are brave," said the wizened seventy-one-year-old doctor. "Everyone else has been bought off or is too scared of losing their new lifestyles. I was tortured during the Cultural Revolution and sewed up bleeding students during the Tianammen Square killings. My children are abroad. What are they going to do to an old man who has seen everything?" Jiang was essentially correct. He was later taken into custody after writing another open letter, this one calling for a revision of the government's verdict on the Tiananmen Square massacre. But he was released after a few months.

Not wanting to appear like it was caving in to a geriatric surgeon, the party waited sixteen more days to acknowledge the seriousness of the epidemic. And still, it never owned up to its lies. On April 20, the government sacked the health minister and the mayor of Beijing for their failure to deal with the crisis. Millions of people were then quarantined. Every airport was fitted with infrared devices designed to weed out feverish travelers. Checkpoints sprouted up on highways and byways across the country where drivers had their temperature taken and their cars disinfected. Beijing's streets were transformed from a bustling mass of humanity to a scantly attended Halloween dance where everyone wore the same costume, a white surgical mask. Stores, parks, and restaurants were empty. During the height of the scare, Mei and I spent a glorious day carrying Dali around the Forbidden City. On average, twenty thousand tourists visit the two-square-mile home to China's emperors every day; but on that day, only forty of us were there. By the time it abated, SARS had killed nearly eight hundred people and infected more than eight thousand, most of them in China, Hong Kong, and Vietnam. Western experts predicted that the SARS epidemic would teach China that openness was the way of the future. In reality, the party took away a different lesson: that it needed to control information all the more tightly.

My family was lucky. Neither Mei nor I lost any friends or colleagues, and Dali continued to get stronger as the months went by. On his first birthday, in tune with tradition, we put him in the middle of a circle of objects—a stethoscope, tools, Chinese and American money, a book, a paintbrush, a calligraphy brush, kitchen implements, a toy truck—to see which he would choose. The Chinese belief is that his choice would give an indication of Dali's career path. Dali squirmed across the floor and picked up an American one dollar bill. Mei noted that it was the smallest denomination in the pile.

35

HIGH TIDES

On a wintry afternoon in late 2003, I received a phone call from a man who identified himself only as a musician. His voice sounded elderly. "A friend of mine has seen you during a press conference on TV," he said. "He wanted me to pass along greetings to you." Shortly after, I met the musician in the lobby of one of Beijing's marble-and-glass hotels. By this time I had already guessed who had asked him to call me: Liu Gang.

For the first time since we parted at a dank eatery following the June 4, 1989, crackdown just days before his arrest, I arranged to see Liu Gang. As the day approached, I became increasingly uneasy. Was he going to seek vengeance? Did I really want to confront this troubling bit of my past?

I drove to his apartment complex, a gated compound on Beijing's east side, feeling queasy as I parked, and climbed to his third-floor walk-up. I rang the doorbell and Liu Gang answered it. I looked him in his eyes, and they were friendly, almost twinkling. It was a lot to absorb, meeting a guy who was thrown in jail because of me. He reached out his hand to shake mine; it was the same firm handshake and warm like his eyes. I must have seemed reluctant to enter his apartment because he basically yanked me inside.

Liu Gang had grown a beard and his skin was tan from the southern sun. He had not put on weight, and still had his easy laugh. He had changed his name to put distance between himself and his past as a political prisoner.

I learned that Liu Gang had been sentenced to two and a half years in prison for breaking martial law provisions. In what was basically a show trial, he still put on a spirited defense, arguing that he had not given me access to state secrets. The speech he had read to me so long ago in that car in Beijing was printed in its entirety in the *People's Daily* the very next day. Liu Gang served his sentence in Beijing's infamous Qingcheng Prison. During the first few months he was incarcerated, he was beaten regularly by guards and fellow inmates and forced to stand in "the jet plane" position—bent at the waist, arms out to the sides, one foot off the floor—for hours.

Liu brought out a stack of photographs of his time in jail. He was rail thin, and his head was shaved. Somebody, however, was looking out for him. After months in prison, several high-ranking People's Liberation Army officers—replete with their epaulets and entourage—entered his cell block. After that, the beatings stopped, and Liu Gang was put in charge of a group of prisoners. Though constantly forced to engage in political study, he was allowed to write music and read. In jail, he wrote three hundred pieces of music, which today sit in a drawer in his Beijing home.

Liu Gang was freed in 1991. His wife had divorced him, but he still had a place to live; again, it appeared that someone in the military had protected him. Officers sentenced to more than two and a half years in jail were automatically given dishonorable discharges; Liu's sentence was exactly two and a half years, so he was allowed back into the service at his old salary. Every so often, a cadre would come by to talk with Liu to gauge if jail had adjusted his attitude. Mostly, he was irate for having wasted almost three years of what had been an extremely productive life.

Liu Gang ditched the stifling atmosphere of Beijing, where hard-liners like Premier Li Peng were busy turning back the clock on the reforms, and headed south to Shenzhen. There he joined hundreds of former political prisoners and other casualties of the Tiananmen crackdown seeking anonymity and a chance at a new life. He found work as a day laborer putting up drywall at a Shenzhen mall. Several composers from Hong Kong visited him on the work site. His foreman took an interest in him and gave him a desk job, allowing him to write music. A few commissions came in for small works, and Liu Gang's career took off again.

By 1995, Liu Gang had remarried, this time to another composer. Soon thereafter she bore him a son. He left the military a year later and started working full-time as a freelance composer, eventually making enough money to buy a sprawling two-thousand-square-foot apartment in a quiet Beijing suburb to the east of the city and a similar apartment in the west.

In January 2004, I went to Shenzhen to hear a performance of one of Liu Gang's new pieces: an opera memorializing an obscure victory of Communist forces during World War II. China was going through a nostalgia kick similar to the 1950s fad in the United States in the 1970s. In China, the longing was for the early days of the revolution and the fervent idealism of the past. By riding this wave of reminiscence, Liu Gang was both enriching himself and currying favor with the party.

I arrived the afternoon before opening night to check out the rehearsal. The concert was to be held in the Shenzhen Opera House—a cavernous box covered in blue glass. A top conductor from Shanghai had been brought in to conduct for Liu, but the two had been at loggerheads all week; Liu, who wanted to make changes in the score, could not reach the conductor, who had brought his lover to Shenzhen and turned off his phone at night. I walked into the hall as Liu Gang and the conductor squared off.

Standing in the orchestra pit, Liu Gang picked up the score and slammed it on the stage. "I can't find you at night," he yelled. "You're off with your little honey."

"You should have made these changes before," the conductor retorted.

"You're irresponsible!" Liu Gang countered. "You're too busy fucking."

The conductor grabbed the tall chair he had been using for the rehearsal and tossed it into the seats toward Liu Gang. It was a good throw for a small man, landing one seat from Liu Gang.

"What's your meaning?" Liu Gang yelled. This phrase gets lost in translation, but in Chinese it is the traditional precursor to a fight.

At this point the entire hall—symphony, chorus, and onlookers—was in an uproar. Liu Gang was forced to apologize for starting the fight and then went outside to smoke a cigarette and cool down. An older woman, whom he introduced to me as Teacher Wang, approached him.

"We Chinese have a common disease," she said to Liu Gang as he fumed and she placed her hand on his arm. "We don't do things responsibly. We agree to do things and then do them badly. In the West, this would never happen. If you hired a conductor, he would prepare. But what can you do? He hasn't prepared, but you can't explode like that because his symphony and his people don't know what the real picture is. You just have to take it." Liu Gang finished his cigarette and went back into the theater to continue the rehearsal.

That night, thousands flocked to the performance. No one in the audience had paid for their tickets; they had been handed out to government work units and state-owned companies by the city propaganda bureau. Liu Gang worked the crowd in the VIP room, where old Communists, with enormous flowers pinned to the lapels of their shiny polyester Mao suits, sipped tea. The mayor of a small city arrived wearing white shoes and smoking a cigarette from an enormously long holder. Then the show began.

As the audience munched on sunflower seeds and boisterously cleared their throats, two narrators walked to the front of the stage and waxed nostalgic about the old days when "the high tide of the revolution—each wave higher than the last—washed over China."

One narrator, sporting a prominent toupee, went on: "The Chinese people were being bit by wild animals."

Enter the strings.

"The blood of our race covered the land."

Enter the wind instruments.

"It was do or die for the Chinese people."

Enter drums and horns.

Next a woman with very big hair in an ill-fitting dress festooned with flowers approached the mike. "Under the glorious leadership of the Chinese Communist Party, we won our victory and became free forever," she said breathlessly. More strings. A crescendo.

"We became forever free, forever victorious," she screeched.

The toupee piped up: "Forever free, forever victorious."

The orchestra joined in, the conductor jerking spasmodically.

Three tenors sang a jaunty ditty about "killing the midget Jap bastards," a real crowd pleaser. A chorus of middle-aged women then launched into an airy tune about marksmanship with the chorus "gun 'em down, gun 'em down, watch the blood flow out of their eyes." The crowd swayed with the beat. The show went on like this for more than two hours, during which I counted fifteen uses of the expression "the high tide of the revolution—each wave higher than the last—washed over China." This was slightly odd because in Chinese *high tide* also means "orgasm." The show ended. I met Liu Gang afterward for dinner.

"What's with all the high tides?" I asked Liu Gang, over a feast of stir-fried frogs legs and baked cuttlefish.

"I wrote most of that stuff. The lyricist didn't know what he was doing," he said with a wry smile. "It's all a joke, a big necessary joke.

"Before I went to prison, I was pure-hearted," he continued. "But inside, my political commissars taught me how to lie. They taught me how to be insincere. So I learned it and learned it well, and that's how I play it now.

"You know my father returned from the United States in 1949 to join the building of a new China and suffered for his decision for forty years," Liu said. "Mao jailed him. Then he died. What was his crime? Loving China. When I got out of jail, I made a decision. I wasn't going to suffer again. I wasn't going to work for anyone but myself anymore. It's about me now. Forget the nation, the people, the party, the big issues of the day. It's about me."

Collaboration was necessary for an easy life, and Liu Gang had more than an easy life, he was thriving. He had recently composed music to commemorate the 110th anniversary of the birth of Chairman Mao, the man responsible for destroying his father, and had planned the theme song to a propaganda documentary on the party's glorious handling of SARS. Having reached such a level of cynicism and deep understanding of the Communist system, he only wanted to make as much money off it as possible.

Liu Gang said his main goal in life was to secure a place for his son in a music school in the United States—a not-so-subtle transference of his own dreams and desires onto the next generation and a way to complete the circle started by his father. A short text message from his son came to him over dinner after the show. "Father, Mother tells me that your show tonight was a success. I hope that when I am older I will be able to write and produce a symphony just like you. Son."

36

THUGS' REVOLUTION

Like Liu Gang, Book Idiot Zhou was trying to make the best possible life within a system that he loathed.

In early April 2005, Zhou and I returned to his ancestral village. No longer Production Brigade 7 of Shen Kitchen Commune, it had been renamed Li Zao (or Li's Kitchen). The Qingming Festival—during which Chinese traditionally honor their ancestors—was upon us, and Zhou planned to sweep the graves of his parents and grandparents.

We stayed at the home of Sheng Hongyuan, Zhou's business partner in the Dongtai county seat, about ten miles from Li's Kitchen. Sheng lived on the top floor of a three-story building that he owned. Downstairs was a car repair shop, a singles dating service, and a car wash. Following Zhou's lead, Sheng had also bought a white car, a Honda made in Guangzhou.

The next morning, Zhou got his white VW Bora polished at the car wash for the ride home to Li Zao. He also bought a stack of ceremonial paper money to burn for the dead. Driving into his village, Zhou had the air of a conquering hero returning home. He had put on a tie for the occasion. We coasted up to the brick house he had built three decades earlier after harvesting more than seven tons of grass, parked the car in the small courtyard, and headed out for a stroll.

The village was not badly off for a rural backwater. Every courtyard had a motorcycle. Many of the men and women had jobs in factories rather than in the fields, freeing them from the vagaries of Mother Nature. Zhou began pointing people out, repeating the same words like a mantra:

"Fate is strange." We passed a wizened woman who looked to be in her sixties, but was actually Zhou's age—fifty.

"I had a crush on her when we were young," he said. "She was the daughter of a party guy. Her mother looked down on our family because we were poor. Her mother came over to our house and left in a huff, saying, 'The holes were so big in their walls that a cow could walk through the house.' She ended up marrying a local farmer. He gets drunk and beats her."

We met the elderly parents of the first man killed in Zhou's village during the Cultural Revolution. A band of Red Guards murdered him because he used to paint portraits of Buddhist saints. We then said hello to the mother of the party secretary who had tried to bamboozle Zhou into marrying his twenty-two-year-old lover. The party secretary had died young. Fate is strange.

"Hello, Professor Zhou," said the old woman who, at eighty-nine, lived alone and was so bent that she stood barely four feet tall. "Tell my grandson to come home, please." The woman was working in her vegetable patch, a kerchief tied around her head.

"I hired her grandson," Zhou said when we were out of earshot. "I hired the son of the man who had tried to keep me down on the farm." To Zhou's great satisfaction, he had given the boy the job before his father died.

Fate *is* strange, I thought, as we walked the dirt paths of Li's Kitchen, smiling at the sunburned faces of the farmers who greeted Zhou with a mixture of curiosity, envy, and respect, but determination counts for more. Destiny didn't pull Zhou out of this place. He had clawed out on his own. He had not only survived, he had prospered.

Zhou and I wandered back to his house for the ritual honoring his ancestors. Along the north wall of the thirty-by-twelve-foot structure hung photographs of his grandparents, his parents, and his birth mother, the borrowed belly, all of these relatives now dead. In the center of the wall was a big poster of Chairman Mao. "That was the tenant's addition," Zhou said.

Zhou began the ceremony by burning paper and incense to appease the ghost of the house so that it would allow the souls of his ancestors to enter and share a meal with their descendant. He placed two small, neatly cut piles of paper money on each side of the doorsill and lit them along with the incense. The house filled with smoke and floating ashes from the burning paper—currency for use in the afterlife. Not quite three decades ago, Zhou had been part of a gang that had beaten people for burning paper money and honoring the dead. Today he was doing the same thing.

Zhou stuck eleven pairs of chopsticks into a big platter of rice and placed it on the table facing the photographs. A cousin brought over a bowl of fruit and a stew of bean curd and radishes to complete the memorial meal. Zhou lit more money and incense and placed it on the floor in front of the table. He then dropped a paper mat at his feet, kneeled on it, and bowed four times to the photos.

The smoke forced us outside. Zhou led me to an embankment of the San Cang River, one hundred yards away. There, in a small stand of trees, he found a mound, the grave of his father. Next to that was the gray tombstone that marked where Big Mama lay. He dug up several tufts of grass, placed them on top of each other in a mound, patted them down, lit more paper money, and kowtowed again.

We walked back to the village and went to the home of one of Zhou's longtime friends, where we lunched on stir-fried vegetables, ham and green peppers, hot fried clams, and the bean curd and radish stew that had played a supporting role in Zhou's sacrifice. Things were pretty good in Li Zao but not good enough to waste food on the ancestors.

The next morning, Zhou took me to Dongtai's city center to see another fellow villager who had made good: Boss Wang. With his perfectly bald pate and ill-fitting double-breasted suit, Wang could have played the part of the baddie in a kung fu flick. Boss Wang, who had made his money in real estate, had spent the weekend in Shanghai with the leaders of several organized crime families. The gangsters, who made the bulk of their profits in prostitution, had wanted to launder their ill-gotten gains through real estate deals. Smaller cities such as Dongtai and its neighbor, Yancheng, were just entering a boom period in land sales, so the time was ripe to invest. Boss Wang had an angle on a large chunk of Yancheng farmland, and his Shanghai associates wanted in.

With a soaring soprano laugh, Boss Wang told a tale straight from hip-hop heaven. He had spent the weekend at a private club where his gangland hosts gave him a choice of sixty women who were displayed naked in a room. He chose twenty, and spent the weekend popping Viagra and smoking methamphetamine, a combination increasingly popular among China's jet set.

"Of course, there's no free lunch," Wang said, screeching and squeezing his legs together. "They want my land."

"Doesn't the Shanghai city government know about this club?" I asked.

Boss Wang cackled. "They are investors." Zhou was not in the least bit surprised.

Over time, I would have thought that Zhou's views on the party would have mellowed. After all, by paying off party functionaries, Zhou had carved out a good business for himself. By 2005, Zhou was making more than sixty thousand dollars a year, even more than Daybreak Song. But I was wrong.

On the way back to Nanjing, Zhou and I took a detour to Fengyang, a small farming town in southern Anhui near the provincial border with Jiangsu. Fengyang was the birthplace of Zhu Yuanzhang, the first Ming Dynasty emperor. Chairman Mao lionized him as a peasant hero, though more objective historians have portrayed him as a bandit king.

During the Great Leap Forward, 20 percent of Fengyang's population died of starvation, and in 1960 the local government documented sixty-three instances of cannibalism, including the case of a couple who strangled their eight-year-old son in order to eat him. In 1978, a famine of equal proportions was brewing, but this time Fengyang's peasants were no longer willing to trust the government; they demanded that the collective land be turned over to them to farm. The land was ceded, thus starting a trend that would lead to the dismantling of the communes, the end of the Maoist era, and the beginning of the transformation that continues today.

Zhou stopped his Bora at the tomb of the Ming founder's parents. We strolled down a walkway flanked by thirty-two pairs of Ming Dynasty stone horses, various stone gremlins, and officials, all six feet tall, and two giant turtles carved from marble.

"Let's look at China from the Marxist perspective," Zhou said. "Let's give the Chinese government the benefit of the doubt. Why did the slave society overthrow primitive society? Because its economy was more advanced and it was richer. The same is true for why feudal society overthrew slave society and why capitalist society replaced feudal society. But then we come to Mao. Who was Mao? Who did he represent?"

Having come to the end of the path, we faced an earthen mound. A light breeze found its way through the skinny pines growing on the knoll. The graves had long since been robbed.

"Did Mao represent economic forces stronger than capitalism? No. Did he represent anything progressive? No. He represented the most backward forces in China. He didn't even represent the working class. He represented thugs. It wasn't a Communist revolution. It was a thugs' revolution. That's our real history."

37

MY PLACE IN THE PROCESSION

Nainai, my wife Mei's grandmother, died in 2003 on Valentine's Day, "lover's day" as it is known by the Chinese, who have grown fond of the Western holiday. Nainai was born in 1919, the year of the sheep. She died in a sheep year, in a sheep month, on a sheep day, and, it was said, during a sheep hour. She had completed seven cycles of the twelve-year zodiac. The local shaman said it was a very good day to die.

Mei and I traveled from Beijing to the funeral in Chengjiang, a small town in Yunnan on the shores of Touching Gods Lake where Nainai had lived out the last twenty years of her life. We sat around the family table on stools, lunching on simple foods: stir-fried greens, meat, and rice. Nainai had her bowl as well, placed by a grandson at the foot of her coffin. A wick, soaked in peanut oil, had burned near the open casket for the three days since her death. It was eerie and poignant to eat a last supper for the dead with the body right at my back. But it made sense. For the family I married into, the world revolved around the dinner table. Nainai had been a great cook. So too was Mei's father, Zhang Minqiang, and all of his sisters. What better way to see her from this world to the next than with a meal?

The next morning, donning a white-and-red cotton headdress, I took my place in the funeral procession, kowtowing to Nainai's casket as we wound our way through the lakeside town to a mountainside burial site. I was struck by the enduring power of ancestors in my new family's life. More than fifty family members and scores of friends had come to pay their respects.

Over the past fifty years, the Chinese government has contrived to weaken what it calls superstition, religion and other spiritual traditions, in favor of promoting communism, science, and now its peculiar form of man-eat-man capitalism. Nainai's life was a microcosm of that struggle.

Nainai's given name was Wang Manfen. She had spent her entire life in Yunnan Province, venturing out only a few times: to Hong Kong when Mei worked there, to Thailand with her daughters, to Beijing to see us, and to the southern city of Hangzhou, famed for its aromatic green teas and traditional pavilions.

A tiny woman with a disarming smile, Nainai was tough. When she stayed with us in Beijing, she shunned the soft couch, preferring the comfort of the floor, where she slept on top of a blanket. When she was young, Nainai was forced by her parents to bind her feet, but she undid the cloth when she was a teenager. Before the revolution in 1949, she had shared her husband with his mistress, who would come over for "accounting" lessons behind closed doors while Nainai cooked dinner at the other end of the house. Nainai's father and a brother were businessmen and landowners. After the revolution, they were executed.

Throughout the famine-plagued Great Leap Forward, Nainai kept her family fed by picking weeds and wild mushrooms. During our visit to Hangzhou, as we were walking to a Buddhist temple, Nainai pointed to some dusty greens in a ditch by the side of the road. "See those weeds?" she said. "I've eaten those. Very bitter."

Nainai's paltry income as a teacher supported her family. Her philandering husband had long since run afoul of the Communists. In the 1950s, he had been demoted from an accountant to a lowly shop clerk; by the Cultural Revolution he had been exiled to the countryside for reeducation.

One day in the fall of 1966, Nainai devoted a lesson to the moral values of Imperial China: respect for elders, education, study, culture, and morality. Within days, Red Guards had festooned her house with posters accusing her of propagating feudalism, capitalism, and revisionism. Beaten for weeks, she attempted suicide by poking herself in the head with an ice pick, leaving a long, thin scar just below her hairline. In the middle of one interrogation, Nainai jumped from the top floor of a three-story building, breaking both her legs and her back.

Red Guards, some of them former students of hers, came to the hospital room where she was recovering to continue the struggle sessions, shouting at her as she lay there, shaking with fear and reeking of excrement and urine.

For decades afterward, Nainai lived among those who had tortured her. She saw them regularly on the street, but said nothing: they were a mundane reminder of a horrific episode still unresolved. Throughout the Cultural Revolution, the power of Nainai's personality held Mei's family together, her endurance standing as a model for the others.

Nainai, once attacked for being a product of feudal China, adapted easily to the newer, more open China that evolved during the last years of her life. She accepted me, a foreigner, into her family, which smoothed my interactions with my other new relatives. On the day of her funeral, I was given a seat at the head table. Nainai would have wanted it that way, my father-in-law said.

For decades, China's government derided funerals and other traditions as vestiges of a feudal past. After 1978, restrictions on them were eased. But to this day, Communist officials laugh uncomfortably when speaking about such rituals. Their discomfort with belief has complicated their efforts to understand not only their own people but also the rest of the world. Even former president Jiang Zemin has expressed befuddlement that so many Western scientists, people he respects, could believe in God.

Nainai didn't suffer from that confusion. She planned her funeral carefully, picking out a simple gray suit to be buried in. She had set aside money for it because she wanted to leave this world, as she said, "looking good." The night she died, she asked for her small jewelry box and distributed her baubles among her family. She made those assembled around her promise to take care of her only remaining brother, a seventy-eight-year-old farmer. The family agreed to give him forty dollars a month until he dies.

After the luncheon, Nainai's casket was slid into a colorful bier, each side decorated with the image of a Taoist saint. Not everyone gets a box like this—only those who have lived long lives. Twelve laborers, hired for the task, lifted the casket onto their shoulders as two men tossed lit firecrackers to ward off malevolent ghosts. Dressed in white sheets and headresses, we lined up behind the casket, Mei's father in the lead. Mei's elder brother carried Nainai's picture, framed in black. In all, there were about two hundred of us snaking through Chengjiang's streets, past butcher shops with pig carcasses hanging in the sun, ancient houses with dainty etchings engraved on windowsills, and new slapped-together buildings, their small white tiles gray with dust. Passersby stared at the procession, gaping at the foreigner in its midst.

Before our climb to the burial site, we halted at an intersection. Making a circle around Nainai's casket, we all knelt down on bunches of straw tied into bows by an elderly neighbor; the straw was to pad our knees against the sharp gravel in the road. Three times we circled the casket; three times we kowtowed. Then the laborers began hauling the casket up to the cemetery, the men with the firecrackers following behind. As we climbed, we could see the ragtag houses of Chengjiang and the silver lake stretching to the west. We took a shortcut and came out ahead of the coffin. We had to wait. It's bad luck to beat a casket to the grave.

After an hour's walk, we entered the woods and trod a dirt path to Nainai's final resting place on a bluff overlooking her home. A shaman blessed the site while the workers jerry-rigged a pulley system to lower the coffin into the grave. The names of thirty-one descendants and relatives, including Mei, me, and Dali, had been engraved on her tombstone. Finally, her casket was lowered into the ground. We clasped our hands behind our backs and a laborer filled them with dirt, which we dropped onto the coffin. In times past, relatives carried earth near the deceased's home to the grave and this was a way of evoking that tradition.

Suddenly, the spell was broken. The shaman complained that something was wrong with the grave. The lines weren't straight, he said, the *feng shui* out of kilter. Relatives grumbled that he was just angling for a few extra bucks. The work proceeded apace and was finally finished when the laborers arranged fifteen pieces of carved stone into a mini mausoleum on top of the grave.

The Chinese call the funerals of those who die quickly after a long life "happy funerals," just as they call morning sickness "happy nausea." Back at Nainai's house, the women gathered and drank sugar water in celebration of her long life.

CONCLUSION: THE CHINESE DREAM

On a balmy October evening in 2004, I found myself in Shenzhen—the first place I passed through when I entered China in 1980. Back then, Shenzhen was a network of villages, mostly rice paddies and ramshackle factories. Now it had a population of 7 million people, a glinting skyline of glass-encased skyscrapers, and a ferocious upward mobility rivaling its neighbor, Hong Kong.

Shenzhen was one of the first economic zones created by the party in the late 1970s. The concept was so revolutionary that for decades Chinese needed a special visa to go there. But Shenzhen was more than just a boomtown. For millennia, China was a society of people with fixed addresses, ordered that way so the emperor would know where his people lived when the time came to marshal them into giant brigades to build vast public works projects like the imperial tombs, the Grand Canal, and the Great Wall. When the Communists came to power, they continued this tradition; people only moved when the party said so.

Shenzhen was something different, a society of modern-day nomads. The city was filled with Chinese from everywhere. The cabbies were Hunanese; the factory girls from Sichuan; the call girls from Manchuria; the businessmen from every corner of the country.

I walked with a Chinese friend to a soup joint about ten blocks from my hotel. On the street, the crowd moved with purpose, men and women in business suits, chatting on cell phones, hailing cabs, dodging hookers and hawkers and beggars with leashed monkeys. My friend, David Li, had returned from his adopted home of Salt Lake City to seek his fortune in Shenzhen. Already on his third career, he had started his professional life as an archaeologist in Hunan, practiced Chinese medicine in Salt Lake, and had returned to China to write a software program that would act like a virtual Chinese healer—diagnosing illnesses, prescribing herbs and acupuncture. Like the rest of the residents of this city, he was chasing a dream.

"You know," David mused as he scanned the crowd, "perhaps this is it. China is always going to be this messy." His words contained much truth. Chinese officials like to speak of their country as "in transition," the implication being that China will one day mature into a well-oiled superpower. My friend was saying that life here would continue to be a mishmash—part totalitarian, part free-wheeling; part button-down corporate, part jeans-and-T-shirt startup; part Communist, part capitalist; part conformist, part wild.

But even with my friend's belief that China had reached its apex, he had nonetheless voted with his feet. A naturalized American, he had chosen to stake his future on the country of his birth. His dream was not the American Dream; it was a Chinese Dream.

Daybreak Song was also taking part in China's great experiment in, of all places, Rome. That Song could make a living writing about international soccer underscored the changes in a generation that just two decades earlier was ignorant of virtually everything beyond China's shores. Why did foreign soccer resonate so deeply among the Chinese? There was nothing particularly Chinese about the game, Song used to say. In fact, soccer's guiding principle—asking eleven people to cooperate to score goals—was anathema to the Chinese way.

"We're the most individualistic people in the world. A lone Chinese is as powerful as a dragon," Song had told me, quoting an old proverb, "but three Chinese together can't even match a bug."

To Song, China's love affair with soccer was a metaphor for its obsession with modernity. China desperately wanted to become a modern country, just as China desperately wanted to have a good soccer team. In endeavoring to become modern, China has studied many political models—from Marx to Milton Friedman—and combined them in the strangest possible ways, just as it has studied many model teams—Brazilian, English, Italian, and South Korean—to improve its soccer. In reality, any model might have led China to where it was now, many, no doubt, a lot faster than communism.

Little Guan did not have any models to study as she made her way from White Pasture Commune to e-commerce. Although she never moved from Hefei, her spirit traveled far and wide in search of meaning. Her decision to junk her assigned job in the capital, drop her dream to study overseas, and stay in an industrial backwater for the sake of her family marked the triumph of love over the gangster state. Though she described herself as easily satisfied, a hen happy with a handful of grain, I disagreed.

Little Guan spent the best years of her life struggling for her ideals. To do that in China was an awesome feat. Her life as a child and young adult were completely foreign to anything I could imagine—even after years in China. But, like many of our classmates, her life had become increasingly recognizable to me. In an e-mail not long ago, she enthused about her new business ventures, going on to tell me what she wanted next from life.

"I've decided to look for someone to marry, someone around my age. I could cook him fish and sweet-and-sour pork ribs. In return, he could massage my back. I want the kind of relationship where we can pour each other a cup of tea or milk and place it within easy reach of each other."

Of all the dreamers and schemers I had met, I felt the deepest connection to Book Idiot Zhou. His foray into the urine business was a parable about pragmatism and will, taking the bad and making good of it. It was like the way China had recycled the so-called bad apples of his generation, the "rightists," and given them another chance.

Zhou lived a schizophrenic life. He was a businessman dreaming of being a scholar. Having completed his book on the history of the Chinese toilet, he was preparing to write a biography of Mao Zedong, one that would eviscerate the Great Helmsman. On a visit to one of his apartments in Bengbu, I discovered a massive library devoted to the dictator: newspaper files, boxes of books, and eye-high stacks of documents. Zhou's fascination with the chairman was not unusual. The consensus among my classmates was that Chairman Mao, despite his success in fashioning a nation state from a crumbling, humiliated medieval empire, took China on a decades-long detour. And yet Mao was everywhere—his portrait in Tiananmen Square and his mug on every *yuan* note, his calligraphy adorning the gate of every major university, the party he created still at the pinnacle of power.

Zhou was deeply pessimistic, but his spirit, too, seemed indomitable.

Without faith in the legal system, he was suing a business partner for unpaid bills. He believed the Communist Party would probably rule China for generations, yet he itched to topple its deity, Mao. He railed against corruption but paid people off. Zhou had benefited from the changes wrought by Deng Xiaoping, yet he knew that China would have been a better place if the Communists had never seized power.

And then there was me, an American who had come of age in China, witnessed its first tentative openings to the West, and seen its army slaughter innocent youth. Like Daybreak Song, I had felt the pain of exile only to return again to watch China's astonishing transformation. I found the love of my life in China, had my first child there, and grew to know it more intimately than I know my own country.

When I first arrived in China in 1980, the average Chinese produced three hundred dollars' worth of goods a year. The country's prime atmospheric was still fear—of the authorities, teachers, and each other. I had watched that society die as affluence and access to information transformed the Chinese and had begun to alter, albeit more slowly, the party, too. By the time I left China in 2005, the gross domestic product had increased a whopping sixfold over 1980. But fear had not been replaced by freedom. Instead a restless unease coursed through society. The Chinese word for it was *fuzao*, an apprehension tinged with a titillating sense of opportunity. No wonder so many of my classmates worried about the future. And, at the same time, no wonder my friend, David Li, was willing to bet his future on China.

Finally there was Big Bluffer Ye—my most enigmatic classmate, a climber, a party man. For centuries, the Chinese viewed their place in the world with an enormous sense of entitlement. The Chinese call their country *Zhongguo*, the "Middle Kingdom," a term coined by emperors who ruled all that was worth ruling "under heaven." The Chinese Communist Party longed to re-create a modern Middle Kingdom, to once again find itself at the center of the world.

Ye was by no means an aging Brezhnev staring at the wall while the state around him collapsed. He was smart, pragmatic, and focused on results. If someone had a good moneymaking idea, Ye's instinct was not that of a Communist cadre of the past: shut it down. Ye welcomed experiments, providing he and his party got a cut. Yet faced with a vacuum in belief and values, Ye and his comrades have sought to fill it with food, drink, clothes, and electronics—the goodies on display on Hunan Road. But this love of stuff, which helped bring China to where it is today, will not bring China where it wants to go tomorrow.

For centuries, Chinese debated what it was to be a good person, a good citizen: What was the Good, the Virtuous, and the Right? Fifty-plus years of Communist censorship and political campaigns have silenced those debates, and it is still unclear whether the country has the ability to revive the tradition of asking these timeless questions.

China has had a great run since the Tiananmen Square crackdown, almost two decades of political stability, and a rate of economic growth unparalleled in modern history, but that is coming to an end. Peasants and workers are increasingly restive. The social contract hashed out by Deng—you can get rich if you keep your mouth shut—is fraying because too few people have won their share of the bargain.

China will also grow old before it has grown rich, an unintended consequence of its one-child policy. By 2050, the number of people sixty-five and older will rise from around 7 percent to nearly one-quarter of the population. China's environmental problems—every major river and all its major lakes are significantly polluted, its seas are depleted, and parts of the country have disappeared from satellite weather maps because the air is so thick with haze—are the world's worst. The current vacuum in everyday morality hampers everything from public safety to education to the stock exchange.

And then there's China's younger generation. My classmates might have missed high school, but they gained enormous wisdom in the fields and factories during the Cultural Revolution. Their children have shied away from real-life experience, coddled by their parents and lost in their books and the virtual reality of Internet chat rooms. "I am worried about these children," Little Guan said to me once. "They don't understand how the world works."

The last time I was in Nanjing, I saw Big Bluffer Ye on Hunan Road, climbing out of his Audi 6. I didn't wave to him, I just watched. Wearing a dark-blue suit, a flashy watch, his hair slicked back, he ducked into the Lion's King Dainty Community Restaurant.

The crowds were out and the lights were on at the Light Art Tunnel. I stopped by an eatery famed for its dumplings and had a few plates. I strolled south, passing a massive neon sign that read: "Welcome to Hunan

Road, Nationwide Demonstration Point for the Establishment of a Civilized City."

I continued south, crossing Shanxi Road by way of a spotless underground passageway lined with flat-screen TVs pumping out frenetic techno beats as African-American break-dancers advertised mobile phones. I came out above ground, between two enormous new skyscrapers on opposite sides of the street. Workers were putting the finishing touches on the taller one, which featured signs heralding the opening of the Galaxy Department Store.

The energy of Nanjing, of all of China, amazed me. It was awe-inspiring, scary, sexy, ridiculous, sad, and wondrous. It made me afraid for China, though proud to have been around to witness the changes. A few blocks south I chanced upon Ninghai Street, and my pace slowed as I ambled through the quiet of this old neighborhood in the Drum Tower District, where the fury of Shanxi Road gives way to a tranquility of sorts. The big houses of this street were built in the 1930s, solid, well-made, Western-style mansions, a few with the soaring eaves of a traditional Chinese abode. Cherry blossoms were peeking out over the tall solid gray gates built to keep prying eyes from staring in. A breeze passed through, rustling a stand of bamboo in someone's backyard. I stopped at a street corner to admire a particularly beautiful cherry tree stretching skyward—every branch aflame in white blossoms—when an old man approached and stabbed the air with a long wooden pipe.

"It's been a cold spring," he grumbled. "The flowers will be blooming for a long time."

ACKNOWLEDGMENTS

Without the support of my classmates, friends, and family, this book would never have been written. My Chinese classmates opened their hearts, homes, and lives to me. In a country that still distrusts foreigners, especially foreign reporters, their willingness to share their worlds with me made this book what it is.

In Beijing, Ed Gargan helped me hatch the idea and Phil Pan watched it grow. Jia Minna, Jin Ling, Wang Dong, Zhang Jing, and Zhou Min provided me with timely research assistance. Li Xiguang and the journalism department at Tsinghua University provided critical help as well. In Shanghai, Peter Goodman shared his apartment and his fine wine. In Nanjing, Chen Ling and Ying Haikang kept me laughing.

My agent, Gail Ross, got the idea quickly and sold it. The Alicia Patterson Foundation helped fund part of the research, and my employer, the *Washington Post*, graciously gave me the time off to do it. My editor, Vanessa Mobley, provided sage guidance throughout the whole process.

In Los Angeles, the Pacific Council and the University of Southern California gave me further financial support and a place to hang my hat. Peter Fuhrman taught me the meaning of twenty-five years of the greatest friendship; he read three drafts of the book, pushed me to give more of myself, and let me mess up his home for three months. John D. Pomfret, Nicholas Meyer, and Laura Hohnhold gave me invaluable suggestions about writing. Willie Brent and Seth Faison, two of the most insightful China-watchers, helped me enormously as well. Thanks also go to Philip Short for his timely and critical advice.

Three men did the most to push me to China. Seymour Topping, then managing editor of the *New York Times*, helped me to get into China the first time, and later to land my first reporter's job. The late Nate Polowetsky, then foreign editor of the AP, sent me to China to cover Tiananmen. The *Post*'s Phil Bennett helped guide me through a third stay.

A couple, Ed Norton and Ann McBride, helped tie me to China forever—introducing me to my wife, Zhang Mei, and providing me with a model for how to live a productive life.

And most important of all, Zhang Mei tolerated my obsession for two years, providing me with the priceless insights into China, storytelling, and life. I count myself lucky to know her.

Negril, Jamaica
April 23, 2006

CREDITS

Page vii. John Pomfret
1. Zhou Lianchun
2. Zhou Lianchun
3. John Pomfret
4. Guan Yongxing
5. Guan Yongxing
6. Guan Yongxing
7. Guan Yongxing
8. Wu Xiaoqing
9. Wu Xiaoqing
10. John Pomfret
11. Yang Su
12. John Pomfret
13. John Pomfret
14. Ye Hao
15. John Pomfret
16. John Pomfret
17. John Pomfret
18. John Pomfret
19. John Pomfret
20. John Pomfret
21. John Pomfret
22. AP/Wide World Images
23. Phil Bennett
Page 318. John Pomfret

INDEX

ABOUT THE AUTHOR

JOHN POMFRET is an editor at the *Washington Post*. Formerly the *Post*'s Beijing bureau chief, he now edits the *Post*'s Outlook section. Pomfret was awarded the Osborn Elliott Prize for Journalism by the Asia Society in 2003 and the Shorenstein Award by Harvard and Stanford universities in 2007; both awards are given to journalists for their coverage of Asia. He lives with his wife and family in Maryland.

Fifty-three history majors from Nanjing University's Class of '82 gather to commemorate their 20th reunion, May 2002